THE COMPLETE BABY ZEKE

The Diary of a Chicken Jockey, Books 10 to 12

(**Collected Baby Zeke**, Vol. II, Books 10-12)

By,

DR. BLOCK

Copyright © 2019-2020 by Dr. Block and Eclectic Esquire Media, LLC

ISBN: 978-1-951728-44-1

No part of this publication may be reproduced, distributed, or transmitted in any form or by any means, without the prior written permission of the publisher, except in the case of brief quotations embodied in critical reviews and certain other noncommercial uses permitted by copyright law.

This UNOFFICIAL Minecraft-inspired book is an original work of fan fiction which is neither sanctioned nor approved by the makers of Minecraft.

Minecraft is a registered trademark of, and owned by, Mojang AB, and its respective owners, which do not sponsor, authorize, or endorse this book. All characters, names, places, and other aspects of the game described herein are trademarked and owned by their respective owners.

Published by Eclectic Esquire Media, LLC
P.O. Box 235094
Encinitas, CA 92023-5094
Information and inquiries: *www.drblockbooks.com*

Table of Contents

Introduction 1

BOOK 10 – RETURN OF THE WARRIOR 3

Chapter 1 4
Chapter 2 8
Chapter 3 13
Chapter 4 16
Chapter 5 25
Chapter 6 29
Chapter 7 38
Chapter 8 44
Chapter 9 46
Chapter 10 48
Chapter 11 52
Chapter 12 64
Chapter 13 69
Chapter 14 77
Chapter 15 83

Chapter 16 93
Chapter 17 98
Chapter 18 102
Chapter 19 107
Chapter 20 115
Chapter 21 119
Chapter 22 126
Chapter 23 133
Chapter 24 139
Chapter 25 144
Chapter 26 152
Chapter 27 155
Chapter 28 158
Chapter 29 162
Chapter 30 167

BOOK 11 – REBELLION 172
Chapter 1 173
Chapter 2 185
Chapter 3 190
Chapter 4 199
Chapter 5 204
Chapter 6 209

Chapter 7..214

Chapter 8..221

Chapter 9..225

Chapter 10..229

Chapter 11..232

Chapter 12..238

Chapter 13..244

Chapter 14..248

Chapter 15..252

Chapter 16..257

Chapter 17..264

Chapter 18..273

Chapter 19..282

Chapter 20..288

Chapter 21..295

Chapter 22..303

Chapter 23..311

Chapter 24..316

Chapter 25..323

BOOK 12 – REVENGE OF THE HUSK 329

Chapter 1..330

Chapter 2..339

Chapter 3..349

Chapter 4 354

Chapter 5 359

Chapter 6 363

Chapter 7 369

Chapter 8 375

Chapter 9 381

Chapter 10 386

Chapter 11 396

Chapter 12 403

Chapter 13 408

Chapter 14 420

Chapter 15 427

Chapter 16 431

Chapter 17 437

Chapter 18 444

Chapter 19 447

Chapter 20 457

Chapter 21 470

A Note from Dr. Block 473

Introduction

Hello there.

I just wanted to write a brief introduction to let you know a little bit about this collection of books. If you are reading this, I will assume you have already read the first nine books in the *Baby Zeke* series. If you haven't, then stop what you are doing and head over to your favorite bookstore and grab a copy of *The Complete Baby Zeke, Volume I: Books 1-9*.

The books in this current volume (i.e., books 10, 11, and 12) are each standalone stories, but you should read them in order because some characters other than Baby Zeke, appear in more than one book. However, the adventure in each book is completed by the end of the book, unlike in books 1-9, where the story continued in the next book.

I started writing longer books after I completed the first nine books of the *Baby Zeke* series, so the three books combined in this book are nearly as long as the first nine books combined.

That's it. That is all I wanted to say, except: Thank you so much for picking up a copy of my book. I hope you enjoy it a lot.

        Sincerely,
        Dr. Block

Book 10 – Return of the Warrior

Chapter 1

It has been nearly two years since I completed writing my initial, nine-volume autobiography in which I reveal my early-life struggles and which culminated with me learning from Notch that I was part of some mystical balance. I was the Warrior, while Notch was the Creator, the Ender King was the Protector, and Herobrine was the Destroyer. I probably would never have written my story except for Notch ordering me to do it so that it could be housed in the Great Library of Minecraft.

After I finished the autobiography, I was approached by a publisher asking me if I would like my story to be published and made public knowledge in the realms of Minecraft. I went through the manuscript and deleted the portion about me becoming the Warrior in the Balance. Instead, I ended it with Notch telling Herobrine to leave me and my friends alone and also included the part where the Ender King told me that we were friends. At least, that's the version that was released into the Minecraft realms. I have allowed the full uncensored version to be released into the realm of human players so that they would know my full story.

Fortunately or unfortunately, I will let you be the judge, my autobiography became extremely popular in the Overworld, mainly among villagers. Numerous scholars have argued that my writings have allowed mobs and villagers to have closer, more civil relationships. It certainly hasn't stopped zombies from eating villagers or hostile mobs from attacking villagers and players, but it has led to more understanding between the groups.

Basically, I became a worldwide celebrity.

My fame stretches from the Nether through the Overworld to the End. While this is totally gangsta, it is not necessarily a good thing for living a relaxing life.

For the first year after the publication of my autobiography, I was constantly hounded by autograph seekers and villager parents wanting me to teach their children lessons in life and be their role model. I found this confusing because my autobiography makes it clear that I only did what I did because I had to save my friends. That's the main reason I left out the part about me being the Warrior in the Balance. If that information had become widespread knowledge, it would have potentially made more people ask me for favors ... for good, or for evil.

After a year, my fame began to subside and I was increasingly left alone. That was all right by me. The sales of my autobiography had brought in a decent amount of emeralds which allowed me to purchase some nice things and to establish a farm where I could live with my friends Otis the baby zombie pigman, his chicken Bob, and my trusty chicken steed, Harold.

Unfortunately, Zeb had been severely injured when Herobrine exposed him to sunlight during the final battle which I chronicled in volume 9 of my original autobiography. As a result of his severe injuries, Zeb cannot live with us. Instead, he resides in a retirement home for zombies located about one hour's walk from my current home. My home and farm, by the way, is located on the outskirts of the village where we defeated Shadow, the wither skeleton minion of Herobrine.

And so, with all that as background, I have decided to write this new story in my life for your edification. I didn't think I would ever write another autobiographical work given that it took me months to write my first story in 9 volumes, but I thought this new story would be of some interest.

Chapter 2

The story I want to tell you begins like this: I was outside attending to my wheat crop, which I grew for Harold and Bob, and to supplement the diets of the cows I raised for my own food. Otis was tending to the carrot crop, which we fed to the cows as well. Occasionally, I would eat a carrot, because I think they taste good, but the crunchiness of fresh vegetables was painful to my loose, stained and rotten teeth.

As I stood admiring the tall rows of wheat, the wind gently blowing through the seed heads which would soon be ready for harvest, a villager whom I had never seen before, approached me.

Great, I thought, rolling my eyes, *he looks like a groupie*. It was the desperate expression on his face that brought this to my mind.

"Baby Zeke? Are you Baby Zeke?" asked the villager, hopeful desperation evident in his voice.

He was just like most farmer villagers, with a brown robe, brown pants, and gray shoes. However, there was something a little different about him. His hair was cut in a manner that made it very spiky, and he was starting to grow a beard, which was extremely uncommon among villagers. There were a couple of stains on his robe, near the cuffs of his sleeves, like he had been eating mushroom soup and carelessly allowed the sleeves to fall into the bowl.

In response to his question, I sighed and said, "Yes, that's me. What can I do for you?"

The villager grinned and rubbed his hands together with relief. "I need you to help me. I need you to find something of mine which has gone missing."

I shook my head. "My days of adventuring are over. I just want to be a farmer. Can't you find somebody else?"

At that moment, Otis, noticing a stranger had approached, came over and said, "What's this all about?"

The villager jumped in before I could respond. "I need Baby Zeke to find something for me. But he says he doesn't want to."

"What is it you want us to find?" asked Otis.

Us?

"My pet llama has been stolen," said the villager, a look of angst, desperation, and catastrophe crossing his face as tears starting to form in his eyes.

I tossed my hoe to the ground in anger and said, "I'm not a pet detective!"

Otis agreed with me and spat on the ground. "Yeah, you come over here asking us to find a llama? Why don't you just buy a new one?"

The villager got down on his knees and clasped his hands together and implored us, as though he were praying to Notch. "Please! Please help me find my llama. It's very special to me."

"Don't tell me ... you've had it since you were a little boy, right?" Otis said, thick sarcasm dripping like apple pie filling from his voice.

The villager nodded his head and without any words coming out of his mouth began to cry and moan.

I was starting to feel sorry for him. *Maybe I should hear him out?*

"Look, buddy, what's so special about this llama that you would want me to go find it?" I asked.

"Llamas are pretty common and, well, kind of dumb and smelly."

The villager took a moment to regain his composure and stop crying before he said plainly and matter-of-factly, so there could be no mistake about the words coming from his mouth, "I can make diamonds with her hair."

At this point, I did not know whether to believe him or if he was insane. I could tell Otis was having the same struggle inside his mind.

"Are you kidding me? You make diamonds from llama hair?!?" asked Otis.

The villager nodded his head. "Yes. I don't want to give away the secret, but it's pretty easy. You just need my llama's enchanted hair and a few common ingredients and a furnace."

"So, is there a reward if we find this magical llama for you?" asked Otis, greed filling his eyes and his half-rotten, half-pig heart as though he were a villager rather than a baby zombie pigman.

The villager blinked his eyes a few times and said, "I hadn't really thought about that ... hurrr ... but okay. If you find my llama, I promise to shave it and turn all the shaved hair into diamonds and then give them to you."

Otis squinted his eyes and asked, "About how many diamonds are we talking about?"

The villager shrugged. "I don't know, depending on how long the hair is, I can get anywhere from 100 to 200 diamonds from a single shave."

That's a lot of diamonds, I thought to myself. *But, I have enough money. We have a farm. I've had plenty of adventure to last a lifetime. I didn't need this.*

Otis looked over at me, grinned and said, "What do you think, Zeke? It might be fun."

"I don't know, Otis. We had some pretty crazy times battling with Herobrine. I not sure if I want to go on an adventure to find some stolen llama, even if it can make diamonds. And, maybe it wasn't even stolen. Maybe it just ran away."

"Oh no, I'm sure it was stolen," said the villager.

"How do you know that?" I asked.

"Because of the enchanted tombstone left behind in my llama's corral," said the villager.

Chapter 3

I tried to hide my surprise and shock by squinting my eyes at the villager. I asked, "What do you mean, an enchanted tombstone?"

"Well, it's a grave marker. Whoever took my llama put it in her corral. It has my llama's name on it, Sparkles." The villager began to sob before he could finish telling us this, mentioning the name of his missing llama clearly was an emotional moment for him.

"Sparkles" though?

"Okay so there's a tombstone that says 'Sparkles' on it. That is weird and would suggest that the villagers or mobs who took the llama placed it there. I'd have to agree with that," I said.

"That's not all," said the villager. "If you walk up to the tombstone your own name appears on it."

"Oh my Notch! Are you kidding me?" asked Otis, slapping the side of his head as a physical manifestation of his amazement.

The villager shook his head. "No, I am not kidding. Every time I walk up to it, my name, Donald, appears. When I back away from it by at least two blocks, Sparkles' name reappears."

This was extremely curious. It sounded like something Herobrine might do. Even though Notch told Herobrine he had to leave me alone and was not allowed to try to destroy the world for at least ten years, it didn't mean he wouldn't play pranks on other people and steal their diamond-making hairy llamas.

"Has anyone else walked up to the tombstone? Maybe whoever left it only created an enchantment for your name and Sparkles' name?" I asked.

The villager nodded. "My wife and daughter both have walked up to it and their names appear as well, Bertha and Gertrude."

I nodded my head and rubbed my chin in thought. I looked at Otis and shrugged before saying to the villager, "I'm not saying I'll search for this llama for you, but I would like to see this tombstone."

The villager unclasped his hands, jumped up from his kneeling position, ran over to me and hugged me. Since I only came up to his chest, it was a super awkward hug. My face was pressed against his gut. His robe smelled like wet dog fur.

I shoved him away. He didn't seem to care.

"Thank you, Baby Zeke! Thank you. I just knew you would help me. After I read your autobiography, I knew you are a kind-hearted baby zombie."

Everything the villager said was true, of course, except the part about knowing that I would help him. Certainly, I am a kind-hearted baby zombie.... That's what always gets me into trouble.

Chapter 4

The villager gave us directions to his house and I told him that we would meet him there in about thirty minutes. After he left – he was skipping with joy, actually – I went to the chicken coop where Bob and Harold lived, with Otis following close behind.

I knocked on the door of the chicken coop and, peeking through the window next to the door, said, "Hey guys, we need to go check something out. I think we should go in our jockey forms just in case."

Harold and Bob stretched and then Harold said, "It has been quite a while since you've been my jockey, Zeke. I might be a bit out of shape."

"It's okay, Harold. If you want, we can walk there separately but I want to have you by my side just in case things get crazy and I need the extra speed that we have in our jockey formation."

"Same goes for you, Bob," said Otis in a gruff, demanding voice.

The two chickens nodded their understanding and decided to walk alongside of us to the villager's house. I could understand their decision. Although the bond of a chicken and his jockey was a strong one, which is difficult to describe in words and which cannot truly be understood by anyone else, I also realized that a chicken's back can get sore and tired when someone, even a puny baby zombie, sits on it.

Before we left the house, Harold and Bob ate some wheat seeds for breakfast, while Otis and I each had a quick bite of rotten cow flesh and a glass of dirty water.

Dirt adds flavor!

* * *

The walk to the villager's house was uneventful.

I spent the time admiring the beauty of the Overworld, with its flowers, trees, grasses, and animals. We saw a few wild cows and pigs wandering about.

Otis just looked straight ahead, a scowl on his face. He had always been single-minded in his purposes. This made him a good fighter, but caused him to be lacking in some of the social graces. He was not the most polite or thoughtful mob I had ever met. But, he was loyal to a fault.

At one point during our journey, a few chickens clucked somewhere in the distance. "They sound like idiots," I heard Bob whisper to Harold.

Harold nodded his head and rolled his eyes. "Surely, they will be filling the bellies of even the noobiest noob player in no time."

Ah, the secret world of poultry.

When we finally arrived at the villager's house, he welcomed us with a smile and quickly led us to the llama's corral. It was a very nice corral, built with what appeared to be very expensive, finely crafted wood. If the llama really did produce diamonds, I was sure some of them had paid for this magnificent enclosure.

In the center of the corral, next to a large puddle of mud and nearly obscured by a large pile of straw, was a gray brick tombstone on which the word "Sparkles" was plainly visible. I turned to the villager and said, "That must be the tombstone you told us about, right?"

The villager nodded. "Yes. As you can see, it looks like a normal tombstone. But, if you approach it, the name will change. Go ahead. Try it."

I really didn't want to walk into the corral with all the mud and ... well ... llama poop, but I had agreed of my own free will to see the tombstone. Any poop I encountered would be my own fault, I guess.

I looked over at Harold, smiled as though I were a kindly old grandmother, and asked in a friendly voice, "How about I sit on you and you walk in there?"

Harold looked at me and squinted his eyes in anger and said, "Is this why you wanted to come here in jockey formation? Absolutely not." Harold folded his wings in front of his chest. "That muck is disgusting."

Bob looked at Otis and said, "Don't even think about it, playah."

I sighed. I guess I would be the victim. But, before I could walk into the corral, Otis spat on the ground and said, "Stop being such pathetic wimps. I'll go check it out."

Otis strode through the muddy corral, carefully avoiding the visible llama poop, and walked right up to the tombstone. I could hardly believe my eyes, but when Otis had approached within a few paces of the gray monolith, the name "Sparkles" disappeared and was replaced with "Otis"!

Otis looked over his shoulder, an expression of wonder on his face, and said, "Are you seeing this?"

"Yeah, I am," I said.

I decided that I needed to see what would happen when I approached the tombstone. As I entered the corral, my rotten, undead feet squishing in the mud, I thought to myself, *I really need to get some shoes.*

Otis backed away from the tombstone and the word "Sparkles" reappeared on it. Then, when I was close enough, the word on the tombstone shimmered, disappeared, and was replaced with ... "The Warrior"!?!?!?!

I was shocked to see "The Warrior" instead of "Zeke" because I thought that the only people who knew that I had become The Warrior were Notch, the

Ender King, Herobrine, Otis, Bob and Harold. *That narrowed the list of suspects at least, right?*

I backed away from the tombstone as quickly as I could so that no one other than Otis would see that "The Warrior" had appeared on it.

I looked over at Otis. He was both shocked and concerned. "How?" He asked in a soft voice. "How does it work? How could it know you are the ... you know?"

I shook my head in disbelief and said, "I have no idea, but I am beginning to think that maybe we should take this job. There has got to be more to it than just a missing llama."

It was at that moment I looked down and saw a strange object in the mud. I picked it up and inspected it. It was red and about the size of one of my stubby, undead fingers. It had a hinge on one end and a clasp on the other. It was flat on one side and had what looked like a spiky comb on the other. I showed it to Otis and asked, "You have any idea what this is?"

Otis took the object and inspected it closely. He opened the clasp, scrutinized it, and then re-clasped it. He handed the object back to me and said, "Not sure. It looks like you could put something in between the flat part and the spiky part and it would hold it in place."

I nodded my head and rubbed my chin in thought. Otis and I walked out of the corral and back to the villager.

The villager was shifting his weight from foot to foot. He was either very excited or needed to use the bathroom. "See? See, I told you. It changes doesn't it," he said.

I nodded my head. "Yes, it does. Very curious. By the way, do you know what this is?" I handed the small, red object to the villager.

He glanced at it and said, "Sure, it's a hair barrette."

I had never heard such a term. "What's that?"

"Oh, people use them to hold their hair in place. My wife and daughter use them all the time."

I nodded my head. "So, is this barrette one of theirs?"

He looked more closely and said, "I don't think so. All their barrettes are made out of brown wood. You know, villager style. This one's bright red. I've never seen them wear anything red."

I took the barrette back from the villager and said, "Well, then, I think we have our first clue."

Chapter 5

Before we left the villager's house I asked him to draw me a picture of his llama. He did better than that, he gave me a small portrait that had been painted by the local village artist. In fact, he had numerous portraits of his llama hanging around his house. There was something strange though about all of these pictures because there weren't any pictures of his wife and daughter, whom he claimed existed.

The llama had the same basic form as any other llama, however the hair was a strange translucent bluish color, similar to the color of diamond ore.

Before I left the villager's house I asked, "It might help with my investigation, so could you tell me how did you get this amazing diamond-haired llama in the first place?"

The villager suddenly became nervous. Sweat formed on his brow. "Hurrr, it's ... hurrr ... a long story."

I looked over at Otis who had raised one of his decaying eyebrows, indicating his suspicion.

I rubbed my chin and leaned against the wall of the villager's house. "We've got plenty of time," I said.

The villager was wringing his hands and then wiping the sweat from his brow. His nervousness had increased. "It ... hurrr ... well ... hurrr ... I inherited it. A long-lost uncle in a village several days away from here died a year ago and left it to me."

I did not believe this nonsense story for a second, but at least it made some sense to a casual observer.

"Really? What village is that?" I asked, pressing for more information.

The sweat continued to pour from the forehead of the nervous villager. "Hurrr ... it's called ... hurrr ... Apple Blossom Valley Village."

The name rang a bell. I think I had received some fan mail from that village at some point.

"What was your uncle's name?" asked Otis, joining the investigation for the first time.

At this point the villager's nervousness spiked and he began to twitch a little bit and said, "Cletus. Hurrr ... yeah, that's right ... Uncle Cletus. He didn't have any other relatives in the village. They said when he died and turned into a puff of smoke, he dropped nothing other than a piece of paper which bequeathed his diamond producing llama to me, his sole surviving relative."

This guy was amazing. He should be a writer. He really could make stuff up with ease.

I nodded my head and asked, "Can I see that piece paper?"

The villager twitched even more and said, "Unfortunately, after it was read, Sparkles ... hurrr ... ate it."

"That's convenient," said Otis in a suspicious voice.

The villager wiped the sweat from his brow and said, "What do you mean? It's true. Don't you believe me?"

I didn't believe him but I said, "Sure, we believe you. We just want to make sure that you are the true owner of this llama. It seems like a lot of people would want to be in your position. Clearly, someone felt so strongly about owning the llama that they stole her from you."

The villager nodded his head and I noticed that his sweating had decreased. "Yes, yes. Hurrr, so you can see why I want to get her back as soon as possible."

"Sure I can," I said, following it with a wide smile of my rotten stained teeth. "We'll do our best to find your llama, as long as that reward is still coming to us."

"Oh, of course. I'll even give you two shavings of hair if you can find Sparkles within a week. Hurrr, I miss her so much!"

Otis nodded his approval at the doubling of the reward. "We better get moving, if we want the double shave reward," said Otis.

I looked over at him with a sideward glance. "The 'double shave reward'? That sounds stupid."

"Whatever, dude. Let's just get moving and figure out what this barrette has to do with this heist."

Chapter 6

Bob and Harold had been watching this entire exchange, bemused looks on their normally vacant, black-eyed chicken faces. After we were out of earshot of the villager, Harold said, "You know he was lying about how he acquired the llama, right?"

I nodded my head. "It's pretty obvious."

"So, are we still going to look for the llama?" asked Bob.

"Well, I told him we would, and I always keep my promises," I said. "But, first, I want to go talk to Zeb and get his opinion about all this. Maybe he will have some ideas about who took the llama or maybe he'll tell us we should not bother looking."

"Sounds like a good idea," said Harold. "Hop on, Zeke. I'd like to see Zeb too." I hopped on to Harold's back and looked over at Otis and Bob. "So?"

Bob looked at Otis, sighed, and said, "Okay, get on if you must."

"Gee, thanks dude. You're so kind," Otis said in a sarcastic voice as he hopped onto Bob, depositing his weight on the chicken's back a little harder than he needed to.

"Ouch! Watch it," said Bob.

* * *

About thirty minutes later, we arrived at the zombie retirement home, located north of the village in which we lived. Harold and Bob dropped us off some distance from the retirement home because some of the elderly zombies were unable to understand their surroundings the way they could when they were younger, and Harold and Bob feared they might be eaten.

Otis and I walked up to the front door of the retirement home, opened it, and walked inside. The matronly female zombie behind the reception desk greeted us and asked who we would like to see. We told her and she confirmed that Zeb was available to see visitors and directed us to go back to his room.

The retirement home smelled strange. It didn't smell merely of zombies. I am, of course, a zombie, so I don't find the scent of zombies to be offensive. However, the retirement home had a strange smell of impending doom. All of the zombies living there knew they would not be undead for much longer; soon, they would just be dead. They were all waiting to vanish in the puffs of smoke.

Zeb was actually much younger than most of the zombies in the retirement home, but his burn injury had made it more likely that he would die sooner rather than later. It was sad to think about.

The zombie medical doctors – yes, they exist; but that is a story for another time – had given him only a year to live after Herobrine cruelly exposed him to sunlight during the Battle of the High Castle, but Zeb had exceeded expectations and had lived for two years already.

Yes, by Notch's beard, Zeb was a fighter.

We approached the door to Zeb's room, which was slightly ajar. We knocked gently on the door and entered the room. Zeb was reclining in his bed, as he tended to be doing whenever I visited. He was reading a book called, *Legends of the Undead: Zombie Myth and History from the Beginning of Time to the Present.*

"How's the book?" I asked, my undead lips parting into a derpy, rotten smile.

Zeb looked up and smiled in return. "Hello, Zeke and Otis, come in." Zeb set the book down and pushed himself up against his pillow with his hands so that he was sitting a little more upright. "The book is good, though it is very long. I've been reading it for six months and I still have 1000 pages to go, but I've already read 3000 pages."

Otis slapped his forehead. "That's ridiculous. No, it's criminal and insane. Who would want to read a book that is 4000 pages long?"

"I would," Zeb said. "The zombie history is really fascinating, and so are the myths. I saw there was a similar book about zombie pigmen too, Otis. Maybe you should read it. It's only 2500 pages long."

Otis spat on the floor and said, "Forget that. I'll wait for the audiobook."

Zeb laughed and said, "You really should not spit inside this building. It's rude."

Otis rolled his eyes but located a paper towel and cleaned up his spit glob from the floor. Otis never apologized, but he usually did the right thing.

"Zeb," I said, "I was wondering if I could ask your opinion about something?"

Zeb could hear the serious tone of my voice. He stopped laughing at Otis, leveled his gaze at me, and said, "Of course, Zeke. You can talk about anything with me."

"Thanks," I said and then proceeded to tell him all about the diamond-haired llama, the tombstone, the appearance of the words "The Warrior", and the bright red barrette we found in the mud. Once I had finished explaining everything, I asked, "So, what do you think? Who could have taken the llama?"

Zeb sat there and thought for a while, rubbing his chin. He had rubbed his chin a lot the last couple of years, so much so that some of his jaw bone was starting to show through his rotten skin. It was pretty nasty. But, we zombies don't really feel pain so Zeb probably had no idea he had rubbed through to bone.

After about a minute, Zeb said, "It seems like just about anyone might have taken the llama. As you yourself noticed and pointed out when you told me the story, the villager himself may have stolen it to begin with. So, I suppose it could've been stolen back by the person from whom the villager originally took it or it could have been stolen by just about anyone else who wanted to have an easy, inexhaustible supply of diamonds."

I nodded my head. "So, you think it is a hopeless quest, a fool's errand to search for the llama?"

Zeb shook his head and laughed. "Of course not. Clearly, it was someone who was aware of your membership in the four-sided balance of Minecraft, which cannot be too many people. And, judging by that barrette, it was probably a woman, though someone may have dropped it there on purpose to throw you off the track."

I nodded. "Perhaps. But, I'm sure it wasn't Notch or the Ender King. It might have been Herobrine, but you'd think he would have better things to do after Notch scolded him for messing with me. Of course, stealing that villager's llama had nothing to do with me, until now."

Zeb nodded. "Well, there's no way that you can find Notch unless he wants to be found, so I guess you have two places start. You can either go to the End and talk to the Ender King about whether he revealed the secret of the Warrior to anyone or you could go see Herobrine and ask the same questions. I've heard he still lives in his High Castle."

I shuddered at the thought of going through the end nectar in order to meet with the Ender King. "I guess I'll start with Herobrine. It seems more likely that he or someone he knows would make that ridiculous tombstone. The Ender King wouldn't do anything like that, even if he could, which I doubt he can."

Zeb nodded his head. "I agree. It seems fairly likely that the culprit is either a mystical being like

Herobrine, or potentially Entity 303 or maybe a witch or an illager of some type. On the other hand, players have been known to become fairly well-versed in enchantments, so maybe it was a player who wanted a lifetime supply of diamonds?"

Otis shook his head and said sarcastically, "Thanks for narrowing down a list of suspects, Zeb. Now it sounds just about like we are back to where almost anyone could've done it again."

Zeb smiled. He had lost a few teeth the last couple of years, so he looked like a spooky jack-o'-lantern or a witch who never brushed her teeth. "No one said this would be easy, Otis. I'd be surprised if you ever found the llama, but the reward sounds pretty nice. It's up to you guys. I can't go."

I placed a comforting hand on Zeb's shoulder. It was clear that he was sad that he could no longer go on quests with us. Not that this was a "quest," per se. We were just doing detective work, actually.

"Thanks for the advice, Zeb," I said. "We will go find Herobrine and talk to him. If we don't get anywhere, maybe we'll just give up. Still, it would be pretty cool to find the diamond-haired llama and watch the villager make diamonds from its hair."

"I suppose so," said Zeb with a smile. "Have a safe journey."

Otis and I stood up, said our goodbyes to Zeb, and returned to where Harold and Bob were waiting for us.

"So? What's the story morning glory?" asked Bob.

I smirked at his bizarre statement and then told him that tomorrow morning we would set off to Herobrine's High Castle to see if he knew anything about the mysterious tombstone and the stolen, diamond-haired llama.

Then, Bob fainted.

Chapter 7

When Bob revived, he kept shaking his head and saying, "Why? No. Why? No."

Otis walked over and petted Bob's head gently. "Look, buddy, you know that Herobrine is not allowed to mess with us anymore. Notch's orders. So, it won't be so bad."

Bob narrowed his eyes and looked at Otis. "You trust Herobrine? I don't. But, even if I did, I don't want to go back to the site of that ... that massacre."

Harold approached Bob and pecked the ground once before saying, "Bob, I don't really want to go back to that horrible place either, but Zeke told us that he is part of the Balance now and Herobrine has to respect that."

Bob put a wing to his forehead and sighed. "But, the memories of that battle.... I don't know."

"If it gets to be too much, we can wait outside while Zeke and Otis speak with Herobrine, right Zeke?" said Harold.

I smiled. "Sure, buddy, whatever it takes. Besides, we will probably only need to speak with Herobrine for a few minutes. What could go wrong?"

"Netherrack," cursed Otis as he gesticulated wildly with his stubby arms. "What *couldn't* go wrong? We are dealing with Herobrine here!"

I gave Otis the side eye and said through clenched teeth, "Bro, I'm trying to reassure Bob here. Be quiet!"

Otis, realizing that he had once again acted without thinking through the situation or reading the room, looked ashamed and said, "Sorry. Um, Bob, I didn't mean any of that stuff."

Bob rolled his eyes. "Yes, you did, but I will choose to believe Zeke and Harold."

The Bob situation now sorted, we filled our inventories with food and weapons. It was going to be a two- or three-day journey to the High Castle, so we needed to be prepared. We hoped to stay with some friendly villagers we had met in the past year – being a celebrity is great for getting free stuff – but if we had to, we could survive on our own in a cave or rudimentary structure.

I put on my diamond armor to make sure it still fit. It felt a little snug in the waist because of my lack of exercise and overeating of rotten cow meat.

"My armor is a little tight," I said to Otis who was trying on his own armor.

"What? Your head swell so much you can't fit into your helmet?" said Otis attempting to insult me.

I rolled my eyes. Then I noticed that my diamond armor seemed a little less shiny than I had remembered it. I rubbed it a bit with a rag, but it did not change.

Weird. Maybe it always looked like this? Or, maybe my eyesight is going?!? Or ....

I decided I would get back a little at Otis for insulting me. "Anyway, Otis, it is a good thing I am so famous because we should have all sorts of free places to stay." I paused for a moment to make sure Otis was getting upset. "Stick with me, dude, and you will never have to worry about anything."

Otis spat on the ground. "I'm famous too. I wrote a diary."

I laughed. "Yeah, only three volumes. Not nine volumes like mine."

Otis was turning bright red with anger. He tossed his diamond sword on the ground and yelled, "I am just as cool as you; maybe cooler." Then, he flopped down on the ground and hit the dirt with his fists like an angry bald baby.

I didn't mean to make him THIS upset!

"Chill, man, it was just a joke," I said, approaching Otis to comfort him.

Otis looked at me through bloodshot, rage-filled eyes. "It wasn't funny!"

"But...," I started before he interrupted me.

"I've had a hard life. No one understands. That's why I wrote my diaries. Do you think I wanted to reveal my private life to the world? No. I just want some respect!"

Wow! I had no idea Otis was so sad about his life or childhood. I just thought he was a rough and crass pigman. I thought that is how he liked to engage with people. Or, maybe it was how he expressed his respect for others, but he wanted normal respect from everyone else.

I was too old to go back to school to get a psychology degree — yes, there are colleges for zombies, but that is another story — so I just decided to stop being mean to Otis. I liked him. He was my friend, even though he could be a bit mean sometimes.

"Look, bro ... I'm sorry," I said, truly meaning it with every fiber of my rotten, undead being.

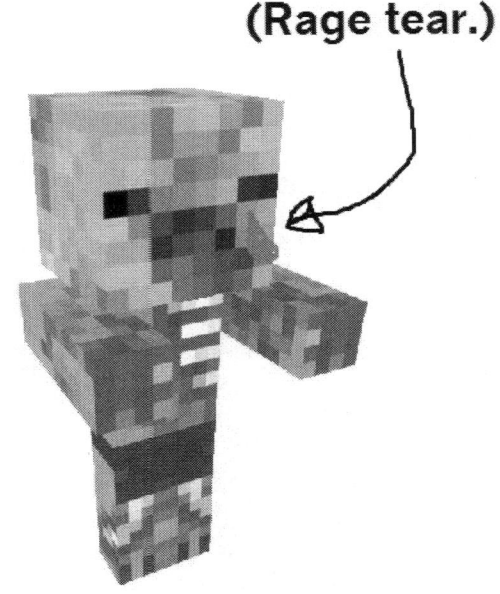

(Rage tear.)

Otis looked up at me and wiped a rage tear from his face. He stood up and stuck out his hand. I took it. We clasped our hands and looked each other in the eyes. No words needed to be said. We understood each other. We were brothers again.

The crisis averted, Otis and I got on our chickens and began our multi-day journey toward the High Castle.

"Ooof," said Harold as I sat on him. "Where is an enderman when you need one?"

"Huh?" I said, confused.

"Teleportation," grunted Harold, "would be nice right now."

"Yeah, Otis, you are heavy," said Bob. "How much stuff is in your inventory?"

Otis grunted. "Probably not enough," he said without any sympathy for Bob's plight.

I laughed. "Let's do this!"

Chapter 8

When we were about ten minutes from our house, we passed by the edge of the nearby village. Unfortunately, some young villagers saw us in jockey formation and rushed over to us.

"Where are you guys going?" asked an excited, wide-eyed young girl.

"Yeah, you going to deliver some justice to bad mobs or something?" asked a young boy, a happy grin on his face.

"No, we are going to search for someone's missing llama," I said.

The two children looked sad and disappointed.

"You ... hurrr ... you are looking for someone's pet?" squeaked the girl.

The boy shook his head sadly. "Wow. I never thought I'd see the day. The ... hurrr ... great Baby Zeke reduced to a pet detective. I thought you were better than that."

"It's not like that," I said. "But, I can't give you any details."

Otis tilted his head back and laughed. "Zeke, it is *exactly* like that. Don't lie."

"I'm not lying," I said angrily. "You know there is more to the story."

"What? We get paid instead of doing it for honor and glory? Lame," said Otis.

The villager children simply shook their heads sadly and walked away without saying another word.

When they were out of earshot, I steered Harold over to Otis. "What in the name of Notch was that? You were the one who wanted to go on this little adventure from the start. Why embarrass me?"

Otis grinned an evil grin. "Don't tell me my diary is less cool or less important than yours *ever* again."

Message received.

I sighed. "Sorry, man. It was a joke, but … yeah … I'm sorry."

Otis grunted his acceptance of my apology, and we continued on our way to the High Castle.

Chapter 9

After a few hours, I was really missing the old days when I would travel with the Ender King and his soldiers using teleportation. Otis was constantly complaining about anything and everything: mob life, pig killing players, insensitive full-sized zombie pigmen who made fun of his short stature ... you get the idea.

Anyway, Harold and Bob soldiered on, transporting Otis and I wherever we wanted to go with no complaints. Though, I did see them exchanging sidelong glances from time to time and they rolled their eyes more than once. I laughed to myself, but said nothing. I wanted to let the chickens have their own secret lives.

In the months since I had learned I was part of the Balance, I had grown apart from Harold. Sure, we lived on the same farm and worked the land together, but it was not the same as the bond we felt when we were jockey and steed, trying to save the world from Herobrine's destructive plot. I missed those days, not the constant sense of impending doom, but the fellowship with my chicken.

Tear. Sniff.

I wiped my eyes, trying to hide the moisture of sadness forming in them. But, Harold noticed. Not the tears themselves, but he could sense my sadness.

"Is everything okay, Zeke?" he asked.

I looked down at him and nodded. "Sure, buddy. I'm just tired that's all. Plus ... well ... I was thinking about the old days. When we were fighting for our lives and running to confront Herobrine." I paused to hold back the tears; I was very emotional. "Anyway, even though our lives were in danger every second of every day ... well ... I miss those days."

Harold twisted his neck around to look at me. He smiled and nodded. "Yeah, I miss those days too."

Chapter 10

Another hour passed.

The sun was moving toward the horizon. Night would be upon us very soon.

We had moved into a thickly-forested region. The leaves of the trees blocked enough of the sun's rays that it was nearly as dark as night.

It was then that we ran into a group of three wandering zombies. All adult-sized, of course. The lead zombie moaned at us, his breath particularly dank and nasty. Even I, a rotten baby zombie, barfed a little in my mouth when I smelled it. As I swallowed back my vomit, the lead zombie said, "Where are you little jockeys going?"

Otis grinned slyly and said, "Let me handle this, Zeke."

I shrugged my shoulders. "Whatever, dude. Go ahead."

Otis urged Bob closer to the lead zombie. "We seek something shiny," said Otis, sounding like a creepy weirdo.

The zombie nodded. "Emeralds?"

"More shiny," said Otis.

The zombie looked confused for a moment, but then said, "Gold?"

Otis slapped his forehead as if the zombie were completely stupid. "No. Shinier still."

The zombie looked even more confused and rubbed his chin in thought. This was a mistake because his rotten chin separated from his body, coming off in his hand. The zombie looked down at his rotten chin in his hand. He looked slightly sad, but then tossed his chin into a nearby bush. Two rabbits sprang from the bush, vomiting from the stench as they ran away from the piece of nasty rotten chin flesh.

The zombie was oblivious to the plight of the rabbits. Then, he snapped his rotten fingers, dislodging a black fingernail in the process. "I've got it. You seek diamonds!"

Otis smiled. "Yes, we do. But, not just any diamonds."

The lead zombie had no response to that, but one of the other zombies said, "Do you seek the mystical diamonds of the Great Sonskew?"

Now it was Otis's turn to look confused. "The Great Sonskew?!? What in the name of Notch is that?"

The zombies all moaned in unison. "He is the greatest zombie who ever lived. They say he had a collection of diamonds and ruled a large portion of the Overworld before Notch allowed players to come and begin killing zombies."

Otis rolled his eyes. "That sounds like a bunch of hooey. When has a zombie ever been a ruler of the Overworld?"

"Unbeliever!" the zombies shouted and moved toward Otis and Bob.

Otis and Bob backed away. "Dude, chill guys! Fine. Whatever. The Great Sonskew is dominant and Notch is lame. But ... look ... have you guys seen a shiny blue llama?"

The zombies paused for a moment. Looked at each other, and then burst into laughter. "You say you seek a blue-haired llama, and you think the Great Sonskew is ridiculous?!? You are a ridiculous fool! Everyone knows llamas only have four colors of hair: brown, gray, white and creamy."

Otis rolled his eyes again and cursed under his breath before looking at me and saying, "Zeke help me out here."

I rolled my eyes and said, "Hey, man, you wanted to handle it."

Otis shook his head and then said to the zombies, "Look, guys, we are looking for a blue-haired llama whose hair can be turned into diamonds. Have you seen it?"

The zombies laughed harder. The lead zombie said, "Wait. Wait. The blue-haired llama can make diamonds? You are stupid and small."

Otis jumped from Bob's back, pulled out his diamond sword, and cut the lead zombie's head off. The zombie's body flashed and disappeared into a puff of smoke before it could even fall to the ground.

The other zombies stared at Otis in horror and moaned in unison, "Why?"

Otis squinted his eyes and then yelled, "Because he body-shamed me!"

The zombies looked confused but did not stay for an explanation. They ran away, moaning in anger.

Chapter 11

After the zombies departed, we continued through the forest. Nothing eventful happened for a few hours until we noticed it was nearing sunset.

"I suppose we should find a cave for the night," I suggested.

"Yeah, unless you want to build a shelter," said Otis. "I'm ready to punch some trees, boy!"

I rolled my eyes before looking around the area. I saw we were near a hill. There was a crack in the hill, which I thought likely led to a cave. "Let's go check out the crack over there on that hillside, and if there's no cave there we can build a small sleeping area if we have to."

The four of us went over to the crack and sure enough, it was the entrance to a cave. The main entry area of the cave was not too big, but easily large enough for the four us to sleep in.

Sometimes it helps to be small, like baby zombies, baby pigmen, and chickens.

There was a narrow passageway leading away from the main area. We quickly sealed it with cobblestone blocks to avoid any surprise visitors during the night.

"I'm going to go find some leaves and sticks to sleep on," said Bob.

"I'll go with you," said Harold.

"Don't stay out too long. The sun is already starting to set," I cautioned them.

"We won't, Dad," said Harold sarcastically. The two chickens rolled their eyes and walked outside of the cave.

I looked at Otis and said, "This cave reminds me of where we first met."

Otis chuckled. "Are you getting all nostalgic on me now, Zeke? Want a tissue?"

I shook my head. "Not nostalgic. It just reminded me of you trying to scare me and Harold while we were seeking shelter in the cave. It wasn't very nice."

Otis shrugged. "I'm not about being nice. I'm about being effective," he said with an intense tone in his voice as he slammed a fist into an open hand.

I smiled. Same old Otis. He would never change. Even though he was kind of annoying to deal with sometimes, that consistency was a good thing. You always knew what you were going to get with Otis.

Otis and I crafted a furnace to cook some food. We also arranged a small sleeping area. By the time we had finished, the chickens had returned with some debris on which they could sleep. I watched as the chickens arranged a little sleeping nest before they came over to where I was standing.

"What's for dinner, Zeke?" asked Harold.

I smiled as I reached into my inventory and pulled out some wheat for the two chickens to eat. "Should I toss it on the ground in front of you or do you want to eat it out of a bowl?"

The two chickens looked offended. "How dare you even ask such a thing? Toss it on the ground," said Bob.

I threw the wheat on the ground and they began pecking at it quite rapidly.

I looked over at Otis and asked, "You want me to roast some rotten flesh for you or do you want to eat it raw?"

Otis shrugged. "What difference does it make? Rotten flesh is pretty nasty either way, but I guess it's our lot in life to eat that stuff. We are of the zombie race, after all."

I shook my head. "I'm going to roast it. I love the smell of roasted rotten flesh, and it should keep away any players who think they can get the drop on us. It seems like players don't really like the smell of burning rotten flesh very much."

I reached into my inventory and pulled out a couple hunks of rotten cow flesh and tossed them on the furnace. They began to sizzle and smoke. I inhaled the noxious odor of decaying and burning flesh into my nostrils. I inhaled deeply and enjoyed the smell as it filled my own rotten lungs.

"It doesn't get any better than this." I said aloud to no one.

Bob looked at me and swore, "Netherrack! That is so nasty. It makes me want to barf up the wheat I just ate."

Harold nodded. "I forgot how gross it is to live in the same area as zombies. It was nice to have our own house away from you guys at the farm."

I looked at the chickens with sympathy but without any understanding because I thought rotten flesh was awesome. "Sorry guys. But a zombie's got to eat, ya feel?"

"Yeah, whatever," said Harold brushing a wing in my direction. "I think Bob and I are going to go to sleep now. Carrying you guys around all day has been tiring."

"That's cool," I said as I pulled the rotten flesh off the furnace. "Want me to bake some cookies before you go to bed?"

Harold looked like he might be sick. "Bake cookies on the same furnace where you just cooked that nasty rotten flesh?!? No."

I laughed. "Whatever. See you in the morning."

I watched as Bob and Harold walked over to their nests and tucked their beaks under their wings and fell asleep.

I cut the rotten flesh in half and extended a hunk of it to Otis on the tip of my diamond sword. Otis grunted as he grabbed the rotten flesh and chewed and swallowed it within about ten seconds.

"You should savor it," I said before taking a bite of the meat.

Succulent! Juicy! Delicious!

Otis spat a piece of rotten flesh that had been stuck in his teeth onto the ground. "Why? It's just rotten flesh."

"I don't know. Aren't you happy just to be alive? After what we had to go through fighting Herobrine a few years ago? I think every day is a gift."

Otis rolled his eyes. "Save me that New Age mumbo-jumbo. Every day is a *struggle*. A struggle for survival and dominance."

I felt sad for Otis. He would never be happy. The only time he ever felt good was when he was in battle defeating someone or something. "If you say so, Otis. If you say so."

"I am going to seal the entrance to the cave with cobblestone so nothing gets in here tonight," said Otis. "And, let's light a few torches so nothing weird spawns in the darkness."

I lit several torches and attached them to the walls while Otis sealed the door.

A few minutes later, Otis and I both lay down on the hard ground inside the cave and fell asleep.

* * *

Several hours into the night, I heard a strange noise. It sounded like a meowing ghast, but I could not tell from where it was coming. At first I thought it was coming from behind the blocked passageway, but then it sounded like it was coming from outside of the cave. A few seconds later it sounded like it was coming from underneath the ground. Finally, it sounded like it was coming from all directions at once.

And then, it stopped.

I reached over and shook Otis's shoulder. "Did you hear that?"

Otis yawned and said angrily, "The only thing I heard is your stupid voice in the middle of the night when I should be sleeping." Otis turned over on his side and went back to sleep.

I stayed awake for another ten or fifteen minutes, waiting for the sound to return, but it never did. I was anxious, the way you are when you wake up from a nightmare and, even though you know it wasn't real, you think it just might actually be. Eventually, though, my fatigue overtook my anxiety and I fell back to sleep.

* * *

No sounds returned during the rest of the night and I was able to sleep until the morning. Harold and Bob were already awake, sitting and staring at me, waiting for me to give them some wheat for breakfast. I reached into my inventory and tossed some wheat in their direction. They both said a quick "thank you" and then pecked their breakfast.

I looked over and saw Otis had already gotten out of bed. He was sharpening his sword.

"You eat yet, Otis?"

He nodded. "I had a loaf bread. Couldn't stand the thought of rotten flesh for breakfast."

I nodded my head. Maybe it had been the rotten flesh that given me some sort of weird auditory hallucination as I digested it during the night. "I think maybe I will have a few cookies and an apple for breakfast."

I reached into my inventory and pulled out a couple cookies and an apple. I sliced the apple into pieces with my diamond sword. My loose, rotten teeth would not allow me to bite directly into an apple. I had about three apple slices and one of the cookies when I said, "I'm going to look around outside for a minute."

I removed the rocks from the exit and stepped outside. What I saw shocked me greatly. Just a few paces in front of the mouth of the cave was a grave marker! A grave marker virtually *identical* to the one that had been in the corral where the llama had been stolen.

I was so shocked I dropped my cookie on the ground. I thought about picking it up and eating it, you know, the five-second rule and all, but I was too shocked to do anything other than approach the grave marker as if I were in a trance. When I was close enough to the marker, "The Warrior" appeared upon it. But that wasn't all. Leaning against the grave marker was a copy of my autobiography with a diamond necklace draped on top of it.

I screamed a high-pitched scream like a little baby. Otis, Bob, and Harold came running out of the cave to see what was the matter. The grave marker stopped them in their tracks.

"Is that what I think it is?" asked Otis.

I nodded wordlessly. I walked toward the gravestone and picked up the book. I inspected the diamond necklace first. Blue diamonds, like I suspected the llama hair would make. I handed the diamonds to Otis. I could tell he was thinking the same thing I had.

I took the book and opened it to the end. It was the version that had been put in the great library of Minecraft, and had not been published to the general public. It had all the information about my role in The Balance and my designation as The Warrior in the Balance of the Four.

"Let me try out that gravestone," said Harold as he slowly approached it. I backed away and my name disappeared from the gravestone. It was blank for a moment and then when Harold got close enough, it said "Harold, battle steed."

Harold clucked with joy. "Battle steed! I like that."

"Hey, what about me?" whined Bob. "Stand aside, Harold."

Harold moved to the side and the gravestone again went blank. Bob approached and the gravestone said, "Bob, steed."

A tear formed in Bob's eyes and he said, "What? I'm not a battle steed?"

Otis chuckled and said, "You are a battle steed to me. What does this stupid enchanted gravestone know anyway?"

Bob sniffed and wiped his beak with his wing. "It seems to know that Zeke's a warrior and that Harold is a battle steed."

"It's just part of the enchantment, I'm sure," I said. "I don't know what the purpose is, but I'm sure it's part of some strange plan."

"Yeah, Bob, the gravestone only said my name. It did not give me any title at all," said Otis. "At least you got a title!"

Bob nodded his head and dried the tears from his eyes. "I guess we are just the supporting actors in this drama, right Otis?"

Otis turned red in the face with anger. "I'm not a supporting actor! I could run this show myself, if I wanted to. Mark my words!"

Harold walked over to Bob and put an arm on his shoulder. "I don't think being called 'battle steed' is actually a good thing. Besides, we've both been through enough together that if I'm a battle steed, you are too. And, anyway, I'd rather just be a plain old chicken than to have to participate in these insane wars."

"Look, all kidding and emotional trauma aside, this is pretty weird," I said, trying to bring everyone back to the situation at hand and away from their own self-doubt.

But, of course, it got weirder.

At that very moment we heard laughter.

A distant, clear laughter.

It was a girl's laughter. Not a little toddler or a woman, but a young girl, probably between twelve or fourteen years old, if I had to guess. Just like the sound of the meowing ghast in the cave, the laughter seemed to come from a specific location for just a moment before it suddenly came from a different direction.

"Do you guys hear that too?" I asked.

By their stunned expressions I could tell they had.

Chapter 12

The laughter didn't last long, just a few seconds. After it stopped, Otis said, "Let's get going. We've still got another day and a half until we get to the High Castle. Besides, I don't want to stay here anymore."

We all agreed with Otis. We quickly packed our things, assumed our chicken and pigman jockey positions, and set off in the direction of the High Castle.

The first couple hours of the day were uneventful. The only unusual incident occurred when a player spotted us from far away, and yelled at us to stop. "I need more XP!" we heard him shout in the distance.

The four of us chuckled in unison and trotted away at top jockey speed. It looked like the player was trying to follow us for a while, but he soon gave up and we did not hear from him again.

* * *

Shortly before noon, we came to a field filled with flowers. Normally, I like looking at fields of flowers, but this field was unsettling. There were flowers in it that I had never seen before.

"Have you ever seen a tulip like this before?" I asked, pointing to what appeared to be a tulip, only it was black.

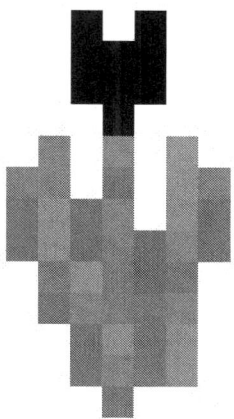

They all said no.

"Do you think maybe it's a flower that only exists in this biome and we've just never seen it before?" I said.

"I don't know, Zeke, I'm pretty sure the flowers of the Overworld are what they are. There aren't very many varieties. This seems suspicious," said Otis.

"I love flowers!" said Bob as he ran into the field of flowers clucking with happiness and breaking a trail as he crushed the stems of the flowers. He stopped for a moment and put his beak to one of the black tulips. "They smell great! Come smell them!"

Bob seemed to be having fun and I assumed any trap would've been sprung by now so I waded into the flower field and smelled them. They did smell nice. I bent down and put my nose to a black tulip. Even with my rotten nostrils, I could smell its strong fragrance. It was an unusual perfume but very lovely.

Otis and Harold followed me in and agreed that the field and, in particular the black tulips, smelled very nice.

"Zeke, you should collect some seeds from the flowers so you can grow them on the farm," suggested Harold.

"We're not florists!" snapped Otis. "I don't waste my time growing flowers. It's bad enough having to grow food for you chickens."

"Otis, you are such a meanie sometimes," I said as I reached down and pulled some seeds out of a flower head. I showed Harold the handful of seeds and smiled. He smiled back.

After tucking the seeds into my inventory, I looked around the field and noticed that I could not see Bob. "Hey, where's Bob?"

Otis and Harold looked around and could not see him either. We called Bob's name a few times but there was no response. We became worried and fanned out to look for him.

Only ten seconds into the search Harold yelled, "He's over here! It looks like he has passed out!" Otis and I ran over to where we saw Harold's wing signaling us, swinging back and forth above the tops of the flowers.

"Is he hurt?" asked Otis, genuine concern in his voice.

"It doesn't look like it. It's like he just fainted," said Harold, poking at Bob with his wing.

At that moment I started to feel a bit woozy myself. I glanced around the field and noticed that there was a fine mist of pollen from the flowers hovering above the field. It smelled of the black tulips.

It was then that I realized there was something in the pollen that induced sleep.

"Guys, I think it's a trap," I muttered right before everything went black.

Chapter 13

The next thing I knew I was walking through a snowy mountain biome. I was following the tracks of a polar bear. Why I had chosen to follow a powerful bear which probably could have torn me to shreds in a single swing, I did not know. Still, it seemed like a good idea at the time.

I knew I was hallucinating or dreaming or having visions because of the strange flowers. Still, it felt entirely real. I felt the snow crunching under my feet. I felt the cold penetrating my rotten bones. It was like I was living in two realities at the same time: One where I had passed out and was sleeping in a field of flowers and another where I was heading for an icy grave.

As I followed the bear tracks, I saw a stray wandering toward me. I knew strays spawned in these biomes. Our paths were going to cross. I was prepared for anything. I reached into my inventory ... but I could not find any weapons!

Hand to hand combat it is, then!

As the stray approached, I could hear his footsteps crunching in the snow. He looked at me with baleful, malign eyes. I was prepared to fight to the death, but he just walked up, gave me a wordless *what's-up-bro* head nod, and continued walking.

Weird.

I let out a sigh of relief and continued following the polar bear tracks until I reached the entrance to its cave. If I had believed this was real, I would never have entered the cave, but knowing that it was a hallucination, I pressed on into the darkness. Still, I felt extremely scared and worried that something very bad was going to happen.

I entered the dark cave and pulled a torch from my inventory and ignited it. The flickering light cast strange shadows against the walls of the cave. I noticed a small alcove cut into the back of the cave. I approached it slowly. I could hear the bear breathing in a slow rhythm. When I got close enough, I held the torch in front of the alcove, and the bear's fiery eyes stared out at me.

"What are you doing in my cave?"

I didn't know polar bears could talk. But, I played it off like I'd been talking to bears since I was a child.

"I don't know. I just followed your tracks here."

The bear looked at me like I was an idiot. "Why did you start following my tracks?"

Why did *I start following his tracks?*

"I don't know. I just woke up and I was following your tracks."

The bear slapped his forehead with his giant white pawn. "Are you daft man? Why would a little puny zombie like you follow the tracks of a big strong polar bear?"

"I already told you. I don't know."

The polar bear scratched the fur on his neck with his claws and said, "Maybe you're supposed to ask me something? Maybe you think I'm some sort of wise old hermit bear or something."

I scrunched up my eyebrows, confused. "Is that possible? Are there wise old hermit bears?"

The bear chuckled a deep chuckle and said, "No. There are not. I was just messing with you."

"I think this has been a worthless trip. I'm sorry to have bothered you," I said.

The bear shrugged his shoulders and said, "No big deal. Just don't bother me again or I might have to make you go away.... Permanently."

The bear did not issue his threat with menace, only in the matter-of-fact way of the world of nature. Kill or be killed.

"Understood," I said as I backed away from the bear and began walking toward the exit of the cave.

But, before I could get to the exit, I saw the Ender King standing in front of me.

"King! It's been a while. Where have you been?"

The King shook his head in disgust at my stupid question and said, "In the End, of course. Where else would I be?"

"I suppose you're right. I don't know why bothered to ask," I said.

"I read your book," said the Ender King. "I thought you captured everything quite well."

"Thanks."

And then without warning, the Ender King turned into Notch!

The amazing part was, I wasn't the least bit surprised. I didn't gasp or say "Oh!" or faint or anything like that. It was like I knew it was going to happen.

"Hi, Notch," I said.

Notch smiled and said, "Zeke. How have you been? Thank you so much for writing your autobiography about the battle to stop Herobrine from destroying the world."

"No problem. It only took me like six or eight months of sitting in a dank room writing when I could've been doing something else. But, I'm not bitter."

I meant it as a joke, but Notch did not laugh. "Zeke, you are part of the Balance. Being part of the Balance carries with it certain responsibilities. The least you could do is write your life down so it can be an example to others."

"It's cool, Notch. It was kind of fun once I got started. Writing the first fifty pages was really difficult, but once I got the hang of it, the words came pretty easily."

Notch smiled and began to open his mouth say something, but before he could, he turned into Herobrine.

Again, I should have been shocked, but I was not.

"Zeke, I see you are off trying to be a goody-goody again. In search of some pathetic llama."

I shook my head sadly. "Herobrine, sometimes people do things just be nice."

Herobrine rolled his eyes and said, "I've never done that. Besides, what's the point of going after someone's pet llama other than to make yourself feel good and try to recapture some of the old glory days when you barely defeated me."

"While I agree you and a llama are very similar, I'm not trying to recapture any old glory. I'm just trying to find something to pass the time."

"Why don't you pass the time on your farm growing wheat for your stupid chickens?"

"Why are you trying to stop me from finding this llama?"

For the briefest of instants, Herobrine looked confused or upset, like this wasn't going according to script.

"I'm not trying to stop you from finding the llama. Go ahead and find it if you want to. I just think it's a waste of time. You could be doing something much more interesting, like mining the Nether or exploring the End, or something like that."

"I'm not sure how interesting any of those things would be, but regardless, we can discuss it tomorrow in person."

Herobrine squinted his eyes and said, "But, we are discussing it in person now."

I shook my head and said, "This is some sort of weird dream or hallucination. You're not really there. But I'll be at your High Castle tomorrow. We can discuss it then."

At that moment Herobrine disappeared and was replaced by an evoker. The evoker began moving his hands and little bubbles appeared. Then three vexes appeared and came after me.

I ran from the cave as fast as I could. As I ran, pursued by the attacking vexes, evoker fangs thrust themselves up from the ground and tried to bite me and kill me.

I don't know why I thought this, but I felt that if I died during this hallucination, then I would die in real life. I kept running, dodging evoker fangs and vexes until I ran to the edge of the snow biome. There was a sheer cliff. The only thing I could do was stand and fight or jump off the cliff.

I was tempted to jump and take my chances.

Instead, I reached into my inventory. This time, my weapons were there! I pulled my diamond sword from my inventory ready to slice the vexes from the air. I stood at the ready. The vexes kept coming towards me but, right when I was about to slash at them, they disappeared!

I suddenly felt very tired and lay down on the snow to go to sleep.

As I drifted off I heard a girl's laughter echoing in my ears.

Chapter 14

When I regained consciousness, there were no more flowers, just a field of green grass. I saw Harold, Otis, and Bob strewn about the field, apparently having passed out just like me. I watched as they also began to wake up. I rubbed my head a few times and then shook it before I stood up and began walking over to Harold. I still felt dizzy, but the world was slowly coming into focus.

"Harold? Harold? Are you all right?"

Harold rubbed his face with a wing and looked at me and nodded his head. "Check on Bob."

I walked over to Bob, who was just now opening his eyes. I knelt down and held his shoulders and asked, "You okay, buddy?"

Bob nodded his head and said, "I think so. That was weird."

"I'm sick of this stuff. I don't like being treated like this," said Otis, who had walked up behind us.

"You okay, Otis?" I asked.

"You think some stupid enchantment that makes me pass out is going to hurt me? No way!"

"I had a weird dream," I said. "What about you guys?"

"I saw nothing. I felt like I was made of smoke floating in complete blackness," said Bob. "I had a feeling I had died and I was being prepared to respawn."

"I saw a llama, standing in a white room. It was the blue llama we seek, but it never moved and we did not communicate in any way," said Harold.

"What about you, Otis?" I asked.

Otis shrugged. "I just saw some piglets. They reminded me of my friends when I was younger. They were playing a game before some players arrived and slaughtered them. If you read my diary, you would know all about it."

"Dude, now is not the time to bring up your anger with me that my nine-book autobiography is better than yours," I said. Before Otis could retort, I quickly added, "I had a strange vision too. There was this weird polar bear in a cave, and then I talked to the Ender King, Notch, and Herobrine before an evoker tried to kill me. But when I faced it down, it gave up and I fell asleep."

"What does all this insanity mean, Zeke?" asked Harold.

I shrugged and shook my head. "I don't know. Can insanity ever mean anything? The only one of us who had a vision anything like what we are doing right now was Harold. The rest of us just had peculiar visions. At least Otis's was tied to something in the past. I've never seen a polar bear. And Bob might have respawned in the past but I'm sure you would not remember it, do you?"

"No, I do not."

Otis grunted and then spat on the ground twice. "This is stupid. It's just Herobrine playing a trick on us, isn't it obvious? Who else could make a field of enchanted flowers and make us go to sleep and have visions?"

"Notch could probably do it," suggested Bob.

Otis snorted forcefully to express his anger. I noticed he had to reverse snort the tip of a booger back into his nose before he started speaking. "Why would Notch do something like that? This is the work of a prankster. Notch might be kind of clueless sometimes and he did, after all, create a world where it's kill or be killed, but he wouldn't do something like this."

"We'll figure this out," said Harold confidently. "We've always managed to figure everything out during our adventures."

Bob's little skinny chicken legs started shaking with fear and he said, "But, Harold, we've always had someone there to help us, like the Ender King. Do you think we can actually figure this out on our own?"

"Of course we can," said Otis. "If it weren't for that stupid Ender King we probably would have defeated Herobrine in book 7 of Zeke's autobiography instead of book 9."

I was getting sick of the bickering and was about to put a stop to it when I looked up in the sky. I noticed that the sun was getting close to setting. It would be dark in less than an hour and a half. "Look at the time! We must have been asleep for six or seven hours!"

Everyone looked up at the sun and saw what I meant. Otis was exasperated. "Well, now it might take us another two days to get to the High Castle. I was hoping we'd put a lot of distance under our feet today."

Bob huffed, pointed at Harold, and said, "You mean *our* feet?"

"Whatever," said Otis. "Distance is distance, no matter how you get there." Bob and Harold did not seem convinced.

I smiled and then nodded my head in agreement with Otis. "Maybe this setback will actually be a boon to us."

"Boon? Seriously? You talk like that?" said Otis.

I rolled my eyes but did not respond to his taunts. "What I mean is, there is a village nearby that was very friendly to me when I was on my book tour a couple of years ago. There are some villager kids there who will probably put us up for the night. We can get a good rest and a good meal and then reassess our plans."

Harold and Bob were extremely happy at the suggestion. They clucked repeatedly and flapped their wings. "Oh boy, a warm bed for a change," said Bob.

"Oh yes. And maybe some freshly harvested wheat," said Harold, drool forming on the edges of his beak.

Otis kicked the ground in frustration. "I think we should just stay in a cave. The less people who know about our mission the better."

I laughed. "Mission? We're just going to recover a llama. Sure, there's some weird stuff related to the llama's disappearance and the llama's hair makes diamonds, but I'm not sure I'd call a 'mission'."

Otis took a couple steps toward me, grabbed my shirt, and pulled my face toward his. As he spoke I could smell his disgusting rotten zombie pigman breath.

Was my breath that bad?

"Listen, Zeke, this *is* a mission. Not only was there a magical gravestone at the corral were the llama was stolen and the llama makes diamonds from its hair, but we've heard a mysterious, invisible little girl laughing twice, and now we have been poisoned in some way and made to pass out for six hours. If this is not a 'mission,' I don't know what is!"

When I gave it some thought, I had to agree that Otis was right. This was a mission.

Chapter 15

We arrived at the village about thirty minutes before sunset. As we walked into the town, several villagers stopped to stare at us. I could see their fearful expressions. It had been nearly two years since I'd been here on my book signing, and I'm sure the same villagers who now regarded me fearfully had lined up excitedly to get my book signed. But, now all they saw was a chicken jockey come to murder them in their sleep.

I waved to them. They cautiously, reluctantly waved back. Their expressions betrayed their continued discomfort.

"It is I, Baby Zeke!"

The villagers looked confused for a moment and then their faces relaxed and they smiled.

"I have your book in my library," said one adult male villager.

"Oh yes. I love that book. And so does my son," said an adult villager woman.

"Thank you," I said. "I was wondering if you could point me in the direction of the Johnson household."

Both of the villagers nodded their heads and pointed in unison to an adjoining street.

"Go down that street there for a distance of five houses and then turn left. Follow that street for a distance of four houses, turn down the next street and the Johnson place is the first house on the right," said the woman.

"Thank you," I said as I gave them a salute with my rotten hand and led the way toward the Johnson house.

As we progressed down the street on our chickens, Otis muttered, "Stupid villagers. They were all super scared of us until they found out you are the great Baby Zeke. Villagers will never like mobs. Never treat us fairly."

I shrugged. "I suppose you're right. When you live in a world where chicken jockeys and pigman jockeys are hostile mobs, for the most part, it stands to reason you would have that stereotype firmly in your brain."

"I guess, but I wish Notch would not have made the world like that. It'd be nice if we could get a chance once in a while to show who we really were," said Otis.

"Getting philosophical on me, eh?" I said.

Otis rolled his eyes. "Just speaking the truth. Philosophy has got nothing to do it."

I looked down and saw Harold and Bob exchanging glances and rolling their eyes at each other. They were the lowest on the food totem pole, and they knew it. They were just living life moment by moment, existing in the now, not concerned about what others thought of them, only survival.

We soon arrived in front of the Johnson house. It was a typical wooden villager house. Simple and functional. I dismounted from Harold and walked up to the front door and knocked. After a few seconds a woman opened the door, saw me, and screamed before slamming the door in my face.

"Told you," said Otis, running the underside of a fingernail against one of his teeth in order to remove the dirt lodged there.

I shook my head and knocked again. The door cracked slightly and the woman looked through the crack with one eyeball. "What do you want?"

"Is this the Johnson residence?"

"Yes," she said cautiously.

"I'm here to see Bill and Ted."

The woman gasped and said, "Why would you want to see my two boys? You're going to try to kill them, aren't you?"

I laughed and said, "No, I'm Baby Zeke. After my book signing in town last year, we hung out. I was passing through town and thought they might want to do something."

The woman opened the door a little farther and said, "Oh, Baby Zeke. I didn't recognize you. I mean, all of you baby zombies look the same, really."

"True, and all the villagers look pretty much the same too. It's a strange, visually monotonous world we live in," I said.

At that moment I heard footsteps running across the floor inside the house and then the door was pulled open. Standing there were Bill and Ted. Bill was about twelve years old, his brother Ted was about ten.

"Baby Zeke!" said Ted. "You're back!"

"Yeah, cool," said Bill.

I smiled. "I'm here with Otis and our chickens. We have been travelling and still have a distance to go before we reach our destination. Do you think we all could come in and maybe spend the night?"

The two boys looked at their mother and said, "Can they? Can they?"

Mrs. Johnson looked concerned. I could tell she didn't want a zombie and a pigman in her house at night. I mean, honestly, who could blame her?

She nervously clutched and released the front of her robe three times before saying, "I guess. We will have to check with your father, but I suppose they could sleep out in the storage shed. We could set up a couple beds in there."

"Yay!" shouted the boys.

I smiled and said, "Thank you."

Behind me Otis was grumbling. I heard him mutter, "Storage shed? Keep the riff-raff out of the house."

I turned around and shot him a look, hoping he would get the hint to shut up. "Isn't that great, Otis? We can stay here tonight in a safe place."

Otis looked up at me with eyes filled with hatred but managed to say, "Yeah. Great."

A few minutes later we were sitting in Bill and Ted's bedroom. I explained to them that we were looking for a missing item, but didn't tell them much more. I left them convinced it was some sort of amazing quest, not just some recovery of a llama. Why should I shatter their vision of me and my greatness?

I noticed they had action figures of me and Otis along with the Ender King sitting on some bookshelves.

"Where did you get those action figures?" I asked.

They looked a little embarrassed but said, "We crafted them ourselves."

Otis walked over and picked up his mini-me and said, "This actually looks pretty good. Maybe you kids should sell these things. It might earn you some emeralds."

Both of the boys smiled so broadly that their entire faces turned into teeth. (Not really, but you get the idea.)

"Really?" said Ted. "That ... hurrr ... would be awesome."

"Yeah, maybe we should do that, Ted," said Bill, an edge of villager greed creeping into his voice.

Otis put the action figure down and returned to where he had been sitting. As he crossed the floor his foot stepped on board that made a hollow sound. The board was underneath a rug so he moved the rug and saw there was a door. He looked at the boys and said, "Is this a Minestagram portal?"

"Yeah, it was just installed about a month ago," said Bill.

I was confused. "I thought only the village where we fought Shadow, Herobrine's minion, had a Minestagram?"

"Oh, yeah, that's where it started," said Bill. "But they got some venture capital investing from some villagers and they've been expanding it to all the villages."

"That must be really expensive," said Harold. "How much does it cost you to have a Minestagram portal?"

Ted smiled and said, "It's free! You just have to look at an advertisement once in a while."

"No such thing as a free lunch," said Bob.

At that moment there was a knocking at the door of the Minestagram portal.

"Cool, someone must have sent us a gram," said Bill walking to the door and lifting it up. His face suddenly looked disappointed and he said, "Oh, it's just an advertisement."

"I've never seen an advertisement," I said. "Let me check it out."

I walked over the door and I saw a square piece of paper that said, "Try the amazing Minecraft series from Dr. Block: *The Diary of a Surfer Villager*. Available now for children ages 9+."

"Interesting. I might have to check out that series," I said. "So that's what an advertisement is? It tells you about stuff you can buy?"

The villagers nodded their heads. "Basically. Sometimes they just want to pass on information or something, but usually it's to get you to buy something."

At that moment, Mr. Johnson knocked on the door and said, "Hi, I'm back from work. I heard Baby Zeke and Otis were in here."

Otis and I stood up and said hello to Mr. Johnson.

"Dinner is just about ready. Do you two like mushroom stew, bread, and apples?"

"Well, we prefer rotten flesh, but that'll do. Thank you," I said.

Mr. Johnson looked uncomfortable and pulled at the collar of his robe. "Um, yeah ... hurrr ... we don't have any rotten flesh. I guess you'll have to go find some of that yourself if you really want it."

"It's okay. We can eat just about anything," said Otis. "We might have to cut it into small pieces, but we will choke it down."

Mr. Johnson looked at Otis suspiciously, but said nothing. He looked at his two boys and said, "Okay, wash up and come to dinner." Then he looked over at me, Otis, and the chickens and said, "If you want to join us for dinner in the dining room, you need to wash up too, otherwise you can just take some food and eat it in the storage shed."

"We'll wash up and join you," I said before Otis could say anything insulting.

* * *

Dinner with the Johnsons was uneventful and we had a pretty good meal. We hung out with Bill and Ted for a couple hours after dinner and then their parents told them they had to go to sleep, so we went out to the storage shed.

It was roomy and warm though not very comfortable. Still, better than a cave. Otis and I each had a quick snack of rotten flesh from our inventories before bed and I gave the chickens a few grains of wheat.

We all said good night to each other and went to sleep. Tomorrow would be a big day. We would arrive at the High Castle.

Chapter 16

I woke up the next morning after a refreshing night of sleep. No bad dreams, no tossing and turning, nothing weird. Especially, no little girl's laughter.

Otis and the chickens woke up shortly after I did, and we all went inside the Johnson household to see about breakfast. Mr. and Mrs. Johnson were in the kitchen preparing bread, cookies, sliced fruit, and even some cooked steak.

"The steak smells good," I said.

Mr. Johnson looked at me and smiled. "I know it isn't rotten, but I thought maybe you'd like some meat for breakfast."

"I'll say," said Otis gruffly. "I ain't no vegetarian."

Bill and Ted were sitting at the table and said, "Come over here, and sit with us."

We sat down and Bill sheepishly removed a copy of my nine-book autobiography from his inventory, held it out to me, and asked, "Would you autograph this for me?"

"Didn't I sign one for you when I was here on my book tour?"

Bill grimaced. "You did, but I dropped it in the mud and it got ruined."

Otis laughed as I signed the book and returned it to Bill.

After he tucked my book away, Bill removed another book from his inventory and handed it to Otis. "Would you sign my copy of your diary?"

Otis appeared to be in a state of shock. He was suddenly proud and happy. I saw tears beginning to form in his eyes but he quickly blinked his eyes to hide his emotion and said, "Sure, kid, give it here. You have a quill?"

Bill pulled a quill from a pocket inside his robe and handed it to Otis. Otis opened to the first page of the book and asked, "Do you want me to write anything special?"

Bill shrugged and said, "I don't know, maybe just 'To Bill: I like your action figures. From, Otis' or something like that?"

Otis nodded and began writing. Here is what he wrote:

> *Bill, it is clear that you have really good taste in Minecraft diaries. The fact that you own mine proves you are a truly intelligent, thoughtful villager. I wish more villagers were like you.*
>
> *Sincerely, Otis, the Pigman*
>
> *P.S. – I think your action figures are really awesome.*

Otis handed the book back to Bill and said, "How about that?"

Bill took a moment to read the inscription and smiled. He looked up at Otis and said, "That's awesome! I'm going to put this right next my Baby Zeke diary."

I could tell Ted was jealous. So I said, "Ted, I'm sure Otis would sign your copy."

"No, it's cool. Bill and I can read the same book. I don't have enough money to buy a copy of it."

At that moment Otis shyly reached into his inventory and pulled out a brand new copy of his diary. "Ted, I don't normally tell people this, but I carry a few spare copies around just in case. I will sign one for you too."

Ted got really excited and screamed with happiness. "Hurray! You're the best, Otis."

"Even better than Zeke?" Otis asked hopefully.

Ted looked back and forth between us and said, "Hurrr, I guess you guys are about equally cool."

Very diplomatic for such a young villager.

"I'll take that," said Otis as he began writing in Ted's diary. Here's what he wrote:

> *Ted, you seem like pretty awesome kid. I hope that you do not grow up to be a greedy, annoying villager like so many of you are. Everyone always wanted me to change, but I never did. Always be yourself.*
>
> *Sincerely, Otis, the Pigman.*

Otis handed the book back to Ted who read the inscription and smiled. "Thanks, man."

The gift exchange completed, we ate a delicious breakfast with the Johnson family. After about twenty minutes, Mr. Johnson stood up and said, "Well, I need to leave and open the store. The players should be starting to come around looking for trades. I'll see how much money I can make today."

We all waved to Mr. Johnson. Bill and Ted hugged him goodbye and Mrs. Johnson gave him a peck on the cheek.

Mr. Johnson walked to the front door and opened it. But he didn't step outside. He just stood there staring. After a few seconds he turned around and said to all of us, "You have to see this."

Chapter 17

The tone of Mr. Johnson's voice indicated that he was astonished, concerned, and maybe a little scared. We all stood up and walked over to the door. What I saw shook me to the very core of my undead, rotten soul.

In the front yard, just a few steps from the door, was a grave marker! The grave marker was just like the other two we had encountered. Surrounding the grave marker were some diamonds. But, the most shocking thing of all was the path of diamonds leading from the grave marker through the streets of the village.

"I don't believe this," said Otis.

I walked up to the grave marker, and as expected, it said, "The Warrior." Then I backed away quickly before the villagers could see the words on the grave marker and said, "Mr. Johnson, I bet if you walk up to the grave marker it will show your name."

He looked at me with a strange expression on his face but decided he would try it. When he approached, the grave marker read "Ben Johnson."

He gasped and then backed away and his name disappeared.

Mr. Johnson looked at me and said, "What is the meaning of this? What evil have you brought to this house?"

"We've been looking for something and ever since we started our search, someone has been messing with us, putting these gravestones here and there. We don't know who's doing it."

"It's obviously Herobrine," said Ted confidently.

"I don't know," I said. "It seems different. That doesn't necessarily seem malicious, the way it would if he was doing it. It just seems .... bizarre."

"By the way, have any of you heard the strange, disembodied laughter of a young girl around here?" asked Otis.

Why, Otis? Why?

Everyone looked at him in shock. Mrs. Johnson grasped the front of her robe and said, "You have been seeing gravestones and hearing disembodied laughter everywhere you go, and you come to our house?!?

What kind of mobs are you to put us in this sort of danger? What manner of evil have you brought upon us?"

"I can assure you, there is no danger," I said.

But Mr. and Mrs. Johnson did not believe me. I couldn't blame them. "I think you and your chickens better leave immediately," said Mr. Johnson. "I appreciate what you did for the world of Minecraft a few years ago, but I can't let you endanger my family."

"But, in the name of Notch, there's no – ."

Mr. Johnson cut me off with a raised hand and said sternly, "Get out. Now."

Bill and Ted grabbed their parents' robes and pulled on them and said, "No! Baby Zeke is cool. And so is Otis. Let them stay!"

"Kids, it's okay. I totally understand why your parents want us to leave. If I were in their places, I'd want us to leave too," I said sadly. "I hope you can forgive us someday."

Bill and Ted nodded their heads. "Of course we can," said Bill.

"Thank you," I said. I looked at Mr. and Mrs. Johnson, hoping they might be able to show me a little bit of kindness, but they didn't. I understood. They were protecting their children.

I looked at Otis and Harold and Bob and said, "You guys have everything?"

They all nodded to me.

"Well, then, let's follow those diamonds and see where they lead," I said as I hopped on Harold.

Chapter 18

As we followed the diamond-paved path through the streets of the village, we saw dozens of greedy villagers using pickaxes to dislodge the diamonds from the cobblestone streets where they were embedded.

I heard one villager say to another, "Hurrr, this is the easiest money I've ever made!"

"Yeah, so much better than making trades with players," said another.

"Stupid villagers," mumbled Otis under his breath.

We followed the trail and soon realized that it was leading in a direction away from the High Castle. We looked out into the distance and the trail went on as far as we could see, eventually disappearing into a nearby forest.

"I don't think we should follow these diamonds much further," said Harold. "Wasn't the point of this little adventure to get to the High Castle and talk to Herobrine?"

I nodded my head and said, "That's true, but obviously whoever made this trail put that grave marker in front of the Johnson's house, and that's probably the same person who stole the llama we are after."

"This is stupid," said Otis. "It's probably Herobrine and he is probably trying to lead us away from the High Castle because that's where he has the llama. He probably made all these diamonds the other day by shaving the llama."

"That can't be right," I said. "The villager who hired us said the llama could only make a few hundred diamonds per shaving. This path consists of at least several thousand diamonds."

"And who knows how far it goes once it enters the forest," said Bob, fluffing up his feathers while he spoke.

Otis pondered for a moment before saying, "I have to admit, the idea of following a trail made of diamonds and, well, maybe pulling them out as we went along, sounds pretty lucrative, but I'm a bit concerned about the misdirection here."

I thought for a moment. I looked at the gleaming trail of diamonds extending into the forest and thought that it would probably be worth taking a risk to follow the trail, at least for a while. "How about this guys? We follow the trail for half the day, and if it hasn't led us to a clue by lunchtime, we can break off and head to the High Castle. Deal?"

The three of them looked at each other and shrugged their shoulders a little bit. "I suppose that sounds like a good idea. Anyway, you're in charge, aren't you? You're 'the Warrior' after all," said Otis, his voice dripping with sarcasm.

I sighed. "If you want me to be the leader, I'll be the leader. You just have to listen to me."

Otis rolled his eyes but said, "Fine then. Be the leader."

I hopped back on to Harold and we continued along the diamond trail. Every time we stopped to rest, Otis pried a few diamonds out of the path and put them into his inventory. I looked at him taking the diamonds and shook my head.

"What?" he said. "This is what people do in the world of Minecraft, they take resources and make things. Why should I pass up pre-made diamonds?"

"I don't care. I just think it's funny that you like diamonds so much."

"I'm gonna make a bunch of diamond armor suits and sell them to players. Maybe the trades could provide us with all the wheat we need so we don't have to grow it ourselves. Farming is stupid."

"There's nothing wrong with being a farmer," I said.

"Yeah, farming is cool!" said Harold.

Otis looked at the chicken with hate in his eyes. "You only say that because you don't have to do any farming. You just sit around and peck your feathers and eat free food all day long."

Bob stood up and walked over to Otis, who was just putting another diamond into his inventory. Bob poked Otis's chest with the tip of his wing and said, "Do not talk to my friend like that! You do it again, and you're walking the whole way. No more free rides."

Otis paused for a moment and, apparently realizing what a fool he'd been or maybe just worried about getting sore feet, said, "I'm sorry. I apologize. I'm just stressed out. We haven't done this sort of thing in a couple of years, and I forgot how tiring and stressful it can be."

Bob's face softened as Otis's apology issued from his mouth. The apology seemed genuine. Bob said, "That's okay. If Harold forgives you, I forgive you."

Otis looked over at Harold, blinking his eyes and hoping for forgiveness. Harold pursed his lips and tapped his foot on the ground and after a few seconds said, "I guess I can forgive you ... this time. Don't let it happen again."

Otis smiled and said, "I'll try not to. I'm a bit hot-blooded you know."

Bob, Harold, and I all said in unison, "We know."

Chapter 19

We walked for another twenty minutes before we entered the edges of the forest. The tree cover was not particularly thick, so there was no danger of hostile nighttime mobs lurking at this time of day. We continued along the diamond trail, marveling at how many diamonds had been embedded in the ground.

"It wouldn't surprise me if all the diamond ore in the world had been used up to make this path," said Bob.

"Oh, this has to be some sort of enchanted path," said Harold. "There is no way that someone mined the amount of ore necessary to make all these diamonds."

"I know, I was just making an observation about how amazing this all is," said Bob.

Otis, who was walking alongside Bob because Bob said he wanted a break from carrying him, was beginning to breathe heavily due to the weight of the hundreds of diamonds he had now tucked into his inventory.

"Can we take a break guys?" said Otis, huffing and puffing.

We stopped and I said, "You need to get rid of some of those diamonds. You're going to slow us down. Bob won't even let you ride on him anymore."

Otis raised a hand and pushed at the air in front of him in a dismissive gesture. "So what. I'll happily carry all these diamonds back home. I'm gonna be set for life when we reach the end of this path."

During our rest break, we all had a little bit of water and a snack. I had some rotten pig flesh, which was greatly offensive to Otis. He had some rotten cow flesh. The chickens were able to eat some old bread.

As we again began walking along the diamond path, further into the forest, a chilly wind came up, and made us feel the chill in our bones. I sat astride Harold, whom I could feel shivering beneath me.

"What's with that icy wind?" asked Harold.

"It does seem a bit unusual for this time of day. Especially a sunny day. It feels like a nighttime wind," I said.

As we continued, the wind got stronger and stronger, but never so strong we felt like we could not continue. I would describe it as a stiff breeze, rather than a gale or a hurricane.

The sun was approaching midday, which was our self-imposed deadline to find a clue or an end to the diamond trail. It appeared as though we would not find anything of use to us and would have to turn back to the village and then move on to the High Castle.

I looked ahead and saw that the diamond path moved up a nearby hill. I turned around and said, "Let's get to the top of that hill and see what we can from its vantage point. If we don't see anything useful, we can eat lunch and then turn around."

Everyone agreed with my suggestion and we made it to the top of the hill. The hill had almost no trees on it and the surrounding area was plainly visible. Incredibly, the diamond path continued beyond the hill to the horizon, appearing infinite in length.

"This is so strange," I said. "I can't believe it continues so far. Oh well, we agreed we'd stop and turn back, so let's eat lunch and then turn around."

I dismounted Harold and sat down on the ground. Everyone else sat down and we had an enjoyable lunch, talking about old times and what it was going to be like to see Herobrine again, this time on what we assumed would be friendlier terms.

The wind continued to blow so we propped ourselves against a rock which offered a buffer against the wind. It felt good to lean up against the rock which had been warmed by the rays of sun. I looked over and saw Harold and Bob curled up with their eyes closed, resting. Taking a nap sounded like a good idea and I decided I would close my eyes for a few minutes before we turned back. Otis himself was continuing to pry diamonds up from the pathway. I smiled to myself about how silly he was and then closed my eyes.

* * *

I wasn't sure how long I had been asleep, but when I woke up I heard Otis yelling, "Let go of me! Let go of me!"

"Fine," said a gruff voice. I looked and saw Otis being shoved from behind, and then he stumbled to the ground, almost landing in my lap. I turned my eyes to see who had done the shoving.

It was a pillager! He stood there holding his crossbow and laughing.

"Who falls asleep in the Overworld without having a shelter! You guys are just a couple of stupid noobs."

I stood up and pulled my diamond sword from my inventory. Unfortunately, I wasn't wearing my diamond armor. In fact, I wasn't wearing any armor, just regular clothes. *Maybe I was a noob?* Nevertheless, I bravely said, "You think you can take all four of us? Who's the fool now?"

Actually, I still was the fool because at that moment two more pillagers and three vindicators emerged from behind trees. The vindicators menacingly held their iron axes while the pillagers readied their crossbows.

"We were told you would be here," said one of the illagers.

He was told?

"Who told you that? No one knew we were coming here, except some people in the village."

"I'll never tell," he snarled.

"You guys must want my diamonds, right?" said Otis. "There's plenty more in this road. Get them yourself."

All six of the thugs laughed at us. "We don't care about diamonds. We're being paid very well for this. We've been hired to assassinate you."

And with that, the vindicators moved in with their axes while the pillagers remained back to shoot us with crossbows if we tried to escape. I quickly jumped on Harold's back and dashed toward the nearest vindicator, and with rapid precision that I had forgotten I was capable of, I chopped his head off in one clean blow. He disappeared in a puff of smoke, dropping only his axe.

The other illagers seemed surprised at my dominance. One of them said, "Just a lucky shot. Even noobs can get a critical hit once in a while. Let's get them."

Otis had pulled out his diamond sword but he was moving very slowly due to the weight of all the diamonds in his inventory. He shook his head and cursed, "Netherrack," before dropping all of his diamonds on the ground. He leapt onto Bob's back and the two of us, Baby Zeke the chicken jockey and Otis the pigman jockey, charged the two vindicators. It was a quick battle. They were no match for our speed.

Only now, that the vindicators were dead, the pillagers had a clean shot at us with their crossbows. I looked over and saw them squeezing the triggers of their crossbows. I yelled to my friends, "Run as fast as you can! Take cover!"

Harold and I went one direction; Bob and Otis another. The pillagers selected their targets and pulled their crossbow triggers. It was only after they fired that they realized what we had done to them. We had fled in opposite directions, causing the pillagers to fire their weapons across each other. Two of the pillagers died instantly as the crossbow bolts entered their hearts. The third pillager's bolt, which had been aimed at me, missed and landed with a THUNK in the trunk of a tree.

You may not know this, but reloading a crossbow takes some time. You have to put the end on the ground, put your foot in a stirrup, and then pull on the string to notch it in a holder before you can load another bolt. Those few seconds were all we needed. We closed in on the remaining pillager and with a few quick blows, killed him. He dropped his crossbow. I looked around and saw another crossbow on the ground.

"Otis, grab that crossbow. I'll get this one."

Otis did as I asked and retrieved the crossbow. "It's heavier than I thought. But it may come in handy," he said, tucking it into his inventory. I tucked the other crossbow into my inventory.

"Who do you think sent those guys?" asked Bob.

I was about to tell him that I had no idea, when I heard a girl's laughter in the background.

Chapter 20

After the mysterious laughter ceased, we began walking down the hill. But, we did not get far because the ground suddenly gave out beneath us without warning. I could feel Harold fall away from me into the darkness.

The two chickens screamed.

Otis said, "Netherrack."

I just wondered what could possibly happen next.

Fortunately, we fell for only about one second before landing with a THUD on some hard rocks. A shaft of light came through the hole down which we had fallen, delineating a jagged oval of light on the ground.

I quickly pulled a couple of torches from my inventory and ignited them. Otis did the same. We attached two torches to nearby walls while each of us held a torch. We looked around and saw silverfish everywhere, scurrying away from us. In one corner of the room, I noticed a silverfish spawner.

"We must be in a stronghold," I said.

Otis nodded. "Yeah, so how the heck did the ground suddenly give way just as we were leaving the hill?"

"It's quite suspicious," said Harold.

"Of course it's suspicious! This has got to be related to all the weird stuff we've been encountering," said Otis.

"You might be right, but maybe it was just a weak spot in the hillside," I said.

Before Otis could answer with some sort of snappy and angry statement, we heard the girl's laughter echoing through the stronghold.

Otis gave me the side eye and said, "You were saying?"

I sighed. "Who is this little girl and what does she want from us?"

In response, the laughter grew suddenly louder and then went completely silent.

"Arrgh," said Otis in frustration. "I hate this kid."

I'd had enough of this as well. "Get your pickaxe, Otis, and let's mine through this wall and get out of this stronghold."

We reached into our inventories and pulled out pickaxes. But, before we could approach the wall and begin mining, the floor beneath our feet gave out again. We fell for a brief moment before landing in the next layer of the stronghold. Our torches remained ignited, and we saw that we had landed inside of a library.

"Why a library? Does she want us to read these books?" said Otis angrily.

"Getting concerned here, Zeke," said Harold. "What if we keep falling?"

"We will probably come out on the other side of the Overworld," said Bob, sounding way too happy about that possibility.

"Bob, you fool, the Overworld is flat. Eventually, we probably will fall into some lava or maybe into endless blank space," said Otis.

Bob suddenly started to shiver with fear. "I don't like lava or endless blank space."

"Don't listen to him, Bob," said Harold, putting a protective wing around Bob's shoulder. "We'll find a way out of this."

At that moment, there was a short burst of the girl's laughter, and we fell down another hole. We just missed falling into a pool of lava! When we recovered from the fall, we saw that we were in the end portal room of the stronghold.

This gave me an idea, and I yelled at my friends, "Quickly, dive into the end portal! The Ender King will know what to do."

At that moment I heard the girl's voice scream, "No!" I could feel the ground beginning to give way beneath my feet but before we could fall into another layer we jumped in the end portal and everything went black.

Chapter 21

That's right, I voluntarily jumped into an end portal. Back into the end nectar. Harold had been through before, so he knew what to expect, but this was Otis and Bob's first time.

I tried to find Bob or Otis in the twilight of the end nectar but could not locate them. I would have turned my head to search for them, but I was paralyzed. In the distance I could see two small endermen floating around, waiting to respawn.

I couldn't make myself breathe. I felt like I was drowning and going to die, but I knew it was going to end ... eventually. I felt sorry for Otis and Bob, who were probably panicking.

I wondered why players voluntarily went to the End to try to kill the Ender Dragon. Why would they subject themselves this horrible nectar? Or, maybe they were spared its horrors for some reason?

Eventually we came out on the other side. We had arrived in the End.

I was breathing heavily, trying to recover from what seemed like hours without air. Bob was screaming hysterically. Otis kept whispering, "Netherrack," to himself over and over again as he began to recover.

"That's the end nectar I wrote about in my autobiography. I told you it was real," I said.

Otis looked at me with evil intent and said, "Well, you have to admit your description of it in your autobiography was a bit extreme."

"What are you talking about, Otis?" said Harold. "It was exactly as he described it in his autobiography."

Otis, still kneeling from the effects of the end nectar, spat on the brownish end stone and said, "Not even. He totally exaggerated. That was no big deal."

But then Bob's hysterical screaming made Otis realize that his false bravado would do nothing to help his friend and loyal steed. Otis managed to get to his feet and stumble over to Bob and gave him a hug until he finally stopped screaming.

"The horror. The horror," muttered Bob between screams.

As Bob's screaming subsided, a group of endermen began to surround us. They approached us with menace, their purple eyes glowing. One of them said, "Now, you will die."

But I was chill. I buffed my fingernails on the front of my shirt and said, "Don't you recognize me?"

The endermen continued to approach and said, "Everyone tries that one. Even new players who come here on creative mode."

I shook my head and said, "Let me help you out a bit." I walked over to Harold and hopped on, assuming my chicken jockey form. A brief moment passed before one of the endermen squealed with delight and said, "Oh my Notch! It's Baby Zeke!"

The group of endermen let out a cheer of joy before surrounding me and patting me on the back.

Meanwhile, Otis sat hugging Bob and glaring at me. He was clearly jealous of my fame. I knew that without Otis I could not have accomplished what I had, but somehow all the fame came to me. But, what can you do? Otis needed to get over it.

After the cheering and congratulating were over, one of the endermen said, "I'd better go alert the Ender King that you've arrived."

"There is no need for that," said a girl's voice. "I'll take him to the King myself!"

I looked over and there stood the Ender Princess, with her little red bow in her hair, just like I remembered her.

"Savannah!" I yelled as I rushed over to her to give her a hug.

As I hugged her, the other endermen gasped and quickly surrounded us and ripped me away from the Ender Princess.

"You are not permitted to touch the Princess!" said one of the enderman. "It is forbidden to all!"

Savannah looked embarrassed and said to the bossy enderman, "It's okay, Frederick, this is how they do things in the Overworld."

The bossy enderman named Frederick looked disgusted. "Those in the Overworld are immoral. That is why the Great Notch has separated them from us at the beginning of creation."

The Ender Princess rolled her eyes. "Look, Zeke is my friend and if he wants to hug me, it's okay. If you don't like it, take it up with my dad."

Frederick still looked upset, but he backed away at the mention of the Ender King. Frederick then bowed mechanically to the Ender Princess and said, "As you wish, Your Highness."

Although Frederick was saying all the right words, I sensed some menace in his voice. It was as if he were biding his time until the right moment came for him to contradict or embarrass the Ender Princess. I did not like Frederick. Not one little bit.

Savannah turned away from Frederick and looked at me and smiled. Harold had approached and she said, "Harold! It's good to see you."

Harold bowed and spread his wings in a gesture of submission to the Princess. "And it is nice to see you again, Princess."

Savannah giggled and then looked a few feet behind us and saw Otis and Bob standing there. "Bob. Otis. Come closer and say hi," said Savannah.

Otis rolled his eyes and grudgingly walked forward. Bob hopped unlike his normal chicken walk, the excitement of traveling through the nectar and now meeting the Princess was too much for him.

"It's nice to see you, Princess Savannah," said Bob politely. "I've heard so much about you."

Savannah giggled and said, "I heard about you too. I think you might have been the best character in Zeke's autobiography." Bob blushed at the compliment.

Otis grunted and said, "What about me? Everyone would be dead without me."

Savannah laughed and said, "You were pretty awesome too, Otis. But, actually, I think everyone would be dead without my dad."

Otis considered her statement and then began to nod his head. "I think, Princess, you may be correct. I knew that Baby Zeke should not have been the center of the story." Otis looked at me with a sly grin. I didn't say anything or do anything. I thought I'd let him have his fun and his little moment in the sun.

"Well," said Savannah, "shall we go see my father?"

Yes," I said, "but can we go directly to the palace instead of through that weird passageway we went through last time?"

"Sure. Now that you are a celebrity and not something to be exterminated, like most who visit the End from the Overworld, we can move about freely."

Chapter 22

Savannah led us through the rather dull landscape of the End for about ten minutes. Our trip to the palace would have been much quicker had we not been stopped repeatedly by fans wanting to meet me and, to a lesser extent, Otis.

When we finally arrived at the gates of the Ender palace, four guards stood at attention holding their diamond swords out to create a barrier of diamond sword points that prevented anyone from passing.

"Who dares follow Princess Savannah into the palace?" asked one of the guards.

"It is I, Baby Zeke, the Warrior."

It felt good to say that!

The ender soldiers' eyes all grew very wide and then they squinted as they look at me more closely. The soldiers looked slightly confused and slightly awed. One of them asked the Princess, "Is this true, Your Highness?"

Savannah smiled and said, "Yes. It is Baby Zeke, Otis and their chicken steeds, Harold and Bob."

The soldier turned to his men and said, "At ease."

The soldiers put their swords into their inventories and backed away though they continued to look at me with awe in their eyes. Honestly, it was rather embarrassing to have them looked at me like that. I'm sure any one of them could've easily defeated me in a one-on-one fight, but I guess my legend precedes me everywhere I go.

Does that sound pretentious? Or, is it just truth?

The ender soldiers opened the gate to the palace and let us pass. As we walked through the thick walls surrounding the palace, a servant appeared to greet us.

The servant was wearing a scarf and an embroidered robe. As you might suspect, the fabrics were purple and black with small shiny diamond flecks sewn into them.

"I am Reginald, head of the Ender King's servants," he announced. "I understand Princess Savannah has brought Baby Zeke himself and his posse to meet with the Ender King."

"I'm not part of anyone's posse!" said Otis angrily.

"Yeah!" added Bob.

The servant looked aghast. Clearly, he was not used to anyone questioning his statements, certainly not visitors from the Overworld. The servant stood up straight and appeared disgusted by what Otis and Bob had said. "I declare that anyone who follows a great leader is a member of that leader's posse. Another word could be follower. I consider myself to be part of the Ender King's posse. What is wrong with that?"

"I'll tell you what's wrong with that," said Otis pointing a stubby rotten finger at Reginald's face. "If you are a member of a posse, it implies that you have no free will of your own. I'm the king of free will, bro. In fact, you can call me 'Free Willy' if you want to."

Otis was too much. Everyone started laughing. Reginald was slapping his knee and saying, "Free Willy! Ha."

Otis, of course, was being a bad sport about all this. He quickly pulled his diamond sword out of his inventory and rushed toward Reginald, clearly intent to murder him. I dove at Otis's feet to try to stop him. My tiny stubby arms just reached his foot, but I could not maintain my grasp as he pulled it away from me.

My rotten fingers attempted to grasp his ankle, but he slipped through. Otis raised his sword high in the air preparing to bring the blow down upon Reginald. Reginald, who had finally realized that his life was about to end, put his hands in front of his face and screamed, "No!"

As the blade on Otis's sword slashed toward Reginald's midsection, a tiny black hand suddenly materialized around Otis's sword arm stopping its progress dead. I followed the long black arm to which the tiny black hand was attached and saw that it was connected to the Ender King himself!

"Same old Otis, I see," growled the Ender King.

Otis looked up at the King and shouted, "Let me go! I need to kill this guy."

The Ender King lifted Otis's tiny baby pigman body high into the air and held him in front of his face. "You will not be killing anyone in my palace. If you kill someone here, it will be the end of you."

I honestly expected Otis to talk back to the Ender King. But, Otis surprised me with his momentary reasonableness when he refrained from speaking and simply nodded his head. He then said in a quiet voice, "I'm sorry. Will you put me down now, please?"

The Ender King held Otis in the air for a few more seconds to assert his dominance and then set him down on the ground. Otis returned his diamond sword to his inventory and then looked over Reginald and said, "I'm sorry I tried to kill you. Don't laugh at me anymore."

Reginald, who was down on his knees shivering with fear, said, "You are so uncouth. But, I have to respect your passion. At least you believe in something. Even if it is just yourself. Almost no one believes in anything these days."

I wasn't sure exactly what Reginald meant. It sounded like he was lost in some strange thought pattern that his near-death experience had brought into his brain.

Otis's murderous rage put on hold, at least for a while, the Ender King looked at us all and said, "Come with me. You too, Savannah." The Ender King then turned around and began walking toward a solid oak door. We all followed the King, with Reginald bringing up the rear. The King opened the wooden door and stood to the side so everyone could enter. We walked in and then the King stopped Reginald before he entered the room. "Reginald, please prepare the dining hall for lunch. We will eat in an hour. Be sure to have some rotten flesh available."

Reginald sneered in disgust at the mention of rotten flesh, but he was a true servant and bowed briefly to the King and said, "It shall be done, my King." Reginald then took two steps backwards before turning around and walking away.

The King entered the room and shut the door behind him. There was a large wooden table in center of the room surrounded by twenty oaken chairs. "Take a seat," he said.

After we had found our places, the King looked at me and asked with serious concern in his voice, "Why are you here? Is something wrong with the Balance?"

My face flushed with embarrassment before I responded. "No, um, not at all. Actually, we're here by accident."

The Ender King had a confused expression. "Why would you come here by accident? I know how much you hate the end nectar."

"I've kind of gotten used to it, though I still hate it. Anyway, we were wandering around a stronghold and had to dive into an end portal in order to escape."

The Ender King's look of confusion was replaced with one of shock. "Whoa! You are obviously leaving out a few important details. What were you doing in a stronghold and why did you have to dive into the end portal in order to survive?"

"We were looking for a llama," said Bob with a childlike voice.

The Ender King's look of shock was again replaced with a look of confusion. "I need to sit down. I can tell this is going to be a long story."

Otis laughed derisively. "Yeah. It is going to be a long story, and I'm going to let The Warrior tell you all about it."

Chapter 23

When I finished telling the Ender King about the missing diamond-haired llama, the grave markers, the strange laughter, the sleep-inducing flowers, and the diamond road leading us away from the village before we fell into the stronghold, the Ender King said, "That's insane!"

I nodded. "I just want to find the llama. Either to help out this villager or at least to figure out why the llama exists in the first place. And, to tell the truth, I guess I wanted a little excitement again, but nothing quite as life-threatening as our adventures together to defeat Herobrine. But, now it's starting to look a little more dangerous than I had expected."

"Who do you think the girl is, Daddy?" asked Savannah.

The Ender King shook his head. "I have no idea. Some of these traps sound like something Herobrine would do, but I was there when Notch himself told

Herobrine to leave Zeke alone. This concerns me greatly."

"Why?" asked Savannah.

The Ender King sighed. "You are still so young, Savannah. If there is a strange force that is able to do these things and it is something other than Herobrine, then what is it? Is it a player who has somehow mastered enchantments and other unknown powers? Is it a group of villagers? Is it a griefer or team of griefers? Or is it some unknown entity that has manifested itself recently within the world of Minecraft?"

"Could an unknown entity actually emerge?" I asked. "I thought everything had been created by Notch?"

"Notch did not create Herobrine. Notch did not create Entity 303. No one knows where they came from," said the Ender King. "Maybe this is a new manifestation of evil in the world."

"Or maybe it's just a manifestation of lameness," said Otis. "Everything so far has been amateur hour. The only thing weird is the laughter. Everything else is just your basic run-of-the-mill distractions. Magical grave markers, diamond roads, enchanted flowers. It's tiresome."

I looked at Otis sideways and said, "It didn't seem tiresome when you are screaming like a baby as we were falling through the stronghold."

Otis stood up in his chair so he appeared tall. He leaned over the table and pointed a finger at me and said, "I was not screaming."

"Tell yourself all the lies you want, Otis. We all know what happened. We were there," I said.

Otis jumped onto the table and ran towards me ready for a fight. But before he could get me the Ender King's arm shot out and grabbed him by the neck, lifted him roughly into the air, and slammed him back down into his chair. "Seriously, Otis. Do I need to send you back to the Overworld so the rest of us can talk this out like adults? Or maybe you just need a timeout. I could send you on a voyage on an end ship out to an end island for a while if you'd like."

Otis crossed his stubby little arms in front of his chest and pouted. "I'll stay here. I'll deal with Zeke later."

The King looked at Otis and said, "You need some anger management classes. We have some at the local high school in the evenings. I'm sure I could convince the teacher to let you attend."

Otis's face turned bright red with anger. I could tell he wanted to explode and yell horrible mean things at the Ender King, but that would just prove the Ender King correct. Otis's strong will overcame his rage and he sat there silently, his decaying lips squeezed together to prevent any words from coming out of his mouth.

The Ender King continued to stare at Otis to make sure that he had finally decided to be silent. After about five seconds, the Ender King turned back to me. "So what now, Zeke? Do you want me to send some of my soldiers to go with you? Do you need help finding the source of this laughter or tracking down the llama?"

I shook my head. "I don't think so. Now that we know we're dealing with someone or something that would be willing to harm us as opposed just playing jokes on us, we will be more alert."

"Well, at least we can give you a good meal and get you back to the Overworld in one piece," said the Ender King smiling.

"Daddy, can I go with Zeke and everyone to the Overworld? I didn't get to go the last time you went," said Savannah.

The Ender King considered momentarily and then said, "I'm not sure you're ready, honey."

Savannah put on her pouty face and said, "Please, Daddy. Pretty please with chorus fruit jelly on top."

The Ender King thought about it for a moment and then said, "I suppose you can go if you let me send two ender soldiers with you as an escort."

"We can protect her. We don't need any of your soldiers," said Otis.

The Ender King's head snapped around and he stared at Otis. "You can't even protect yourself. Either my soldiers come with her or she doesn't go at all."

I could tell Otis wanted to say something insulting again but he kept quiet.

"Thank you, Daddy. That would be awesome," said Savannah. "Thank you."

The Ender King smiled softly at his daughter. "It's hard for me to believe you're old enough to go to the Overworld now," he said with a tear forming in his eyes. "I want to give you something to keep with you. It's a small Redstone device. If you're ever in trouble up there push it. I'll be able to locate you and teleport to your location within a few seconds. But don't press unless it's an absolute emergency." The Ender King teleported to his daughter's side and pulled a small box out of his inventory and handed it to her. She held onto it and looked at it before tucking it into her inventory.

"Do you think I might actually need this?"

The Ender King's face looked grim. "I hope not, but you might. I suspect my soldiers can handle just about anything, but you never know."

Chapter 24

After we had our meal – the rotten flesh was among the best I had ever tasted. I'm not sure where the Ender King found it, but it was delicious – the Ender King led us to the portal room of the Palace. When we entered the room, I was astonished. Before me were at least fifty portals. They looked essentially like an end portal you might find in the Overworld, but instead of a black center area, the colors varied.

Then Ender King smiled when he said, "You all are very privileged. It has been many generations since any mobs from the Overworld have seen the Ender King's portal room."

"What's with all the different colors?" asked Otis.

"Each portal goes to a different location in the Overworld or the Nether. We designate them by color so they're easy to tell apart."

"I didn't know you guys had anything colorful down here. If it wasn't black, tan, or purple, I figured you guys had no idea," said Otis.

"Oh, we understand color. We just don't like to be gaudy," said the King.

"So, which one are we going to use?" I asked.

"I hope it's the pink one," said Bob.

"I hope it's the orange one," said Harold.

Otis and I looked at the chickens and then locked eyes with each other. We could each tell what the other was thinking: Chickens are weird.

"Well, since you want to go see Herobrine, you should take the yellow-tinted portal. It will get you within about a twenty-minute walk of his High Castle," said the King.

Otis grunted. "Twenty minutes? You can't get it inside the High Castle with all your fancy technology?"

"Otis, do you think it's wise to just materialize inside of Herobrine's home? And besides, how would we install the portal inside his house without him knowing?" said the King.

"Yeah, Otis, use your brain," said Savannah.

I could tell Otis wanted to clap back to Savannah's insult, but he refrained. I'm sure he'd stored the insult in his rotting brain, and he would carry this grudge until he could give her a walloping insult at some point.

"When you enter the portal, you'll transport through the end nectar momentarily and then emerge inside a cave. From there, you can walk to the High Castle," said the King.

Bob shivered. "I don't like the end nectar. It's gross."

"Yeah, can we get to the Overworld without going through the nectar?" asked Otis, trying not to sound scared, even though I could tell he was.

The Ender King shook his head. "I'm afraid that's the only way. For most people from the Overworld it's a one-way voyage to the End. If they don't kill the Ender Dragon, it's over. The end nectar is the medium which connects the Overworld to the End and vice versa. It is the only road."

"I guess I can handle it," said Otis.

"I'm not sure that I can," said Bob, the lower half of his beak quivering.

Harold walked over to Bob and put a wing on his shoulder and said, "Just take a deep breath and keep your eyes closed. Time will pass more quickly that way. And if it gets too scary, just pretend you're hanging out inside of a slime," said Harold.

Bob nodded his head. "I'll be brave."

At that moment Savannah's ender soldier escort arrived. The two soldiers walked up to the King and saluted. One of them said, "My name is John and this is Todd. Reporting for duty, Sir."

"At ease, men," said the Ender King. "You've been chosen to guard my daughter during her trip to the Overworld. If any harm befalls her and you haven't died to protect her, you will regret it. Do you understand?"

The two soldiers clicked their heels together, saluted and said in unison, "We understand!"

The Ender King gave his head a short nod and said, "Good. Fulfill your duty and protect my daughter, and you will receive a great reward. Now go."

Savannah ran over to her father and gave him a long hug. I watched the Ender King fight back a tear as he let his daughter go on her first big adventure.

Savannah let go of her father and then ran toward the edge of the portal and waved at him. "Bye, Daddy. See you later."

He smiled and waved back but said nothing. His emotions would not allow him speak.

I hopped on Harold and Otis hopped on Bob. We stood at the edge of the yellow-tinted portal. Savannah and the two ender soldiers stood to our right. Savannah said, "On the count of three, we jump."

We all nodded our understanding.

"One. Two. Three."

We jumped in unison, passed through the mist of the strange yellow portal, and then into the end nectar yet again.

Chapter 25

When we emerged from the end portal hidden deep within a cave, Bob screamed once and then took deep, meditative breaths, recovering from the horror of the end nectar. I removed any remaining nectar goo from my body and tried to put the memory of that horrible place out of my mind. Otis and Harold were doing the same thing.

In contrast, John, Todd and Savannah seemed newly energized, like being in contact with the end nectar had made them younger or stronger or maybe both.

"Netherrack, that stuff is so dank," said Otis.

"I realize the end nectar is not something anyone other than ender folk like, but you could be a little more polite," said Savannah.

"Now that your dad's not here, I've got something to say you, little girl," said Otis raising a finger and pointing it at her. Before he could continue, the two ender soldiers surrounded him with their swords drawn and held next to Otis's chest.

"Think very carefully about what you say next. It may be the last words you ever utter," said John.

Otis looked at him and said, "On second thought, I forgot what I wanted to say." But, he continued speaking to the ender soldier sarcastically, "I like how you use your size and speed to dominate me. My intellect and courage obviously outweighs yours, but my tiny little body will not allow me to fight you in a fair fight. So I refrain and yield ... for now."

The ender soldiers put their swords away, and John said, "We only require that you yield until we complete this mission. Once Savannah takes you and The Warrior to meet with Herobrine, we shall leave you to your own devices and return to the End."

Otis waved a hand at John as if he were batting away a pesky fly and said, "Whatever."

Savannah led the way out of the cave into the forest hills around the High Castle. It was indeed a short walk to the High Castle, the place where I had nearly died and where the world had nearly come to an end. I was feeling anxious as we approached. Once it came into view, my anxiety tripled. I was starting to have heart palpitations. I was sweating profusely, which is not at all pleasant for those around me. Zombie sweat smells like concentrated decay or death. There's no deodorant in the world that could help me.

I hoped nobody would notice, but judging by the sidelong glances I was getting from the ender soldiers and Savannah, my stink cloud was expanding.

"Zeke," whispered Harold. "You need to take a shower."

"Thanks for the support, buddy," I said sarcastically.

Just then a breeze came up and blew my stink away from the group, I could see the three ender folk relax as the fresh air cleansed their nostrils.

We were now just a short distance away from the entrance to the High Castle. I was examining the walls surrounding the castle when Herobrine himself appeared on the wall!

"Baby Zeke," said Herobrine condescendingly. "To what do I owe this tremendously tremendous honor?"

"Don't be mean," said Savannah.

"Or what," asked Herobrine.

"Or ... well ... I'll tell my dad."

Herobrine laughed a deep belly laugh and then turned back to me. "Like I said earlier, what do you want?"

"I'm here to pick your brain. Some strange things have been happening near our home and I thought you might be involved or at least know who is."

"Why would I be involved?" asked Herobrine, fluttering his eyelids innocently.

"You know why," said Otis roughly. "You're always messing around with people and causing havoc. You are a mean person."

"I am not," said Herobrine shocked. "I am not a person. I am something unique."

"Are you going to let us in, or what?" I asked.

"Fine," said Herobrine. He moved his hands a couple of times and snapped his fingers and then the door to his High Castle opened by itself.

We passed through the door and into a courtyard. We watched as Herobrine walked down the stone steps from the top of his wall and approached us. "Well?"

"Well ... um ... we are looking for a llama," I said. Before I could explain the story, Herobrine began to laugh. He continued laughing until he fell to the ground, grabbing his stomach and rolling around like a bunny rabbit with stomach cramps. I just stood there watching him. He would laugh himself out soon and then I would explain to him why finding the llama mattered.

Over a minute passed before he finally calmed down and stood back up. He said, "That's the most ridiculous thing I've ever heard. Why would you come talk to me because you're looking for a stupid llama?"

"Because the llama's hair can be shaved and converted into diamonds."

Herobrine looked somewhat interested but shrugged his shoulders. "So? It seems like that would be a simple enchantment of some kind. Maybe even a villager came up with it."

"Even if a villager did, the things that have happened to us since we've been searching for the llama could not have been done by a villager."

Herobrine regarded me with suspicion and curiosity. "First, tell me why you are looking for the llama. Then, tell me about these strange happenings."

"There is a villager who lives near us and he had read my book and thought we might help find his missing llama," I said.

Herobrine smirked. "So you're a pet detective now? I thought you were the big, bad Warrior? What a loser."

"Let me finish. Anyway, he tells us he inherited this diamond-haired llama and that it was stolen. I didn't believe his story about the inheritance part. I assume he stole the llama, but he convinced us about the llama and its magical properties."

"Okay, so let's say this diamond-haired llama exists. Big deal. Any idiot can get diamond ore out of the ground if they want it. Why would anyone steal this thing?" asked Herobrine.

"Agreed, I suppose. But that's not the weird thing. There was a grave marker near the missing llama which displays the name of whoever approaches it."

Again Herobrine shrugged. "Simple trickery. I could do something like that when I was a baby."

"There's more," I said. "Since we've been pursuing the llama, we've been led into a field of flowers that put us to sleep and induced weird dreams, we walked upon a road made entirely of diamonds, we've been attacked by a group of illagers, and fallen into the stronghold before passing to the End."

"That actually sounds a bit weird," said Herobrine. "Someone's obviously pretty good at making strange things happen. Maybe it is Entity 303, though these pranks don't seem vicious enough for his taste."

"And there's the girl," said Otis.

Herobrine's head snapped over at Otis and said, "What did you say?"

"A girl. We hear a girl laughing every time one of these weird events occurs. Except for when we jumped into the end portal in the stronghold. Then she yelled 'no' because we were getting away from her."

Herobrine momentarily had a strange, faraway look on his face before he said, "How peculiar. Have you seen this girl?"

I shook my head. "Never. Just her laughter."

"So, Herobrine, any ideas?" asked Harold.

Herobrine stood for a moment contemplating. He rubbed his cheek and brushed under his chin with hand. "Not really. Entity 303 is obviously capable of all these things, but like I said, this seems more like practical jokes, at least until the illager attack near the stronghold. It wasn't me. Not really sure who else would have these powers. Maybe some witch has been studying forbidden ancient texts she found in a long lost treasure chest or something."

I was disappointed that Herobrine had not been of more help, especially after all we went through to get here. But, it was a shot in the dark anyway.

"Show him the thing," said Bob.

I looked Bob and raised an eyebrow. "What are you talking about?"

"You know, the hair thingy. The barrette."

I could not believe I had forgotten. The barrette! It was our only clue.

I fished the barrette out of my inventory and held it out so Herobrine could see it. "We found this in the corral from which the llama was stolen. Any chance you recognize it?"

Herobrine glanced down at the barrette. When he saw it, his eyes grew wide and all the color drained from his face. He looked like a walking corpse. And that's when he said, "The barrette. It … it … belongs to my daughter."

Chapter 26

"Your daughter? You have a daughter!" I said.

I looked around and saw everyone else was as shocked as I. No one had ever heard that Herobrine had a child. And now, it looked as though she were implicated in the kidnapping of the diamond-haired llama.

Herobrine slowly nodded his head. "Yes, I do. Heidi. She's fourteen years old. But she's not supposed to leave the High Castle. I had not seen her in a few days, and now I know why."

Savannah gasped and said, "You don't see your fourteen-year-old daughter for days on end and you don't bother to look for her? What kind of father are you?"

I thought Herobrine was going to do something drastic. Maybe knock her down with his mental powers or cause an explosion or something. But he just looked at her sadly as a tear rolled down his face.

"I'm not much of a father at all. I just hope she's okay."

"I'm fine, father!" came an all-too-familiar voice from on top of the wall. We all looked up and saw Heidi standing there, her fists on her hips and legs slightly apart in a power stance.

"Heidi. What have you done? Where have you been?" pleaded Herobrine.

"I had to save her. I had to rescue her. She shouldn't be treated like that."

"What are you talking about? Who are you talking about?" asked Herobrine, clearly confused.

Heidi crossed her arms in front of her chest and said, "You know. Don't play stupid with me. You're the one who did it."

"Did what? I don't know what you're talking about."

"Yes you do!" yelled Heidi. I could see tears forming in her eyes and beginning to run down her cheeks. "You did this. You turned mom into a magical llama!" Heidi then ran along the wall and disappeared around a corner.

I stared at Herobrine in shock. I wasn't sure my mouth would work, but I tried anyway. "You turned your own wife into a llama?!?"

When Herobrine turned around and looked at me, tears were streaming down his face. "I never did such a thing. A few days after Heidi was born, my beloved Helga disappeared. I thought she'd gotten sick of me and had run away. I just assumed she was gone forever. That's why I locked up ... er, I mean ... confined Heidi to the High Castle because I didn't want to lose her too."

I knew Herobrine could be a conniving, manipulative creep, but I believed him right now. His pain was real. His confusion was real.

"But, if you didn't do it, then who did?" I asked.

Herobrine wiped his forearm across his face to dry his tears. He set his jaw. In a deep stern voice he said, "That's what we are going to find out."

Chapter 27

We spent the next ten minutes searching the High Castle for Heidi. The ender soldiers and Savannah teleported all over the High Castle and Herobrine searched inside the Castle's various secret passages. Harold and I, assisted by Bob and Otis, ran along the walls and the exterior passageways, looking for any clue where Heidi might have gone. But, we found nothing.

When we had completed our searches, we rendezvoused in the main courtyard and reported that none of us have been able to find Heidi.

"Now that I know Helga is alive and Heidi is with her, we have to find them," said Herobrine. "I have to reunite my family."

"Does she have any place she likes to hide out?" asked Savannah. "Sometimes when I'm angry at my dad I go down to the Ender Hall of Heroes and look at the famous ender folk who are in my family line. It makes me feel better."

"I'm ashamed to say that I don't know my daughter very well. If she's not in the Castle, which she does not appear to be, I really have no idea where she might have gone," said Herobrine dejectedly.

I looked around the courtyard, hoping to see some sort of clue or secret passage that even Herobrine did not know about, but it was futile, as I knew it would be. I shook my head in disgust. I'd never find the llama. And now, even if I did, I couldn't return it to the villager. After all, the llama was Helga, the wife of Herobrine. He'd want to return her to her original form. If he could....

I thought about telling Herobrine that we were done with our search and that we would return to our farm, but then I remembered, I'm the Warrior. The Warrior fights the battles that are necessary to fight. I realized that Herobrine had locked away his sadness for fourteen years, and now that the old wound had been reopened, if he couldn't find his wife, he would likely turn into a horrible person, doing irreparable damage to Minecraft. He might even ignore Notch's order not to try to destroy the world for the next ten years and just go ahead and do it.

And that's when I knew. I knew where Heidi had gone. It was so obvious. I don't know why I hadn't thought of it sooner.

I turned and looked at everyone and said, "I know where she is."

Chapter 28

The hard part was getting there.

When you have only been someplace in a dream, finding it in real life takes some doing. Fortunately, Herobrine had a complete map of the Overworld, showing all its biomes. There was a snowy tundra biome about a day's walk away. Herobrine confirmed that his daughter could teleport like he did. So, with the aid of the teleportation power of the ender soldiers and Savannah, we could get there in less than an hour.

* * *

As we entered the cold, snowy tundra biome, I pulled a blanket from my inventory and wrapped it around me, draping it over Harold so that he could stay warm as he carried me into the snow. We walked slowly up the side of a mountain until we arrived at a plateau. The same plateau where I had fought for my life before waking up from the dream I now know was caused by Heidi creating a field of enchanted flowers.

I looked in the distance and saw the entrance to the polar bear's cave. I pointed at the cave and said, "In there."

We slowly approached the entrance to the cave, wary of possible booby-traps or attacking polar bears.

We entered the cave and found Heidi and the diamond-haired llama, or should I say, Helga, sitting next to a warm fire. The llama was on the ground, its legs folded underneath it, the way llamas tend to sit. Heidi was leaning against the llama's fur while the llama licked Heidi's hair. It was a tender moment for sure.

Heidi and the llama did not notice us when we entered the cave, but soon the llama's ears pricked skyward and her head turned toward us. She regarded us calmly until she saw Herobrine was amongst us. Her eyes became steely and her expression filled with hate. She did the only thing a llama could do to express distaste; she spit on him.

Herobrine didn't even try to wipe the spit away. He knew he should have searched for her. At that moment, he became as weak as a baby. He collapsed to his knees and cried. Heaving sobs of grief flowed from unknown depths of his soul. It was hard to watch. It was as though he was mourning a death or the loss of everything.

I watched as the llama's eyes softened before she stood up. Heidi stood up too and began to approach Herobrine, her shoulders set for confrontation. But, the llama stood in front of her and looked at her and shook her head to indicate that she should back off. Heidi stood there, still angry, with her arms folded across her chest, but she did not approach any closer.

Herobrine did not see any of this. His head was bowed and tears were streaming out of his eyes. He was crying so hard that boogers flowed from his nose, and he did not care. He did not notice as the llama approached him and then folded her legs and sat down in front of him. He looked up and saw the creature, who had once been his wife, sitting in front of him. His crying stopped for a moment and then it became even more filled with despair. I began to cry. We all did, even Otis. He wasn't even trying to hide it. It was the saddest thing any of us had ever seen.

And then the llama put her chin on Herobrine's shoulder. Herobrine's sobs slowed, and he reached out and hugged the llama around its neck. He squeezed it tightly and whispered to the llama, "I miss you, Helga. I love you."

And then the miracle happened. The llama began to shimmer. Fireflies of light rose from its body and began to circle around it like a tornado. Herobrine released the llama's neck and stared in awe as the beast was completely engulfed in swirling light. I put my hands over my eyes so I would not go blind from its radiance. I glanced to the side and saw Heidi, her arms now at her sides, her shoulders slack, tears on her face and a smile on her lips.

There was a final flash and then lying on the ground, appearing as though she were asleep, was Helga, wearing a bright blue dress and a golden crown.

Chapter 29

Herobrine and Heidi rushed toward Helga and embraced her tightly. Helga smiled and embraced them in return.

Savannah walked up to me and whispered, "We should give them some time."

I nodded my head and motioned to Otis that we should wait outside the cave. Otis complied and we waited outside in silence until the Herobrine family emerged a few minutes later.

Helga spoke first. "Baby Zeke, thank you for trying to find me. I had heard about your adventures while I was in llama form. It's all anyone could talk about, even the savage villagers who traded me for diamonds." Then she looked at Herobrine and said, "I was secretly cheering for you to defeat my husband who I still hated back then."

I bowed slightly to Mrs. Herobrine and said, "You're welcome, but I really thought I was just going after a magical llama. I didn't realize it was you."

She smiled kindly and said, "Nevertheless, you have a good heart."

Helga tapped Heidi on the shoulder and nodded her head toward me. Heidi resisted, but her mother insisted. "Guys, I'm ... well ... I'm sorry I tried to kill you. I thought maybe you had been hired to take my mom away again." She paused as her face flushed with rage. "And, I was NOT going to let that happen again!"

I was surprised when Otis was the first to say, "Apology accepted. I would have done the same thing."

"Apology accepted," said the two chickens.

"Agreed," I said smiling. "And, Mrs. Herobrine, if you don't mind me asking, who was it that turned you into a diamond-haired llama, anyway?"

Helga sighed. "It was a group of villagers and witches who'd gotten together to try to create a philosopher's stone."

"What's a philosopher's stone?" asked Otis.

"It's a stone that is supposed to change anything it touches into gold," said Savannah.

"Only in my case, they had been trying to create something that would turn anything it touched into diamonds. But, they were unsuccessful. However, when they learned that I had the ability to create diamonds myself, which I've had since I was a young girl growing up in a distant village, they kidnapped me when I was outside the walls of the High Castle gathering flowers to put next to Heidi's crib."

Helga was silent for a moment, reliving that horrible day and all the horrible days that came after it.

"So, you're saying that you were born with the ability to turn things into diamonds?" I asked.

She smiled. "Yes, they call it the diamond touch. Anything I touch will turn into a diamond, if I want it to. If I wanted to turn my husband into a diamond I could do it, but I won't," she said. "At least, not yet...."

"So why did they turn you into a llama then, and not just keep you locked up in a cage or something?" asked Savannah.

"Llamas are docile animals. Easy to control. I think they assumed that if they turned me into a type of livestock, I would not disobey them or run away. Unfortunately, they were correct. Once I was turned into a llama, I lost most of my free will. I still managed to spit on them once in a while, but otherwise I just sat in the corral eating wheat and growing hair that was shaved periodically. It was a terrible existence."

"Are there any other villagers like you?" I asked. "You know, who are born with supernatural powers?"

Helga shrugged noncommittally. "I've heard one or two villagers every century are born with the diamond touch. There are rumors of villagers with other powers, but I've never encountered them."

Herobrine stepped in front of his wife and waved his hands at us. "Okay, that's enough. She doesn't want to talk about this anymore."

"I don't?" said Helga, apparently displeased at the interruption.

Herobrine looked back at his wife and said, "I mean, I just assumed you didn't want to talk about it anymore. I was just trying to protect you."

Helga looked at him and said, "I've taken care of myself for the last fourteen years. I'm glad we have reunited, but you have to let me be my own person from now on. And you can't just lock me away in a room like you did Heidi."

Herobrine looked ... well ... ashamed. I never thought I'd see him look like that, but he did. I wondered at that moment if all the mean things he had done went back to the kidnapping of his wife. He assumed she had run away from him, but it wasn't the case at all.

What would it be like to discover the last fourteen years of your life had been based on a lie? It was too horrible to contemplate.

"Actually, I think we should be going," I said. "Savannah should probably get back to her father, and we need to pay a visit to that villager who hired us. He needs to know that he can't lie to Baby Zeke."

Chapter 30

After we waved good-bye to the Herobrine family, Savannah and her military escort teleported us back to the home of the villager who had hired us.

"I guess we will leave you to take care of these final details," said Savannah with a smile.

I smiled back. "At least you didn't have to use your special box to call your father for help."

Savannah reached into her inventory and pulled out the box. She handed it to me. "Here. Maybe you will need it someday?"

I looked at the box. "Are you sure you want me to have this? I mean, the Ender King gave it to you."

"Take it. I'm sure he has more. Besides, you are the Warrior and he is the Protector. You two should have a direct line of contact, no?"

I reached out and took the box and tucked it in my inventory. "Thanks. But, I hope I'll never need this. If I do, it will be a dark day for Minecraft I am sure."

Savannah hugged me briefly and then attempted to hug Otis. He backed away. "Hugging is stupid," he said.

Savannah giggled. She bent down and scratched Harold and Bob's heads. They clucked their enjoyment.

"Thank you, Princess," said Harold.

"Yes, indeed," said Bob.

Savannah stood up. "It's been fun." She turned to her guards. "Let's get back to the cave and back home." They saluted, and all three enders disappeared.

Once they had left, Otis and I approached the villager's door and knocked. He opened the door and said breathlessly, "Did you find her? Did you find my llama?"

Otis reached up and grabbed the villager's robe and pulled his face down toward his own. "You mean the stolen llama? The stolen llama that turned out to be Herobrine's wife?"

The villager went as white as a sheet. "Herobrine's wife?!?" he said, looking at me.

I nodded my head in confirmation.

"But, I ... hurrr ... I just thought it was a magical llama. I mean, sure, I stole it, but I had no idea." The villager's knees were shaking so hard they were knocking together.

"I would suggest you move away from here and never come back. After Herobrine completes his reunion with his long lost wife, I'm sure he will come for his revenge," I warned.

The villager nodded his head in agreement. "Thank you, Baby Zeke."

"Where's my reward?" asked Otis.

"What do you mean?"

"I mean, we found the llama. It is time for our reward."

The villager was confused. "But, the reward was to shave the llama. She isn't here."

"You had better pay us something. We don't work for free," growled Otis.

The villager looked frightened and then said, "You can take my farm. I'll never be back here. It's yours."

"I ain't no farmer!" yelled Otis. "You need to do better than that!"

"I don't have anything else," whined the villager. "Just this farm and some cows."

Otis spat on the ground. "I'll take the cows, then. At least I can eat those."

At that moment, the villager's wife and daughter appeared at the doorway. "What is all this about?" asked his wife.

Otis looked at her and softened. "Nothing, ma'am. Just talking to your husband. We'll be on our way now." Otis looked at the forlorn villager who would have to exile himself and his family to some far corner of the Overworld and said, "You can keep your filthy cows."

I hopped on Harold and Otis hopped on Bob. We trotted back to our house.

* * *

That evening, after a hearty dinner and a shower, I lay in bed reflecting on our adventure. It was good to get back into the world. To do something to help people, even though there was danger. I had to admit, I missed the adrenalin rush of adventure and battle.

I resolved to be true to what I had become: **The Warrior.**

From now on, the evil doers who lurked within Minecraft had better watch out. Baby Zeke is coming for you!

End of *Baby Zeke,* Book 10 –
Return of the Warrior

Book 11 – Rebellion

AN UNOFFICIAL MINECRAFT BOOK

BOOK ELEVEN

BABY ZEKE
THE DIARY OF A CHICKEN JOCKEY

REBELLION

DR. BLOCK

Chapter 1

Although I had made a commitment to embrace my identity as The Warrior following the recovery of a magical llama, who turned out to be Herobrine's wife, my identity was not embracing me.

I don't mean that my identity was some sort of humanoid object that could physically give me an embrace or a hug or something. No. What I mean is that no tasks suitable for The Warrior of the Balance had come to my attention.

Like, I don't mean to sound arrogant, but, yo, when you are literally one of the four beings in Minecraft keeping everything in alignment, you want to do some meaningful stuff, or else do … nothing.

So, instead of doing amazing, historical stuff, I had been participating in a series of ridiculous, basic nonsense that anyone could have been able to handle.

Let me give you an example. Or two.

For instance, whenever I walk around the village located close to my farm, the villagers — especially the old lady librarian villagers — ask me to help them cross the street.

Don't get me wrong. I'm a nice undead mob, so I'm happy to oblige, but shouldn't they be asking their own grandchildren to do this? Or maybe one of the young male villagers? I mean, it is not like I am trying to earn a merit badge in the Zombie Scouts or anything.

A few weeks ago, I finally thought something worth my time had come my way.

I was sitting inside my house, reading some fan mail, when a very inexperienced player – he was still wearing leather armor – came to my door and asked me to explore an igloo he had located. He said he heard very bizarre noises when he was inside of it but couldn't figure out where they were coming from.

I did not know anything about igloos, so Otis and I accepted the challenge and took Harold and Bob with us in our jockey formations.

After a couple days of travel, Otis complaining the entire time about how cold he was in the snow, we arrived at the igloo.

"I don't hear anything," I said to the player who had accompanied us.

He shivered with fear. "You'll hear it when you get inside."

Otis shook a small undead fist at the player. "This better not be some sort of trick."

"It isn't," I swear said the player with a shaky voice. "I really think it is some sort of demon or something. Maybe Herobrine or Entity 303 created it or something?"

I drew my diamond sword. "You wait here, player. We'll check it out."

We remained in jockey formation as we entered the igloo. It was a small structure. The floor was carpeted and there was a bed in one corner and a crafting table and furnace against a wall, suggesting it was or had recently been occupied.

"Stay alert," I cautioned. Harold and Bob nodded their agreement.

Otis gave me the side eye. "Bruh, I'm not a noob."

I was about to say an epic comeback, when we heard the sounds. It sounded like something trapped and moaning. I would not have assumed it was a demon as the noob player had, but it did not sound friendly.

"Where is it coming from?" I asked.

"Sounds like it is coming from everywhere," said Harold.

"Yeah, I don't like this," said Bob.

"Don't be a wimp," scowled Otis. "There must be a source."

"Unless it is a haunted igloo," added Bob, his scrawny chicken legs quaking.

Bob and his imagination. He had been talking to too many players about the world from which they come. Apparently, hauntings are common in their world. But, there is no such thing as ghosts in Minecraft. At least, I didn't think there were....

"Let's get out of jockey formation and spread out and look around," I suggested as I hopped off of Harold. Otis jumped off Bob.

"There doesn't appear to be anything here," said Harold.

"This bed doesn't even look comfortable," said Otis.

I noticed Bob wandering around on the carpet. His goofy chicken head darting this way and that as he tried to find a clue. Suddenly, he stopped walking and froze in place.

"Guys, I just stepped on something. I think it was a pressure plate," said Bob nervously.

A pressure plate?!? Oh, no. It was probably connected to a booby trap.

"I bet it was that player. He is probably an assassin in disguise!" said Otis, starting for the door with his sword.

I reached out and stopped Otis. "Just, chill. Let's make sure what is going on first."

Otis pushed my hand away, but remained inside the igloo. I walked over to Bob's location and said, "Don't move. I'm going to look around."

I began removing pieces of carpet from the floor to see if I could get a look at what Bob had stepped on. Eventually, I had removed all the pieces around him and found only stone underneath. I carefully lifted the edge of the carpet on which Bob was standing and saw … a trap door!

I breathed a sigh of relief and said, "Bob, you can move. It is just a trap door."

Bob exhaled and then fainted.

"Bob!" yelled Harold, rushing to his side to care for him.

I removed the carpet from the trap door and the moaning sound we had been hearing became much louder. It distinctly sounded like a zombie. I could see a ladder leading down from the trap door.

"Should we check it out?" I asked Otis.

"Of course. You aren't scared, are you?"

Of a zombie? I laughed as I broke the trap door. "Harold and Bob, you guys stay up here while Otis and I check it out." Harold and Bob both nodded and then sat down on the ground. I began descending the ladder with Otis following close behind.

It was a long ladder, and it took us about ten seconds to descend its entire length. As we approached the end of the ladder, I could see that it dropped into a stone chamber lit by torchlight. The moaning was very loud now and was unmistakably a zombie.

I jumped off the ladder with my sword at the ready. Otis was immediately behind me. We saw a strange room with a chest, a brewing stand, and two jail cells! Inside one cell was a cleric and inside the other was a zombie villager cleric!

I rushed to the cell holding the villager. "What is going on here?"

He looked at me, relief passing over his eyes. "Have you come to rescue me?"

"Yes, but why are you here in the first place?" I asked.

"A griefer kidnapped me and another cleric from our village a few weeks ago. He put us down here and has been doing experiments on us. Examining the effects of various potions and ...." the villager paused,

I could tell he had been horribly traumatized. "Hurrr, anyway, he turned my neighbor into a zombie villager a couple days ago and then abruptly departed. I've had to live with the moaning since then."

I smashed the door to the villager's jail cell to free him. He looked at me with sad eyes and said softly, "Thank you."

"No problem, but I wish we could cure your friend, but I don't have any golden apples or weakness potions."

Otis chuckled. "That is where you are wrong, Zeke. There are some weakness potions on this brewing stand and a golden apple in this chest."

"Awesome!"

The villager looked at me strangely. "Zeke? Hurrr ... are you the famous Baby Zeke?"

I smiled. (I wish I hadn't because one of my few remaining teeth suddenly fell out of my undead mouth.) "Yes, sir, in the undead flesh."

The villager suddenly reached into his inventory and pulled out a copy of my nine-book autobiography. "Can I have your autograph?"

"Seriously?" said Otis.

I took the book and quickly autographed it. I handed it back to the villager. "Here. Now, let's cure your friend."

Otis tossed a splash potion of weakness on the zombie cleric. Once it was clear the potion had taken effect, he held a golden apple through the bars of the cell so that the zombie villager could eat it. The zombie gobbled it down as though it were villager brains. Suddenly, there were red sparks and after a few awful, painful moments, he transformed into a normal villager. Then, I broke open his jail cell.

The cleric rushed toward his friend. "Luke, you are cured."

Luke smiled. "Yes, Justin, I am."

"And, you won't believe this, but it was Baby Zeke who cured you!"

"Oy, what about me? Otis?"

"Oh, yeah," said Justin. "Otis helped too."

Luke looked at both of us thankfully and, as he reached into his inventory, asked, "Baby Zeke, can I have your autograph?"

Otis growled. "I've had enough. I'll see you on the surface."

I signed Luke's copy of my book, put the few remaining weakness potions into my inventory, and we climbed back up the ladder. We saw the villagers on their way and explained what had happened to the leather-clad noob.

"So, it was just a zombie villager all this time?" he said somewhat embarrassed.

"Yeah, and if you weren't such a noob and would have explored a bit, we wouldn't have had to come on this wild goose chase to the frozen world of lameness," said Otis.

The noob scratched his head. "Sorry. I won't make that mistake again."

Otis laughed. "I bet you won't, if you live long enough to make it."

"Come on, guys, let's get back into jockey formation and head home," I said.

I climbed onto Harold and Otis sat astride Bob. As we walked away, leaving the noob alone with his thoughts, Otis called back to him, "Don't get eaten by a polar bear, Noob."

So, I think you will agree with me that the igloo adventure was cool and all, but not something worthy of The Warrior. I'm not trying to flex, or anything, but even a noob could have handled that situation.

A few hours later – it had taken him *that long* to calm down – Otis said, "You know, we need to get paid. I thought we would be having more lucrative adventures more often, but it seems we are going to have to keep farming. And you know I hate farming. I only managed to grab a few gold ingots from the chest in that igloo."

I shrugged. "Look, man, I've been putting myself out there to do more Warrior stuff, but the universe isn't providing. I guess I need to work on my manifesting."

Otis slapped his face with this stumpy undead pig hand and said, "That manifesting stuff is self-help nonsense. If you want something, you have to take it."

Oh, boy. I think Otis has an idea.

"What did you have in mind?"

"Look, Zeke, as much as I hate to admit it, you are super famous. All the players know who you are." He paused for a second thinking how to phrase his next words. "I was thinking we should have some meet and greets. We can charge players emeralds or diamonds, and then we can just buy whatever we need from the local villagers."

I shook my head. "It seems kind of stupid. Making money off your fame. Shouldn't we be doing a service for the world?"

Otis spat on the ground. As we were still in a snowy biome, the spit quickly turned a little glob of ice. "We've already done enough for the world. It's time for the world to pay us back. If those players are willing to pay to be in your presence, why shouldn't we profit?"

"We?"

I could see Otis become angry. "You know you'd be dead without me. I get a slice of the pie."

I chuckled. "Alright, if you want to set up some meet and greets, I will participate. But don't make me do any marketing."

Otis grinned greedily. He rubbed his hands together as if he was already counting the wealth. "Leave it to me, Zeke. Leave it to me."

Chapter 2

It didn't take long for Otis to arrange several meet and greets. *Greed is strong in that one.*

Honestly, the meet and greets weren't too bad. All the players seemed genuinely awestruck when they met me. I always felt bad about taking money for the privilege of meeting me, since the meetings also benefited me in that they really stroked my ego. But, the meeting did take time away from me when I could be doing other things like farming or sleeping, so I guess it was an equivalent exchange. The players didn't seem to mind.

There were even a few mobs who paid money to talk to me, though they weren't as awestruck as the players. They usually wanted something from me other than my autograph.

I especially recall one husk who visited. He paid me ten emeralds for an hour of my time. The first thing out of his mouth was, "I want to be like you.

How can I get in contact with Herobrine so I can engage him in an epic battle and defeat him?"

I shook my head in disbelief. "Why would you want to do that? I almost died fighting Herobrine."

The husk smiled at me. "But you didn't. And, neither will I. Defeating Herobrine is the quickest path to fame. Everyone knows that."

"Well, I don't know where Herobrine is," I lied. "Maybe you could go to the End and defeat the Ender Dragon or something? I don't think any husk has ever done that."

The husk shrugged. "Any stupid player can kill the Ender Dragon. I want something that's unique. Something that I can be known for. That way, I can hold meet and greets too and make a bunch of money."

I got angry. "You think that's what this is all about! I didn't fight Herobrine because it was some sort of long-term investment strategy! I fought Herobrine to save my friends, to save my life, to save Minecraft."

The husk laughed. "Sure, you did. Great act."

I stood up and pointed to the door. "Get out before I do something I will regret. I do not want to talk to you anymore."

The husk stood up and indignantly pointed his dry, dusty, undead finger at me. "I paid you ten emeralds for your time. And you're going to give it to me!"

Oh, no he didn't!

I reached into my inventory and pulled out ten emeralds and threw them at the husk. "You can have your emeralds back. The last five minutes was free. Now, get out!"

The husk stared at me with fire in his eyes but bent down and retrieved his emeralds before skulking away.

A moment later Otis rushed into the room. "Why is he leaving already? Didn't he pay for an hour?"

"I gave him back his money. He was a freak."

Otis rushed up to me and grabbed my shirt and shook it. "You can't just send paying customers away. We'll go broke."

I pushed Otis' hands off my chest. "We will never go broke. This is Minecraft, get it? If we need something we only need to *mine* raw materials and then *craft* the item. Or, we can grow it."

Otis snorted. "That sounds like 'WorkCraft' to me. These meet and greets will put us on easy street. All you have to do is sit there and talk."

I shook my head. "I'm not so sure anymore. I don't know if I want to do this."

Otis looked angry and said, "But, I've already booked a meet and greet with one more player for today. At least talk to him. He paid three diamonds."

I nodded. "Okay, if you already booked someone I just can't send him away. But after that, I'm done ... at least for a while."

Otis sighed. "Fine. We've made quite a bit of income in the past couple weeks. It should sustain us for quite some time."

I nodded. "Whatever. Anyway, send in the player."

Chapter 3

I sat down at my table and waited for the player to come in. When he entered, I saw that he had been in the world of Minecraft for quite some time. He had a full set of diamond armor and diamond sword. He had a few scars on his face, probably from an encounter with a sword-wielding mob or maybe a berry bush.

"Sit down, player. What do you want to talk about?"

The player walked up to the table, tucked his sword into his inventory, and sat down. "I don't know. I heard about these meet and greets and just thought I'd want to meet and greet."

I chuckled. "That was worth three diamonds?"

The player shrugged. "I don't know. I'm hoping it will be. I read all your diaries and thought they were pretty cool. I just wondered what you are really like. I mean, you could never have written everything down in your books, right?"

I nodded my head and smiled. "Well, that's for sure. I just tried to hit the highlights. No one wants to read about what I eat for breakfast everyday or what I wear when I go to sleep."

The player laughed. "That would be pretty mundane." The player paused for a moment. "Anyway, I guess I was just wondering what's been going on lately in your role as The Warrior in the Balance. Any new diaries coming out discussing your adventures?"

I shrugged. "Did you read the one about the llama?"

The player nodded his head. "Yeah, that was crazy. What were the odds of the llama turning out to be Herobrine's long-lost wife?!? If I didn't know any better, I would assume you were making the whole thing up!"

"I know, right? But, anyway, since you asked, nothing else of note has happened." I paused for a moment. "I don't know. Maybe it's for the best. Being The Warrior is pretty stressful sometimes."

The player rested his elbows on the table and put his head in his hands. "I bet it is. Just being a player in this world is pretty stressful, what with all the creepers and skeletons and zombies ... I mean, um, no offense."

"None taken. We all have a role to play in this great drama of life, I suppose." I paused for a moment. It was a bit awkward. "Anyway, you seem pretty dominant. Have you done anything interesting lately?"

The player smiled. I could see hints of arrogance and viciousness in it. "I've just returned from the End."

I nodded. "So, you must have killed the Ender Dragon then?" I was sad when I said it. I recalled the valiant young ender dragons – Tom78 and Asher – who had helped me defeat Herobrine's minion, Shadow. They must have been called upon to grow to the full-sized Ender Dragon and battle a player.

"I did indeed. In fact, this is my fifth time to the End and back."

Wow! He has killed the Ender Dragon five times!

"That is a lot. Haven't you gotten ... well ... bored of that?"

He shrugged. "Oh, maybe a little. I'm working on a new ... um ... project that should keep me entertained for a while. But, I am not here to discuss my project. I wanted to ask about the end nectar you wrote about. I've never experienced that in my travels to the end."

"Yeah, I've never met a player who has." I paused and rubbed my chin. "I guess maybe only mobs must travel to the End through the nectar; players get a shortcut?"

The player nodded his head and was about to say something else when I heard a strange beeping noise. I looked around the room but could not tell from where it was coming.

The player was looking around too. "Don't tell me you guys have cell phones in Minecraft now?"

"What's a cell phone?"

The player laughed. "Never mind. But the beeping, it sounds like a device we have in our world. People communicate with it."

That's when I realized. It had to be. It could not have been anything else.

I reached into my inventory, dug around, and found the redstone device that Princess Savannah had given me after we had rescued the llama. Sure enough, a little red light on it was blinking and there was a beeping noise coming from it.

Ingenious.

"What is that thing?" asked the player, mesmerized.

"It's a communication device the Ender King gave me. I didn't know it could do this though. I thought I could only call him with it."

The player's eyes got wide and then narrowed into slits. "The Ender King? The Protector, right?"

I nodded my head.

The player came closer in order to examine the device. "What if you flicked that little switch? Maybe the beeping is like an alarm or something you're supposed to turn off?"

I knew the switch was to call the Ender King to my location. At least, that was its purpose when Princess Savannah had given it to me. I didn't want to flip the switch just because it was beeping. But, there didn't seem to be any other way to stop the beeping other than to destroy the device. And, as sure as the sun is square, I was not going to destroy it.

I reached down and flipped the switch. The beeping stopped. And then, nothing happened ... for two seconds.

Suddenly an enderman – not the Ender King – appeared in front of me. The player screamed in fright, recovered his composure, and sat back down in the seat. The enderman looked at him curiously, as if he might have recognized him, but ultimately ignored him. He turned and looked directly at me. "Baby Zeke?"

I nodded my head, unable to speak at the surprise of his appearance.

"Good. You need to come with me. Immediately."

"Why?"

The enderman looked at the player and pointed to the door of the house. "You need to leave. Now."

"But, it is just getting exciting! Let me stay."

"Get out, player," said Otis, who had just stepped into the doorway.

"Ah man, I know this is going to be part of a new Baby Zeke diary. Can I come along?" begged the player.

I looked at him and shook my head. "I can already tell this is not something you will want to be a part of. I feel it in my undead bones. We will have to cut our session short. Do you want your diamonds back?"

The player shook his head. "No, it's cool. But, if this becomes a diary adventure, will you be sure to mention me in it?"

I nodded my head. "What's your name anyway?"

"My name is Jason." And with that, the player turned and walked away.

Otis approached the enderman and said, "What's wrong?"

The enderman started to shake ... not with fear, but with rage. "There has been a rebellion in the End. The Ender King's servant, Frederick, is working with a dominant griefer to kill everyone and take over the End."

I was shocked. I had not liked Frederick when we met while I was in the End recently. I even wrote about that in my most recent diary volume. "I knew it. I didn't like that guy when I met him. He was mean to Savannah."

The enderman nodded his head. "He and the griefer are holding the Ender King prisoner!"

"What do you mean? Is there a ransom?" asked Otis.

The enderman shook his head. "No, they threatened to kill him if there was any resistance. But of course, everyone's resisting. Princess Savannah is leading the army against the rebellion."

"Is the Ender King still alive?" I asked, almost not wanting to the answer.

"As far as anyone knows, he is. But we have no time to lose. Princess Savannah sent me to bring you and Otis to help her."

I nodded my head sternly. "Of course. Let us fill our inventories and get our chicken steeds ready. We need five minutes." I said.

The enderman nodded his head. "Understood. I'll wait here."

Chapter 4

Otis and I rushed to Harold and Bob's chicken coop. We knocked on the door a couple times before bursting in. We did not have time for being polite.

Harold and Bob were each sleeping in their nests. They looked up groggily at us. Harold said, "What do you want? We were taking naps."

"It's an emergency. We need to go to the End right away," I said.

"Did someone lose their chorus fruit or something? Can't this wait," said Harold, still bitter from being awakened rudely.

"No it can't. The Ender King has been kidnapped!" I said.

Harold and Bob's eyes opened wide in shock. They both stood up immediately.

"Hop on Otis. Let's do this," said Bob.

"Same goes for you, Zeke," said Harold.

"We don't need to go in jockey formation right now," said Otis gruffly. "You guys just find some food to take with us. So you don't starve."

I nodded my head. "Yes, get some food and whatever else you think you'll need and meet us outside as soon as possible. We still have to pack our own inventories. There is an enderman out there waiting for us."

Harold and Bob quickly went to work preparing for the journey. Otis and I left the chicken coop and ran back to our house to pack weapons and food.

I had been drying rotten cow flesh into jerky so that I could store more meat in my inventory. I packed every slice that I had. I packed a few cookies, some water, and a few loaves of bread that I could feed to Harold and Bob as a treat.

Next, I packed several pickaxes, swords, bows, and arrows. I had a few TNT blocks and pressure plates sitting around, so I packed those too. Maybe landmines would come in handy at some point?

Otis emerged from his room fully armored head to toe in diamond armor. He had a diamond sword in one hand and a crossbow in the other.

"Where did you get that crossbow?" I asked.

"Oh, I ran into a pillager in the forest a couple weeks ago. He tried to kill me. He lost," said Otis with a grin.

I rolled my eyes. Same old Otis. "Well, it sounds like we are going to need your aggression once we get to the End. Are you all packed?"

"I sure am. Let's go save our friend."

We walked out of our house and met the enderman, Bob, and Harold. I looked at the enderman said, "What now? Is there an end portal nearby?"

"I transited through the cave portals. Princess Savannah said you'd been there before, when you were searching for the llama."

I nodded my head. "So, we can just use the cave portals then?"

The enderman shook his head. "All the portals in the cave arrive in locations controlled by enemy forces. The only reason I got through was that I had pretended to be a spy so I could get access and jump in. We'll have to build a new end portal."

Otis raised his arms in the air and yelled, "But we won't know where it comes out in the End? What if we transit into a terrible place? Or, right in the midst of the enemy?"

The enderman looked sad. "We will just have to risk it. Using the existing end portals would be certain death."

My heart was starting to beat faster. Even though I was undead, I felt the excitement and adrenaline a life-threatening adventure coursing through my veins. A proper adventure for The Warrior. "So, do you have all the pieces for an end portal?" I asked. "Or do we have to go find a stronghold?"

The enderman nodded his head. "Yes, I was prepared for this contingency."

The enderman reached into his inventory and pulled out end portal blocks and eyes of ender. He quickly assembled everything, and after he had placed the final piece, it glowed to life.

I looked over at Harold and Bob and Otis. "I know you aren't looking forward to going through the end nectar again, but we must."

They all three leveled their gazes at me. "It's not a problem, Zeke," said Bob. "I don't mind suffering a little if it's to save a friend."

Otis and Harold nodded their heads in agreement.

I felt a tear of pride coming into my eyes. I wiped it away quickly before anyone could notice, pretending that I had an itch. "Well then, shall we go?"

Without a word we all stood on the edge of the end portal, staring at the swirling inky blackness in its center. The enderman looked at us and said, "On the count of three, jump in all at once. That way, we all should arrive in the End at the same time."

He didn't have to tell me. I knew the drill. I'd been to the End more times and I ever really wanted to be, and now I was going into the midst of a battle royale. This wasn't going to be fun.

"One. Two. Three."

Chapter 5

The transit through the end nectar was its typical claustrophobia- and paranoia-inducing process. I floated there, unable to breathe or speak. Unable to move my body. At one point the enderman who had come to fetch us passed in front of me. He looked so happy. He looked like a fish gracefully swimming through the waters of a crystal clear lake in an unspoiled biome. I could tell he wanted to stay in the end nectar forever.

But, all good things – and, in my case, all horrible things – must come to an end, one way or another.

We suddenly appeared on the dull brown soil of the End. At first, I thought we had arrived in a perfect location. I could not see anyone, friend or foe. Otis, Harold, and Bob had were slowly recovering from the journey through the nectar. At least Bob didn't scream hysterically like he did the last time he went through the nectar. He merely looked completely shell-shocked.

I was just about to suggest we all walk to the top of a nearby hill to get our bearings when I heard a menacing voice behind us.

"What have we here? Overworlders? You don't belong here."

We all turned around and saw pillager standing before us leveling his crossbow at me and Otis. "I could say the same for you," said Otis. "By the way, the last time I met once of you guys, I acquired this." Otis removed the crossbow from his inventory and shook it in the air, taunting the pillager.

The pillager raised his crossbow and shot at Otis. But Otis was too fast. He ducked down on one knee as the crossbow bolt whizzed over his head. He leveled his own crossbow at the pillager and shot him right to the heart.

The pillager collapsed to the ground, but wasn't dead. I jumped up and ran over to him as quickly as I could and slashed at him twice with my sword. He grunted in pain, and then disappeared into a puff of smoke, dropping his crossbow and a couple of arrows. I grabbed the crossbow and arrows and tucked them into my inventory. I looked over at the enderman. "Pillagers? What are they doing here?"

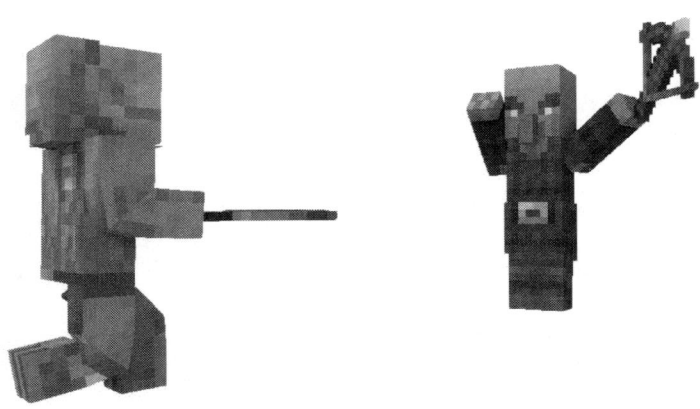

The enderman shook his head sadly. "The griefer recruited them to help with the rebellion against the Ender King. He brought a whole army of pillagers, as well as some evokers and vindicators. They love killing."

"Wait here a minute. Let me get the lay of the land," I said as I scrambled up a nearby hill. I cautiously looked over the hill to see if there were any additional any enemy forces. Fortunately, I didn't see anything. In the distance I saw a few endermen teleporting from here to there, but I couldn't tell whose side they were on. I went back down the hill.

"It seems like the coast is clear. But, are there any enderman who are helping Frederick and the griefer, or do we only have to worry about illagers?"

The enderman nodded his head as rage filled his purple eyes. "Almost every servant working in the Palace has betrayed the King and the Royal family. I don't really know why. The few who remained loyal have been killed or captured. It was a miracle that Princess Savannah escaped. Most of the common people are on the side of the Ender King, but they don't have many weapons. The illagers are going from town to town, rounding everyone up to put them into prison camps. Rumor has it that once Frederick and the griefer secure the main island, they will go to the outer end islands and round up all the endermen there."

Otis kicked the ground and spat. "Netherrack. How in the name of Notch are two jockeys supposed to defeat an army like that?"

"Yeah, and if most of the endermen don't have any weapons, how can they fight back?" asked Bob.

I had to admit, it was a conundrum. I was The Warrior, sure, but I couldn't single-handedly kill all these people. It had to be a team effort. *But where could we get a team?*

"Where is Princess Savannah now?" asked Harold.

The enderman smiled. "She's in a chamber deep beneath the Ender Dragon's mountain. I didn't even know it existed until Princess Savannah led a small group of us there as we escaped the Palace."

I nodded my head. "Can you get us there? I'd like to discuss everything with the Princess. Maybe we can figure out a plan."

The enderman smiled. "I thought you'd never ask. Why don't you get in your jockey formations to make it easier for me to teleport you there?"

Otis hopped on Bob and I hopped on Harold. It felt good to be back in jockey formation. It had been a few months. The last time was when we went to investigate that igloo.

The enderman walked in between us and tapped me and Otis on the shoulders. And then we teleported to the underground chamber beneath the Ender Dragon's mountain.

Chapter 6

When we materialized in the chamber, we appeared amid activity bordering on chaos.

Ender soldiers were running and teleporting to and fro.

There were some young ender children sitting in a corner crying and being comforted by an older ender woman.

I heard an ender doctor yell, "Bring some chorus fruit and an ender pearl. We're losing him."

I hopped off of Harold and Otis hopped off Bob. We looked at each other in stunned silence. I saw the enderman who had teleported us there look around the room frantically and then point. "There is Princess Savannah now. Follow me."

As we approached Savannah, I watched her barking orders to various soldiers. "What's happening in the eastern front?"

An ender soldier shook his head. "Frederick and his illager army have taken most of the eastern part of the island."

She shook her head. "I can't believe he's done so much so quickly. What about the northern part of the island?"

Another soldier spoke this time. "A substantial illager force has invaded, but so far has failed to capture much ground. But ... there have been thousands of civilian casualties."

Savannah's head slumped down. She put her hand to her forehead, rubbing it like she had a terrible headache. I felt bad for her. A teenager, even a Princess, shouldn't be put in a position like this. And with her father kidnapped too? Oof, it was dreadful.

When we were near Savannah, the ender soldier leading us suddenly stood at attention saluted her back and announced, "Your Highness. I have brought Baby Zeke and Otis, as you requested."

Savannah turned around quickly. She smiled briefly and then her grim countenance returned. She walked up to us and gave us each a quick, emotionless hug. "Have you heard what's happening?" she asked.

I nodded my head. "It sounds terrible. But I'm here to do whatever is necessary."

"You're darn right," growled Otis. "I'm ready to crush some pillager skulls."

Savannah managed a slight giggle at Otis' typically over-dramatic statement. "Well, if it comes to that, I'm sure you'll do well. We're hoping that we can somehow manage to put down the rebellion with the smallest loss of life."

"Savannah, what is this I hear about your father being kidnapped?" I asked.

I saw tears beginning to form in Savannah's bright purple eyes. But she blinked a few times and they went away.

"Frederick was serving dinner. Without any warning, the griefer and a few dozen pillagers surrounded us." She paused for a moment trying to control her rage. "Frederick, that traitor, must have let them into the Palace via some sort of secret passage. They restrained my father before he was able to teleport away to safety. I managed to escape when my servant, Billie, distracted a pillager." Savannah paused and sniffed. "The pillager killed her while I ran."

"So, where is your father now? Let's go get him," growled Otis.

Savannah shook her head. "He is somewhere in the Palace. I have no idea where. Frederick and his forces have it too well guarded. We have to neutralize the forces out here before we even attempt an attack on the Palace."

I thought for a moment. I could see the logic in Savannah's strategic choice, but I also had a concern. "That makes sense, but what do you think Frederick and the griefer will do if they're cornered in the Palace? Do you think they're going to let your father go?"

I could tell by the horrified look on Savannah's face she had not thought about that possibility. "What are you saying, Zeke?"

"I'm saying, if I were a horrible, evil person and had kidnapped the King of a realm I was trying to conquer, I would never let that King get away ... ever. Either I take over the realm and he becomes my figurehead ruler who did everything I told him to, or ... I'm sorry to say this ... I kill him."

Savannah gasped, but she knew I was right. "Well, then, what can we do? Just surrender the End so that my father can live? He wouldn't want that."

I nodded my head. "Of course, he wouldn't. He's the Protector. He would gladly lay down his life in order to free the End. But I don't think that's necessary."

Otis squinted his eyes at me. "You have a plan?"

I smiled. "Of course I do. I'm The Warrior."

"So you say," said Otis as he rolled his eyes, coughed, and then spit on the ground. "What's your plan?"

Chapter 7

"Well, I was trying to think about what the Ender King might do. He is the greatest strategic genius I've ever known," I said.

"That's what I've been trying to do, too," said Savannah. "Honoring my father's teachings."

"I recall that he always went *toward* the danger. There's no reason to run away from it. It's like if a tree is falling. The safest place is to be right next to the trunk because you only need to take one or two steps in any direction to avoid the falling tree. But, if you are far away from the trunk, it is more uncertain and one of the outer branches on the tree can crush you."

Otis coughed and sounded like he was gagging on his decomposing zombie pigman tongue. "Get to the point. These analogies hurt my brain."

"Well, I don't want to damage it too much. It's pretty darn small as it is," I said.

Otis pulled his diamond sword, stepped to me, and held it to my throat. "Do you want to say that again?"

An ender soldier reached out, grabbed Otis, and stripped him of his sword, tossing it to the ground. "Do not threaten The Warrior again."

"Some Warrior. I'm way more dominant than he is. Have you read my diary?" said Otis, never missing an opportunity to market his life story.

"I have not. And I do not intend to," said the enderman matter-of-factly.

Otis grunted with anger but said nothing more. He reached down and picked up his sword.

"May I continue?" I asked Otis.

Otis crossed his arms in front of his chest and said, "Be my guest."

"And so, in light of my tree analogy" – I paused to glare at Otis – "we need to go directly into the Palace. They will not be expecting it. But first, we need an army. A big army."

Savannah shook her head. "I can't spare anyone. We're too busy fighting the pillagers. There's thousands of them. And not to mention the ravagers, vindicators, and evokers." Savannah twitched. "I'm trying to save my people from extinction!"

"I understand, that's why we are going to bring the army from the Overworld."

Harold looked at me with a confused expression. "How are we going to do that, Zeke?"

I smiled. "We aren't going to do it, Otis and Bob are."

Bob pumped his wing into the air and said, "Yes!"

Otis gave me the side eye and asked, "How are we supposed to raise an army?"

"You're persuasive. Besides, you are friends with that husk jockey girl, right? Sandy was her name, wasn't it?"

Otis blushed slightly. I think he liked Sandy. "I suppose. I met her at the zombie retirement home while I was visiting Zeb. She was visiting her great-grandmother. She seems cool and dominant."

"Wait. A husk jockey girl is named Sandy? Kind of a basic name for a dried up zombie, no?" said Savannah.

"Her brother's name is Husky, if you can believe it," responded Otis.

"Anyway," I said, "let's focus. Didn't Sandy tell you how much all the husks hate the illagers, especially pillagers? How they would raid the deserts killing every husk in sight just for fun."

Otis punched fist into his open hand. "Yes, now that you mention it, I do remember her saying that."

"I think if you go find Sandy and ask her to bring a husk army, she will do it. Or, at least, she will know the right husk to ask."

Otis grinned with menace. "I'm sure she will. We might even be able to get some more mobs to come with us. Skeletons and spiders. I lived with a spider family for a while before we met. I bet they could organize some troops."

I could tell Otis was finally getting into it. The idea of bringing an army and killing a bunch of illagers was stirring his blood. He was feeling good about it. I had not seen him look this happy in months.

"And, I know an armored skeleton named J.T. who lives in a cave near our farm," said Bob. "Maybe he can get some of his people to join us?"

"Excellent," I said before looking at Savannah and asking, "Do you have any more of those redstone communication things?"

Savannah nodded. "Just a few. Why?"

"Give one to Otis. Otis can muster the army at the cave we teleported to when you helped us find the missing llama. One of those portals goes directly into the Palace, right?"

She nodded her head. "Sure, it's labeled with a letter 'P' on the side of the portal frame."

"Perfect," I said. "So here's the idea. Otis will recruit as large an army as he can. He'll have to do it in the next twenty-four hours. Then, we will distract Frederick, the griefer, and the illager forces, pulling as many away from the Palace as possible. Once we have them where we want them, we will use the redstone communicator as a signal for Otis and his army to enter the end portal and infiltrate the Palace. Then, it'll be kill or be killed. The die will be cast. We will either emerge victorious or dead."

"I like this plan Zeke. It's perfect," said Otis.

Savannah wasn't so sure. "This seems kind of like an all or nothing plan, Zeke. If Otis's army is overwhelmed and we can't distract the illagers or defeat enough of them, the End ... and my father ... will be lost."

I nodded my head. "Yes, it is very risky. But it's either that or fight a war of attrition which it doesn't look like the endermen are going to win."

Savannah thought about it for a few moments and then said, "Okay, let's do it." She looked at Otis and Bob. "Go with my servant, Krit. He'll get you to the Overworld. After that, it's up to you."

Otis stood at attention and saluted the Princess. "We will not fail you. Give me twenty-four hours, and I'll give you the biggest army you have ever seen."

I looked at Otis. "Make sure everyone knows how to fight. The moment they appear in the Palace, it'll be hand-to-hand combat. Once you materialize, find or capture someone who looks like they know what's up. Make them take you to the Ender King. Everyone else is expendable, including you."

I couldn't believe I was saying these things. I felt like a vicious monster. I felt like I was Herobrine.

But I wasn't marking people for death just for fun and laughs, I was making strategic choices about who could live and who could die in order to save the End from Frederick's rebellion and, with any luck, to save the Protector in the Balance as well. I didn't like doing it. But it had to be done.

Otis flashed me a vicious smile. "Understood."

I watched as Krit led Otis and Bob away. When they had gone, I looked at Harold. "You ready for this, buddy?"

"Probably not. But, that never stopped us before."

I forced a laugh to try, in vain, to lighten the mood, and patted Harold on the head. Then I looked Savannah. "Now it's time for phase two of the plan. Distraction."

Chapter 8

"Savannah, when I was here a long time ago, I met the young ender dragons who were preparing to become the full-sized Ender Dragon. They are still around, right?" I asked.

A pained expression crossed Savannah's face. "A few of them are. The griefer and his pillagers have been killing the Ender Dragon over and over again. Every time the full-sized one is killed, one of the trainees becomes full-sized and must fight." She paused for a moment and sighed. "But their training is incomplete and they are killed even more quickly. I think the plan is to force the ender dragons to become extinct. Then, the traitorous army will have an easy time mopping up the endermen without worrying about being attacked from above."

I was shocked to my core. The thought that the Ender Dragon could actually go extinct made me extremely sad. That a group of evil creatures could exterminate another creature who was just fulfilling its role in the Minecraft ecosystem disturbed me greatly.

"How many are left?"

Savannah shrugged. "Probably two or three dozen. Enough to last maybe a day or two."

I looked down at Harold. "We can't let this happen."

Harold nodded his beak. "I agree, Zeke. What should we do?"

"Well, the second part of my plan was to get the Ender Dragon to constantly shoot fireballs at the pillager forces, but I guess that hasn't worked so far. I think what we need to do is have some more organized attack runs. We can fly the young ender dragons in formation, like a flock of parrots. They can shoot fireballs at the pillagers and then we can follow up the ground assault using endermen."

"That seems like a good idea, Zeke," said Savannah. "I'm just concerned that all the ender dragons could die at once. The pillager crossbows are pretty accurate ... and deadly. I'm not even sure how many shots it would take to kill an undersized ender dragon trainee."

I thought for a moment. "Can't the Ender Dragon be regenerated using end crystals or something like that?"

Savannah nodded. "Sure, but we have to have an end portal from the Overworld to make it work. The crystals have to be placed on the portal, but all of the end portals are in the Palace."

I looked at Harold. Harold looked at me. We smiled. "There's one portal that is not in the Palace. The one we just used."

A huge grin spread across Savannah's face. "That means the next full-sized Ender Dragon that is killed can be regenerated! We might even be able to regenerate it two or three times before the pillagers discover the location of the end portal. That should give us enough time…."

"Do you have any end crystals?" I asked.

"I don't have any with me, but I know where we can get some. I'll send one of my people there right now." Savannah took a few steps away and spoke to an ender soldier who had been standing a short distance away. He nodded his head and saluted the Princess and then teleported away.

"He should be back in a few minutes." I nodded my head. "Excellent. Can you take us to the ender dragon trainees so we can chat with them. Just keep the end crystals here. For now. We'll be back."

"Sure, let's go."

Chapter 9

A few moments later we materialized in the ender dragon training facility. In contrast to the fun-loving behavior of youthful dragons the last time I was here, there was a morose atmosphere, like a black cloud of death had descended upon the chamber, choking all joy from the room. All the dragons were just waiting until they had to grow to full size and go outside to be slaughtered.

When we materialized they all looked at us and rather than greeting Princess enthusiastically, they just blinked a couple times and then went back to their private thoughts.

Savannah stood on top of a couple of blocks and raised her arms in the air. "Dragons. Can I have your attention please? We have a new plan, courtesy of Baby Zeke, The Warrior." She pointed to me as she finished her speech. I noticed the dragons perked up a bit. They'd heard about me. They knew what the Balance was.

Savannah stepped down from the platform and I climbed on top of it. Of course, I was so short I barely could look the dragons in the eye. "Dragons. Princess Savannah has told me about the situation in which you find yourselves. But, we can't just wait for each of you to go out to be killed. We must take the offense."

One of the dragons snorted and said, "What can you do? You are just a tiny baby zombie. There are thousands of pillagers out there killing every full-sized Ender Dragon who takes to the air. We won't last much longer."

"Stop thinking like that," I said forcefully. "Look, we've arranged to have end crystals taken to an end portal so that the current full-sized Ender Dragon can regenerate the next time he is killed. None of you will have to go out there as long as the crystals last."

The dragons perked up immediately. They looked around at each other smiling. A few of them even cheered. It felt good to give them hope for the first time in who knows how long. But we were not through this yet.

I raised my hands in the air to call for silence. "Princess Savannah tells me that there are enough crystals for several regenerations, but not infinite ones. We need to go out there and shrink the size of that pillager force. You all can shoot fireballs right?"

The dragons nodded enthusiastically. But then one of them asked, "I'm sure we can kill quite a few the pillagers, but in the end, won't they be able to take us all out? I mean we're not full-sized ender dragons. We can be killed much more easily." This put a damper on the celebration of the dragons.

"There will be risks, to be sure," I said. "But, I think there are a few things we can do to mitigate those risks. I have several ideas I'll discuss with Princess Savannah, but with respect to you guys, I was thinking we could make some lingering splash potions of weakness, harming, and poison so that during our first pass over the pillagers, we can throw a bunch of them into their forces. Each potion will create an area affecting multiple pillagers. Then, we can come around for a pass and kill the helpless pillagers using your fireballs before returning to the mountain."

The dragons cheered wildly. One of them said, "That's a great idea. Do you have any bottles for collecting our breath for the lingering effect?"

Bottles. Right. I looked at Savannah and raised an undead eyebrow asking if she had some.

"I'll have some brought here immediately," she said. Then she vanished and reappeared about ten seconds later. "The bottles will be here shortly."

"Hip, hip, hooray," cheered the dragons.

Chapter 10

We left the dragons with a few of Savannah's servants who were going to assist them in capturing their breath for the lingering potions. The servants were given instructions on how to brew the various splash potions we would need.

"We will get it done!" said one of the servants.

"How long do you think it will take to brew all of the potions?" Asked Savannah.

"We can do a few dozen an hour, so maybe two hours?" said the servant.

Savannah nodded. "Excellent. We will be back at that time to launch the first wave of attacks."

We then teleported back down to the hidden lair deep underneath the Ender Dragon's mountain. When we arrived, we saw that twelve end crystals were stacked in the center of the room. Standing next to them was an ender soldier. We approached the end crystals and Savannah asked, "Is this all you could find?"

The soldier nodded his head. "Yes, Your Highness. I have some men working on making more. If we are lucky, we can get another four made before these run out."

"So, that means we will likely have four total regeneration cycles?" I asked.

"Yes," said the soldier. "As long as the pillagers don't get more aggressive with their attacking style."

"Understood," I said. I turned to Savannah. "You should have someone teleport the four crystals over to that end portal and be ready to place them the next time the Ender Dragon is killed. Based on what you've told me, it might have to regenerate even before all the potions will be ready for our first attack run."

"I'll do that, Zeke. Plus I'm going to send fifty ender soldiers to guard the end portal. After that first regeneration, someone among the enemy is bound to know what's going on. They will start searching for the end portal. We have to protect it at all costs."

I reached into my inventory and pulled out the four TNT blocks and pressure plates I had packed before I came to the End. I put them on the ground and said, "Tell your soldiers to use these for landmines around the end portal. It could buy them some time."

Savannah smiled grimly. "Great idea." She looked around the room and then addressed the soldier guarding the end crystals. "You heard all that. Round up some men and teleport the first four crystals and the landmine components to the end portal Baby Zeke used to get here. Then, watch the sky. When the Ender Dragon falls again, bring him back to life."

The soldier saluted and teleported away to complete his mission.

Chapter 11

Having sorted out the use of the end crystals, we returned to the cave of the ender dragon trainees. As predicted, we saw the current Ender Dragon fall to his death and then be regenerated. The surprise of the regeneration was such that we could hear the distant pillager army gasp as though with one mouth.

The regenerated Ender Dragon seemed a little more dominant than before he had been killed. The skills he had acquired during his first life remained, and he was thus ever more skillful at using his fireballs and various attacks. I figured this would work to our advantage. If the Ender Dragon was regenerated two or three times, his skill level would increase and it would be more difficult to kill him.

Savannah's servant approached us and said, "I've got 100 potions ready for you. A variety of nasty compounds. All splash potions with the lingering effect."

"Fantastic. Are the dragons ready?" asked Savannah.

The servant nodded his head. "They are."

Savannah looked at me. "You and Harold are going to ride on a Dragon, right?"

Harold perked up. "You mean I get to fly? That would be awesome."

I laughed. "Of course, I wouldn't do this without you. I can't wait to drop some potions on these villagers."

"Totally," said Harold.

"In that case, you should wear these." Savannah reached into her inventory and handed us each a set of elytra wings. I had never seen a pair of elytra wings in person. It was beautiful and finely crafted. "Put these on. If, Notch forbid, the dragons on which you ride are killed, you can glide down to the ground and maybe escape."

I put on the elytra. It felt comfortable. Harold put his on. It was a little ridiculous. The elytra was about the same size he was.

"These are really heavy," complained Harold. "But the dragon's going to be doing all the work, so I guess I can live with it."

I patted Harold on his white-feathered head. "Let's hope we don't need to use these."

We followed Savannah to the staging area. Twenty young dragons had been fitted with cargo carriers. Each dragon had five potions. There were numerous ender soldiers ready to mount the dragons to ride during the attack.

Savannah, Harold, and I walked to three dragons. Savannah looked out into the sky and saw the Ender Dragon was beginning to falter. She turned around and addressed everyone in the room. "The Ender Dragon is about to die again. Once he is regenerated, we attack. Try to fly out of range of the pillagers crossbows. Drop your potions randomly so there's no overlap. Then we will make a second pass and strafe the affected areas with fireballs, killing as many as we can. If you think another pass will help, go ahead and do it. But no more than two. After that, return to the mountain. Understood?"

There were no questions. Everyone cheered. They were finally going to get some vengeance on these evil pillagers.

Harold walked up to the dragon he was going to ride. "My name is Harold. What is yours?"

"My name is Glacier."

"I've never met anyone named Glacier. That's a cool name." Harold paused for a moment before he realized his own unintentional joke. "Ha!"

The dragon rolled his eyes. "Yeah, I've never heard that one before. Get on, bird." Harold hopped on Glacier's back.

I thought it was only polite to introduce myself to the dragon I would be riding. I walked up to his face and said, "Hello, Mr. Dragon. My name is Zeke. What's yours?"

The dragon snorted. "I'm a girl, you fool."

I turned purple with embarrassment. "I'm sorry. I don't have much experience in telling dragons apart."

The dragon rolled her eyes and snorted again. "Whatever. It's fine. My name is Nuance."

I scratched my head. A little piece of rotting flesh came off under my fingernails. I flicked the flesh down to the dirt before saying, "Nuance? That's a peculiar name, isn't it?"

Nuance shrugged. "Actually, it's a common family name. I was about to say that Zeke is a name I had never heard. It sounds harsh on the tongue."

I silently mouthed my name. Zeke. Zeke. It did seem to end rather abruptly when spoken. *Maybe the Dragon had a point?*

"Are you ready to kill these pillagers?" I asked.

Nuance growled with menace. "I've been saving my fireballs up just for them. Just make sure you're accurate with those potions. The more we can kill, the better."

I agreed with that. I hopped on Nuance's back and watched as the Ender Dragon was slowly drained of its life force before crashing down to the barren soil of the End.

And then, I watched in awe as it suddenly roared back to life like a phoenix. It flew straight up into the air and screamed with rage. Then it circled and shot gigantic fireballs at pillager army, killing and wounding many.

"That's our signal! Attack!" ordered Savannah.

Chapter 12

Our squadron of dragons launched into the dark sky of the End. We were blocked from view of the pillagers by the gigantic body of the Ender Dragon. As the Ender Dragon turned to one side, however, our presence was revealed to the pillagers. We heard them scream and shout. We saw them pointing towards us.

I watched as they targeted their crossbows at us, most of the arrows falling short, though a few zipped past us, and a few dragons were hit. But nothing was critical.

Within a few seconds we were over the horde of the pillager army. We began tossing our potions of weakness, harming, and poison down into their mass. Nearly all the potions hit home. The cloud of the lingering effect spreading like a cancer among them.

Those not affected continued to shoot arrows at us. Nuance was hit but continued on. "Are you okay?" I asked.

Nuance nodded her head. "I can take a few of those before it will be a problem."

Nuance banked hard to the left to begin her strafing run. But at that point, a vex, conjured by one of the of evokers among the pillager army, jumped on my back!

It was grabbing at the elytra, trying to pull it off of me. But I was quicker. I pulled out my diamond sword and, thrusting it backward over my shoulder, stabbed the vex in the head. It screamed in pain and backed away.

After a few seconds, it had regained its composure and went for frontal assault, trying to bite my face. But again, I was far too dominant for a single vex. I blocked it with my diamond shield and slashed at it with my diamond sword, killing it.

"Nice work, Zeke," said Nuance.

I nodded my head. "Are you ready to resume the strafing run? Got your fireballs all heated up?"

Nuance nodded her head and began to dive. To get the most lethal effect, she would have to dive low, well into the range of crossbow fire. I crouched against her neck and held on. I felt the warmth as the fireballs climbed up from her stomach and out of her mouth.

I saw as they hit the ground exploding, killing dozens of illagers with each shot. I looked to my sides. I saw that all the dragons were having great success. Harold and Glacier were within shouting distance.

"Harold! How's it going over there?"

"Pretty well, I think. Glacier is a really good shot."

I gave Harold a thumbs-up sign and was about to say something about how good Nuance was when I felt the impact of several crossbow bolts into Nuance at the same time.

"Oof," she moaned.

I could feel the strength in her body going away.

"Nuance? Are you okay?"

"I don't think I can make it, Zeke. It was a pleasure fighting alongside you. Or, I guess I should say, underneath you."

And with that, I felt the life drain completely from Nuance and she flashed red and disappeared.

"Zeke! No!" screamed Harold as he and Glacier continued their attack.

I would have said something to Harold and mourned Nuance, but now I was in the middle of the air with nothing holding me up! In a panic, activated the elytra wings and began gliding away from the pillager army ... but you can only glide so fast.

I was alert for crossbow arrows coming in my direction, and there were many. I was deflecting them with my sword and my shield, but one penetrated my leg, and another my side. I quickly pulled out a potion of harming from my inventory and drank it. It restored my health, but the arrows were still in me.

I looked down at the ground for place to land away from the illager army, but I could not see any clear landing zone. The entire area was covered with illager forces.

This is it, Zeke. You are going to have to fight your way out!

I looked for the biggest opening I could that would give me a chance to prepare for battle. I saw one that was at least thirty blocks from any pillager and zoomed in on it and landed there. I removed the elytra quickly and tossed them in my inventory. I put my shield away and pulled out another sword. I would have to use two-sword technique if I were going to break through enemy lines and return to the Ender Dragon's Mountain.

The pillagers saw me land. But they didn't come after me immediately. Instead, they sent a ravager to take care of the job.

I stood my ground. The ravager charged straight at me. I had no idea what it was thinking. Maybe it thought it would just trample me to death. But I had other ideas.

When the ravager was nearly upon me, I jumped into the air and did a back flip over it. When I was directly above its neck, I slashed my swords across it, severing its head. It flashed red and disappeared.

When I landed back on the ground, I struck a pose of dominance and shouted with rage, "Is that the best you got? You'll have to do better than that to destroy the Warrior."

In response to my taunt, a dozen pillagers screamed and rushed toward me. *Oops!* If they attacked one at a time, I was confident I could defeat them. But, of course, they didn't. They all rushed me at the same time. They would meet with me in the middle and I would be dead.

Fortunately, they had miscalculated. When their sword tips were so close I could have reached out and touched them, I quickly jumped straight up into the air. The pillagers could not stop their momentum in time and they crashed into each other, stabbing each other to death. I landed in triumph on top of their bodies just before they flashed red and disappeared.

I laughed at the top of my lungs. I was trying to use psychological intimidation against the rest of the pillagers, hoping they would think twice against attacking me. If hundreds of them came at me, I didn't stand a chance.

And that was when I heard a slow clapping sound.

I looked around for its source. I didn't see any of the pillagers clapping. I kept looking back and forth but saw nothing.

"Who's clapping? Show yourself!" I demanded.

Several pillagers stood to the side, and I soon saw that it was a player who was clapping. A player clad in diamond armor from head to toe. The same player who had been at my house for a meet and greet just a few hours earlier.

Chapter 13

"Jason? You? You're the griefer?!?"

The griefer smiled with one corner of his mouth. "Brilliant deduction. No wonder you are part of the Balance."

"Seriously? Sarcasm right now? Why are you doing this?"

Fake fan.

The griefer shrugged before pulling out two diamond swords from his inventory and slashing them dramatically in the air. "I've already destroyed so many players' dwellings and accumulated fat stacks of goods on various Minecraft servers, I thought it might be time to step it up a bit. You know, capture an entire realm of Minecraft."

I couldn't believe the audacity of him. "You won't be able to get away with that. The Balance will eventually defeat you." I tried to stand tall and confident, even though I was short, undead, and not entirely sure I believed what I was saying.

The griefer chuckled. "Really? I've already got the Protector locked away, and you're next. That only leaves Notch and Herobrine."

"So, they will restore the Balance."

The griefer put a finger to his lips and tapped them for a moment. He looked like he was thinking. "I doubt it. Notch and Herobrine are polar opposites. That's not really a balance; that's a tug-of-war. It will tear Minecraft apart. Which is exactly what I want."

What is it with these power-hungry maniacs? They are all the same, even though they all seem to think they are unique visionaries.

"But if Minecraft tears itself apart, then what are you going to grief? You won't have anything to do." I don't know why I tried to reason with him using logic, but it seemed like the … um, well … logical thing to do.

The griefer laughed a deep belly laugh, the kind that a maniac would laugh right before telling you something insane. "That's perfect. I'm sick of Minecraft. It's been around for more than ten years and it is still popular in my world. No videogame should last for ten years. I'm through with it."

I held my sword out and pointed it at him for emphasis, even though he was several blocks away. "I don't know what you are talking about when you use the word 'videogame,' but if Minecraft is popular in your world and players want to play it, then why do you want to deprive them of that joy?"

I watched the griefer's face. I could tell he had an answer to my question, but he didn't want to give it to me. Instead, he snapped his fingers and suddenly twenty vexes appeared around me, summoned no doubt by the griefer's evoker minions. The vexes dove toward me and I slashed at them. I killed two of them immediately, but they kept coming and coming. Eventually, the weight of the vexes and the scratches of their claws against my face forced me to the ground. I was struggling, rolling back and forth trying to get them off me, like putting out a fire. *Stop. Drop. And roll.* But it was no use.

A few moments later, I felt the thick viselike hands of several pillagers grabbing me, tying my hands behind my waist, and then picking me up by the collar of my armor.

A pillager held me above the ground and carried me roughly to the griefer.

The pillager held me up so that the griefer could lean in and look me in the eyes. "Baby Zeke, you're no longer the Warrior anymore. You're the Prisoner."

Chapter 14

As I watched the reincarnated Ender Dragon continue to strafe the illager forces, I was tied to a wooden plank and carried into the Ender Palace. The griefer walked in front of me, like a triumphant trophy hunter with his low-paid servants bearing the weight of his kill.

Inside the Ender Palace, the traitorous ender servants bowed before the griefer and then, as I passed in front of them, they pointed and laughed.

You'll get yours, I thought. Otis should be back with his army in a few hours. I didn't care if I died as long as this rebellion was put down.

The pillagers carried me through the reception hall and then into the throne room where Frederick was sitting on the Ender King's throne!

I. Hate. Him.

The griefer walked up to Frederick and bowed. "Your Highness, I have captured the so-called Warrior."

That was it. No one is going to call Frederick "Your Highness" much longer. And, what did he mean, "so-called"?

Frederick stood up and said, "Untie him from the board, but keep his hands bound."

The pillagers did as they were told and soon I was standing and looking face-to-face with the evil enderman traitor. "You realize you're going to go down in history as the worst mob who ever lived, right?" I said, practically spitting venom at Frederick's face.

"You know, Zeke, the winners write the history. Like your diary. If Herobrine had won, you would just be remembered as a pathetic little baby zombie who didn't count for anything." Frederick paused for a moment. "Come to think of it, that still may come to pass."

"Why don't you untie me and we can discuss it? Alone."

"Oh, I know you could defeat me one-on-one. But that's why you won't defeat me, because I have this griefer and his illager army to help me out."

I looked around at the griefer and the handful of pillagers who were in the room with us. "You realize that once they capture the End, they are probably going to kill you and keep it for themselves."

Judging by the shocked look on Frederick's face, I could tell this had not crossed his mind previously. "You are being absurd, Zeke. They need me as the King of the End. I've always wanted to be King. Your buddy, the Protector, wasn't much of a king. All he cared about was being worshiped."

I lunged toward Frederick but because my hands were tied behind me, I lost my balance and flopped on my face. Frederick laughed at me and told one of his servants to pick me up.

Once I was back on my feet, I said, "You'll never be even 10% of the leader the Ender King is. In fact, no one's ever going to call you King. Sure, maybe they will to your face, but they will always know that you are a traitor. They will probably call you Black Frederick."

Frederick looked down at his obsidian body and then back at me. "Well, that would be a completely accurate description of me. All endermen are black. You are an idiot, Zeke."

I grunted with frustration. "You know what I mean. Black is also a symbolic color of evil. So when they call you Black Frederick, they will really be calling you Evil Frederick. Or, Traitorous Frederick. No one will ever even name their children Frederick anymore once I'm through with you."

Frederick put his hand to his forehead and pressed on it slowly and rhythmically. "You are giving me a headache."

"I'm going to give you more than that once I get free."

Frederick shook his head and clucked his tongue. "Take him to his cell."

"As you wish, my King," said the griefer bowing low before Frederick. As he bowed, the griefer turned his head slightly, almost imperceptibly towards me, and winked.

Chapter 15

The griefer and two of his pillager henchmen took me out of the room, down the hall, and down some stairs into the Palace dungeon.

What was strange was that the ceiling seemed exceptionally low. I could tell that new layers of stone had recently been affixed to the ceiling. As a result of the remodel, the ceiling was now too low for an enderman to stand up.

What is the meaning of this alchemy?

I could feel the temperature of the air getting cooler as we descended further into the dungeon and beneath the ground layer of the soil on which the Palace was built. We descended at least sixty blocks into the depths.

As we walked down a hallway of cells, we passed one door that had four pillager guards in front of it. *That had to be the Ender King's cell.* I noted its location as we continued down the hall.

We walked past four other doors, which were unguarded. I didn't know if they were empty or just held lower-value prisoners. Finally, we came to the last cell in the row. The griefer opened the door and then shoved me in. I landed on the ground. Hard.

I looked up at the griefer and squinted my eyes. I made sure he saw every ounce of anger and hatred in me at that moment. "You're going to regret that."

The griefer appeared unconcerned. "Right. We'll see about that."

The two pillagers who had been walking with us entered my cell and shackled my legs to the walls of the room. Then, they untied my hands from behind my back but shackled them together in front of me. I had some additional slack in the shackle, so I could take care of basic tasks like eating and drinking.

"Comfy?" said the griefer with a snide smile.

"I've been in worse spots," I said. "If you let me go now, I won't kill you, but I will have to punish you."

The griefer laughed and shook his head. "By Notch's beard, you never stop, do you? You're so cute when you're angry."

No one calls me cute and gets away with it.

I decided there wasn't much point in trying to engage this evil creep in conversation. If I ever got out of here, he was going to get it. But, assessing my current situation realistically, I wasn't sure I'd ever get out. Even if Otis showed up with an army and they managed to take back the Palace, I was sure someone would come down here to kill me before I could be rescued. Still, I was the Warrior and I wasn't going to curl up into a fetal position and cry like a little baby.

I sat down on the floor and crossed my legs. I rested the backs of my shackled wrists on my knees. I began to meditate.

I could tell the griefer and the two pillagers were standing and staring at me. Maybe they had never seen anything like it. Maybe they just thought I was a fool.

"Go ahead guys, you can go back to the battle," I heard the griefer tell the pillagers. I kept my eyes closed. I heard their footsteps leave the cell and then the griefer walked to the door and shut it. But he remained inside with me.

I kept my eyes closed, meditating. I heard the griefer walk around me a couple times. I could tell he was looking at me. Maybe he was checking the shackles too, just to make sure I wasn't trying a trick.

Eventually, his footsteps stopped and he was standing directly in front of me. "You're a strange duck, Baby Zeke."

I remained in my meditative position with my eyes closed, but I said, "What's a duck?"

The griefer chuckled. "That's right. You don't have ducks in Minecraft, do you?"

"What's a duck?"

"I'm sure we could have been friends under other circumstances. It's too bad you had that redstone communication device. I was truly looking forward to our meet and greet."

I opened my eyes for that one. "Right. If it weren't for that redstone communication device, you'd still be here doing all your horrible griefing while I, the Warrior, remained in the Overworld completely oblivious to everything. That would've been perfect for you, no?"

"Yes, of course. And that was the plan. I had no idea the endermen had such fascinating communication technology. Still, it doesn't change my mind about capturing this realm."

I squinted my eyes at the griefer. "Frederick has no idea what you intend to do. I know you're going to kill him, eventually."

The griefer shrugged. "Maybe. Maybe not. It depends on how he handles himself."

"Can I give you some advice?" I said in all seriousness.

An amused expression passed across the griefer's face. "Why not? It'll probably be the last advice you ever give anyone. Lay it on me."

"Leave Minecraft now. Do whatever it is you players do when you shimmer and disappear. Leave your inventory where it's stored and never return. That is my final warning."

As I spoke, the griefer's eyes got wider and wider, like he was shocked and amazed at the same time. His eyes remained extremely wide as he stared at me, unblinking.

Maybe I had gotten through to him?

But then the griefer blinked his eyes a few times and laughed. He did not say another word, just laughed. He was still laughing when he walked out of my cell and slammed the door, locking me in.

Chapter 16

I was left alone for the next hour. I returned to my meditative pose, hoping that if I quieted my mind a solution would come to me. The way for me to escape, capture Frederick, rescue the Ender King, and defeat the griefer and his army.

Simple.

I had been meditating solidly for one hour, but nothing. I knew the battle was raging outside, but I couldn't hear or see anything for myself. I wondered if the full-sized Ender Dragon was still regenerating, or if the end crystals had run out. Were the young dragons again sacrificing themselves to the crossbows of the pillagers?

It was still a few hours before Otis would arrive with his army. I hoped that Savannah's forces could hold the line against the pillagers long enough to give Otis a chance.

There was a brief knock on the door to my cell and I heard it open. I heard light footsteps walk in and I knew it was an enderman.

I opened my eyes. Standing before me was a young ender servant holding a tray of food. It looked surprisingly good. Some raw cow meat, two slices of watermelon, a loaf of bread, and a bottle of water. I would've preferred more flesh, preferably rotten, but this would be satisfactory.

The ender servant approached and set the food tray down in front of me. When he bent down, I noticed that two pillagers were guarding the door.

While the enderman was still crouched down depositing my tray of food, I whispered to him, "Are you a traitor?"

The enderman looked surprised. He glanced around furtively and then whispered back, "I serve the true king."

I hoped he wasn't just lying to me. Maybe trying to get me to say something that he could report to the griefer in exchange for some sort of reward for his service. I nodded my head but said nothing. When he realized I wasn't going to respond, the enderman whispered again, "I recommend the bread." Then he stood up and slowly walked out of the cell.

One of the pillager guards looked in and said, "Eat your slop, you disgusting undead freak." And then he slammed the door shut.

I may be an undead freak, but at least I wasn't an unthinking minion.

I wondered what the ender servant had meant about the bread. I guess I would figure it out eventually, but I ate the meat first. I am a zombie after all.

After I had finished the meat and washed it down with a watermelon slice and a few sips of water, I turned to the bread. I broke a piece off from the end and ate it. It was very tasty. I broke another piece off, and that's when I saw it.

A piece of paper.

I looked up quickly at the door to the cell to make sure no one was observing me. There was no face in the small window. I pulled the piece of paper out and concealed it behind the loaf of bread, which I held in front of my mouth.

The writing was so tiny I could almost not read it. But it said: "There is a weapon buried in the cell.

Mine down two blocks in the far back right hand corner of your cell. Use it as necessary."

Was this real? It seemed extremely convenient. Was it put there because they knew I was coming? Was this a set up? Or did all the cells have weapons hidden in them?

I put the piece of paper into my mouth and chewed and swallowed it so that it could never be discovered. I tucked the rest of the bread into my inventory, which was otherwise completely empty, having been stripped by the guards when I was captured. I waited a few minutes and then shouted, "I'm done with my dinner."

The door opened and one of the pillagers came in and grabbed the tray. "Sweet dreams, freak."

I waved to the pillager with my shackled hands. "Nighty night." The pillager grunted with disgust and slammed the door.

I returned to my meditative position. I breathed slowly and quietly. Eventually, I heard the pillager guards snoring.

I slowly crawled over to the corner of the room where the note had said the weapon would be. Fortunately, there was just enough slack in my chains that I could reach the final block of the corner of my cell. Unfortunately, I would not be able to get a full strike against it with my fist, so it was going to take two or three times longer than normal to mine the blocks.

As I slowly and methodically punched the blocks, I listened for the snoring sounds of the pillager guards. Fortunately, they never ceased. When the first block came out I tucked it quickly into my inventory. Then, struggling to stretch my body to its maximum length, which isn't very long, I managed to punch the second block below until it disappeared and floated in the air waiting for me to grab and put into my inventory, which I quickly did.

I looked into the hole and sure enough there was a weapon in there!

A wooden sword?!? Weak.

At that moment the door burst open and the griefer stood there pointing at me and laughing. "I knew you would fall for it. I just knew it."

I did not like being laughed at. I quickly reached into the hole and managed to grab the wooden sword. I turned around and tossed it through the air. The griefer was so surprised that he did not have a chance to react. My aim was true, and the tip of the sword lodged in the griefer's neck. That silenced him.

But, it was a wooden sword after all, and he was a high level player. It did almost no damage. He pulled the sword angrily from his neck, tossed it on the ground, and stomped on it until it broke into splinters.

"How dare you throw that sword at me?"

Now was my turn to laugh. "How dare you try to get a laugh at my expense? If it had been a diamond sword, you would be dead right now."

The anger vanished from the griefer's face. He smiled at me grimly. "Touché. I should've known better. It was actually Frederick's idea. He is a vindictive little weasel."

"What's a weasel?"

The griefer slapped his forehead. "I forgot, you don't have weasels in Minecraft either." He paused for a moment thinking of the right animal. "How about this? He's a vindictive little endermite."

I cringed at the analogy. How awful, especially for an enderman, to be compared to an endermite?

"So, now that you have played your prank on me, you're going to let me go free, right?"

The griefer waved his hand in front of his face dismissively. "Yeah, right. Get some sleep."

The griefer turned around and left the cell. A pillager guard stood in the doorway, pretending to snore like he was asleep, the sound I had been hearing that entire time. Then he grinned before slamming the door in my face.

Chapter 17

After the evil griefer left locked the door to my cell, I returned to meditating. I needed to find some way to escape from the cell, no matter what.

I sat in an upright position my hands gently resting on my knees as I cleared my mind.

I sat there, mind clear and receptive, waiting for an idea about how to escape to come to me.

Whatever it was, it needed to be creative. When I had been captured, my inventory had been emptied. I had absolutely nothing left, except a small piece of bread. And if I thought of a plan that needed paper, I was out of luck because I had already eaten it.

I began to feel that my meditation was hopeless. I was shackled in a windowless cell guarded by two pillagers. I had no weapons. I was a tiny baby zombie. *How did I ever become the Warrior?*

Nevertheless, I continued to meditate. I refused to give up. The lives of my friends and all of the endermen were in the balance.

To those to whom much is given, much is expected.

Unfortunately, my meditation wasn't going well. After about fifteen minutes, all I could think about was eating the piece of bread I had tucked away. The thought wouldn't leave my mind. It was distracting me.

I stopped meditating and sighed as I reached into my inventory which held nothing but half a loaf bread. I pulled the bread out and nibbled a piece. I chewed it for a while and then swallowed.

But I swallowed wrong. I started to choke. I was coughing, gasping for breath. *Was I really going to choke to death?*

I coughed and coughed. Even the pillager guards got up and looked in the cell. "What's going on in there?"

I pointed in my throat indicating I was choking. The guards pointed back and laughed, hoping to watch me die.

But then I coughed up the small glob of slimy chewed bread onto the ground.

"Aw shucks," said one of the pillager guards as they both sat back down.

I gave him the evil eye, even though he didn't see it. I looked at the disgusting blob of undigested food that had nearly killed me and was about to flick it into the corner of the room when I had an idea.

I reached out and touched the glob. It was extremely slimy. *Slimy enough, perhaps?*

I put the glob on my wrist just beneath the shackle on my left arm. I rubbed it around and tried to get as much as I could tucked underneath the shackle itself. Then I pulled on the shackle, trying to slide it down my wrist and over my hand.

I pulled as hard as I could while still being very quiet. If I grunted or shook the shackles, the pillager guards would hear what I was doing.

I continued to pull and finally the shackle began to move slightly. I pulled some more, and it slid further. Unfortunately, it was peeling some of my decaying flesh off my wrist and hand as well, but I didn't care. My health would regenerate eventually. All that mattered now was escaping.

After about a minute, I managed to slip the shackle off my wrist completely!!!

I set it quietly onto the floor, and then put my hand on it to make it look as if I was still shackled, just in case the pillagers looked into my cell.

I took another bite of bread and chewed it into a slimy goop. I then worked myself free of the two shackles on my legs.

The final shackle was going to the trickiest. I would have to use my free hand to pull it off. I needed at least one minute without a pillager looking in.

I chewed up my last piece of bread and spit it into my free hand. I rubbed it on my right wrist and was about to begin pulling it when I heard the chair in which the villager guards were sitting scratch against the floor.

I quickly put my feet and left wrist on the shackles to make it look like they were still shackled. If the guard came into my cell, I would be discovered. But, if he just looked in, I hoped I would escape detection.

The pillager guard peeked in through the window. "Comfy in there?"

I held up my one truly shackled wrist and shook the shackle at the guard. "Yeah, I love jewelry."

The pillager chuckled. "You know, it's too bad we had to take you prisoner. You seem like pretty funny zombie."

"Thanks, I appreciate that," I lied. I needed to get him to sit down.

"Anyway, it'll all be over soon. I heard that our army is inching closer to the Ender Dragon's Mountain. Once we capture that, it'll just be a mop up operation."

I shivered inside. "How close are you?"

The pillager guard shrugged. "Not sure exactly. You know how rumors go. Some people are saying we should capture it within the hour, others say it may take another day."

I hoped it was the latter. I still needed time to escape, and Otis needed a few hours to get his army prepared.

"Yeah, rumors usually make a mess of the truth, don't you think?"

The pillager laughed again. "See, you're even wise, not just funny. Oh well. Enjoy your imprisonment." And with that, the pillager guard sat back down.

I waited a few minutes just to make sure he wasn't going to stand up again. I thought I heard him snoring again. I didn't want to fall for that trick again, but since the fake snoring had already been used against me, I didn't think the guards were going to try it again.

The goo on my wrist had gotten dry. Unfortunately, that was my last piece of bread. So I had to spit and drool all over my own wrist in order to re-moisten those slimy bread goo.

My mouth started to dry out. So I imagined eating rotten cow flesh and ... pardon me for this ... villager flesh. That made my mouth salivate and I was able to moisten the goo very thoroughly.

Once it was fully moistened, it didn't take long to slide the final shackle off my wrist.

I crept to the cell door and peeked through the window. I could just make out the pillager guards sitting in chairs. They were both sleeping.

I went to the far corner of the cell where the griefer had hidden the wooden sword just to make fun of me and began punching in the corner. I did it as quietly as possible, and soon was three blocks deep.

I then turned at a right angle aiming for where I believed the Ender King's cell was.

Once I had mined a few blocks in that direction, came back up to my cell, grabbed a torch, got back down in the hole, and sealed myself in with previously-mined blocks.

When someone finally entered my cell, it would seem like I magically disappeared. All they would see would be empty shackles.

As I mined toward the Ender King's cell, I took each block I had mined and put it behind me. That way, if the pillagers began to mine down inside my cell, they wouldn't find an obvious pathway. It would make it much easier for me to do what I need to do. Some would think I had mined straight down. Others will think I mined to the outer wall of the Palace. But someone might figure I was going for the Ender King's cell.

I had to work fast.

* * *

It had been about two minutes since I had escaped from my cell. The mining was slow going because all I had to use as my fist. And my fist was starting to hurt. But I wasn't going to give up. I wasn't going to slow down.

When I had been in my cell, I determined it was six blocks wide. The walls between the cells appeared to be two blocks wide. Since I thought the Ender King's cell the fifth cell in the line from my own, I figured I needed to mine at least thirty-five blocks in order to pop up inside of his cell.

I was on block thirty-five now. I would mine block two more blocks to get into the center of the cell, and then mine up.

The trick was going to be to pop up into the cell when no one was looking. *But what if there were guards inside of the cell?* I'd be seen immediately.

Then, a horrible thought crossed my mind. I didn't have any more bread. How would I get the Ender King out of his shackles, assuming he was shackled. *What if he was inside some sort of obsidian cage? How would I break that?*

I didn't have time to think about it. I would just have to embrace my inner Warrior-ness and react immediately to what I encountered.

I was now at block thirty-seven. I mined up two blocks and knew that I only had one more block to mine before I would pop up into the cell.

I prepared myself mentally. If there was a guard in there, I would go for him first and then take whatever weapon he had and use that to defend myself and free the Ender King. If there were no guards, I would just have to figure it out.

I took a deep breath and punched the final block. As it collapsed into rubble, I saw torchlight. I reached up to the edge and pulled myself into the Ender King's cell.

Chapter 18

I had seen evil before, but nothing prepared me for what I saw inside the Ender King's cell.

The majority of the cell was only two blocks high, not tall enough for an enderman to stand. The only portion that was three blocks high was in the center of the cell. There was a column made of glass blocks. The blocks themselves were filled with water. The Ender King stood inside the column of water-filled glass blocks. Due to the low ceiling, I could only see his legs and torso. I could see his body periodically flash red, taking damage.

He was being tortured.

It took me a moment to figure out that the torture was coming from tiny drops of water dripping on his head.

The Ender King's ankles were bound together with cobwebs, as were his wrists. He could do nothing to stop the torture. He could not teleport away.

It was horrifying.

Fortunately, there were no guards in the cell. The griefer and Frederick must have assumed that there was no way for the Ender King to escape or be freed. That's why all the ceilings were so low in the dungeon. No endermen could teleport to the King's aid because they could not fully materialize in such an enclosed space.

Diabolical!

I vowed right then and there that no matter what else happened I would kill Jason the griefer and Frederick. Even if it meant my life. Even if it meant the lives of the innocent. I was raving. No matter what the cost, the stain of evil they had created needed to be wiped from Minecraft forever.

I walked slowly to the cell door. I peeked out the window. There were still four pillager guards standing outside of it, but they were not paying attention. In fact, it looked like they were playing some sort of game using sticks and rocks. I had never seen it before. But, it had something to do with gambling. After a couple of throws of the sticks and the rocks, someone always looked happy and the rest looked sad. Money changed hands.

Good, I thought to myself, *their vices can keep them distracted.*

I returned to the hole out of which I had crawled and quickly mined down another five blocks. I also doubled the width of the hole. When I was done, I climbed back up into the Ender King's cell.

I then broke away some of the ceiling rock so that the Ender King could see that I was there.

When he saw me his eyes got wide and he smiled. But then when a drop of water landed on his head from the torture device, and he cringed, flashed red, and grimaced in pain.

I held my hand up and indicated that I was about to do something. The Ender King nodded his head.

I went down to one side of the glass blocks and I punched a hole in the glass, draining the water. The water drained into the hole I had just dug, but only filled up about two blocks deep. I then bashed the glass column and ripped the cobwebs off the Ender King's arms and legs.

The Ender King looked relieved. "I am glad to see you, Zeke. I didn't know how much longer I could stand that without going insane," he whispered.

I gave him a thumbs up. I noticed my thumb was starting to look really stubby, all this rock punching was really taking its toll on me.

"Follow me. We have to leave before the pillagers get in here."

The Ender King nodded his head but then said, "They've got it set up so I can't teleport anywhere. They have this low ceiling surrounding this entire area.

I smiled and pointed. "We are going down this hole. We can mine for a while and then get out of here."

"I'm not leaving my Palace. I shall go kill Frederick," whispered the King with a dramatic flourish.

I shook my head. "No, I have a plan. Savannah's in on it too."

A tear came to the King's eyes. "Praise be to Notch that she is still alive. I did not know. Do you know about the rest of my children and my wife?"

I shook my head. "Savannah didn't know either." I paused for a moment as the Ender King processed this information. "But we need to go. Otis is going to be here with an army very shortly, and we need to coordinate our attack."

The Ender King looked relieved though still concerned.

We were just starting to climb into the hole when the door to the cell opened. The pillager who had opened the door saw what was happening and sounded the alarm.

"He's escaping," he said as he raised his crossbow to shoot at us.

I rushed over to him and kicked him in the knee. It was just enough that his shot went wide and missed the Ender King. The Ender King stretched out his long spaghetti arm and grabbed the crossbow from the pillager. He then loaded it and shot the pillager right through the head, killing them. The pillager dropped an iron pickaxe, which I quickly grabbed.

Two more pillagers rushed in. I used the pickaxe against one, killing him. The Ender King shot the other with two crossbow arrows. He momentarily seemed uninjured, but then suddenly flashed red and disappeared into a puff of smoke.

The last pillager entered the cell holding a crossbow in each hand. He aimed for the Ender King and shot both of them. The Ender King ditched one arrow, but was hit by the other in the arm. The King dropped his crossbow he had been holding.

The pillager was trying to reload his crossbows, but I took the iron pickaxe to the pillager with abandon. I hacked at him, taking out my frustration against the griefer and Frederick on this poor pillager. He died in excruciating agony, dropping a crossbow and an iron sword. I put the crossbow in my inventory along with the iron sword. I would need the pickaxe to mine our escape.

I grabbed a couple of torches from the walls of the cell and we went down into the hole, followed quickly by the Ender King.

Using the pickaxe, I mined down at a slight angle which I believed would bring us to the Palace walls. I was right. Five minutes later we were standing in a hole overlooking the plains between the Palace and the Ender Dragon's Mountain.

In an ominous sign, the pillager army did indeed appear to be within a short distance of the mountain itself, just as the guard to my cell had suggested.

"We don't have much time," said the Ender King.

"Agreed. Can you teleport me to the mountain? Do you have enough strength left?"

The Ender King looked down at me. "There's plenty of strength left, Zeke. The pain of torture is nothing compared to the pain I feel at the deaths of my people at the hands of a traitor who now sits on the throne of the End."

I felt the same way. The Ender King reached out and grabbed my shoulder. And we teleported to the Ender Dragon's Mountain.

We first appeared in the training area for the young ender dragons. To my shock, only eight young dragons remained. Nevertheless, when they saw the Ender King they cheered wildly. One of them was Glacier, who had survived the initial attack and apparently had not been called yet to transform into the full-sized Ender Dragon. "My King, you are alive. Praise be to Notch."

"My jockey, you are alive," said Harold, who rushed to me. "Hop on."

I smiled and stroked Harold's head. "Later. We don't need to be in jockey formation right now."

The Ender King nodded his head. "It's all thanks to Baby Zeke. I don't know how he did it, but he rescued me."

Glacier looked at me and said, "Thank you so much, Baby Zeke. I expect you will be writing this down in your next diary. I can't wait to read it."

I nodded my head and said, "If we survive, I'll put it in a diary. If we survive."

The King looked at me. "Did you say Savannah was near?"

"Yes, since she's not here I assume she's in your secret stronghold deep within the mountain."

The Ender King grinned. "Yes, I installed that all by myself shortly after becoming king many years ago. I wanted a place where I could be alone to think about things. But, I also made sure it would have military capabilities in the event of an invasion of the End." The Ender King paused and looked sad for a moment. "I never thought the invasion would be orchestrated from within my own Palace."

I shook my head sadly. "I'm sorry, King. But we can still beat them. Let's go talk to your daughter."

The Ender King reached out and grabbed my shoulder and we teleported down to the secret stronghold.

Chapter 19

When the Ender King and I materialized in the secret underground stronghold, there was a great commotion. Endermen rushing from here to there. We saw princess Savannah speaking with the Ender General.

We stood there for a moment, taking in the scene. I looked at the Ender King and could see tears welling up in his eyes as he saw his daughter. But rather than rushing to her side immediately, he was watching her work. Watching her be a royal leader. His tears were as much from joy of seeing her alive as from pride of seeing her in the role she was born to play.

But after a few seconds, the endermen began to realize who was standing in the room. They let out a cheer of thanksgiving. The cheer made Savannah and the Ender General turn around.

The Ender General immediately stood at attention and saluted the King, while tears of joy streamed down his face.

Savannah teleported to her father's side and gave him a hug. All pretense of royalty was gone. She was just a little girl who was glad to see her daddy. She cried heaving sobs of tears while she hugged him. The Ender King, unable to restrain his emotion, cried as well.

After a few seconds, there wasn't a dry in the room. My own eyes were virtual swamps of decaying eyeball meat mixed with tears.

After about fifteen seconds, the Ender King gently moved his daughter away from him. He looked at her lovingly and said, "I'm glad to see you too, Savannah. And nothing would give me greater pleasure than to go sit in a room and talk to you for the next five days uninterrupted, but we have work to do."

Savannah nodded her head and wiped her tears from her face. "We already have a plan, Daddy."

The King nodded. "Baby Zeke told me a little bit about it. How much longer do we have until Otis returns?"

"Well, we gave him twenty-four hours to acquire an army. He only has about one hour left. He is supposed to be ready to transit to the End at any moment after the twenty-four hours has expired," said Savannah.

The King looked at me. "I don't mean to be rude, but I recall Otis as being somewhat of a wildcard. Do you think he can really raise an army?"

I nodded my head confidently. "I'm sure he'll raise an army. Whether it's a few hundred or a few thousand strong will be the real question. I'm sure he'll have enough troops to provide a substantial distraction, at the very least. Whether they can actually retake the Palace, I have no idea."

The Ender General had by this time approached our group. "Yes, my King, we have troops in the area to assist in the distraction of the pillager forces, but they are severely outnumbered. If Otis does not return with a very large army, I fear that this will only be a temporary delay in the conquest of the End."

The Ender King nodded seriously. "That's what I pay you for, General, to tell it like it is."

"We can't give up yet!" I said.

The Ender King looked at me like I was a fool. "We are not giving up, Zeke. I was just getting an assessment of the situation." The King paused for a moment and turned to his daughter. "How many troops do we have in the outer end islands?"

"I'm not precisely sure, but it's at least 10,000, if you add up all the garrisons."

The King nodded. "Good, have them be here within the next half hour."

Savannah leaned over to an ender soldier who was standing nearby and whispered the commands to direct all the soldiers to come.

The King looked at the General. "If we had those 10,000 soldiers here, would the pillagers still outnumber us?"

The General thought for a moment before responding. "It'll be close. They probably would still outnumber us, but our soldiers are better fighters one-on-one."

The King squinted his eyes and tapped his chin for a bit. "I don't want to be just a little better, I want to overwhelm them. What about the rest of the troops on the main island?"

"I don't know about that, Daddy. The only substantial force of troops we have left is in the north of the island, holding back a pillager force in order to protect all the civilians. We probably have about 15,000 troops up there, but if they leave, a hundred thousand endermen will very likely lose their lives."

I was thinking how horrible it would be to be the King of an entire realm. I wondered why there was no king of the Overworld. I mean, Herobrine thought he was some sort of King of the Overworld, but not like the Ender King was in his own realm, someone who was respected and obeyed. I supposed it would be difficult to find a leader who could unite the diverse mobs and NPCs of the Overworld.

The King looked at the General. "Is there any way we can evacuate all the civilians in the north at the same time we brought the troops here?"

The General took a deep breath and sighed. "We could try, but I think we would fail."

The King thought for a moment. "In that case, direct half of the troops in the north to come. That should get us to about 17,500 additional troops here. A coordinated push against the pillagers near the Ender Dragon's Mountain, combined with the surprise invasion of the Palace, should tip the balance."

I looked at the King. "So, King, what should I do? I am at your disposal."

The King looked at me with a vicious grin. "Oh, you're going to help me."

"Of course, Your Highness. Help you with what?"

"You and I are going to kill Frederick and the griefer."

I rubbed my hands together with glee. "If it's the last thing I do, King. If it's the last thing I do."

Chapter 20

Savannah, the General, and I informed the Ender King of all the details of the plan. How we planned to mount the final assault using the young ender dragons to drop potions on the ground forces directly against the pillager army, hoping to distract them and pull more forces away from the Palace. Then, we would activate the redstone communication device and Otis would come through with his troops into the Palace's portal room, fanning out from there and killing anyone who got in his way.

"Of course, we told him that you would be in prison and that he should try to look for you," I said softly. "If he knew that he didn't have to do that, he would be much more efficient at killing the enemy."

The King nodded his head. "We can fix that easily enough. We will just have one of our soldiers teleport into the portal room at the same time as Otis arrives. He can inform him that there are no more rules of engagement. The only rule is to kill anyone he sees who does not immediately surrender."

I smiled. "Otis will love hearing that."

"He is a bit violent, isn't he?"

"He had a rough childhood and probably could use therapy," I said. "Unfortunately, he uses violence as his therapy."

The King shook his head sadly. "That's no way to live. But, in times of war and rebellion, such people can be an advantage to those in power."

"I suppose so. It seems like that is what some people in power do, right? Manipulate the most prominent traits in everyone. That's why Frederick thinks he is the King. The griefer flattered him and made him believe that he would actually let Frederick run the show."

"Indeed," said the King through gritted teeth. He paused for a moment and looked at Savannah and the General. "Zeke, I need to speak with Savannah and the General in private to firm up our plans for this assault. After that, I want to talk to you about what we're going to do."

"No problem, King. I'll be here when you get back."

"Why don't you get something to eat?" suggested Savannah. "There's some fresh food in the cafeteria."

I had not realized how hungry I was. My stomach grumbled at the offer. "Any chance there is some rotten cow flesh?"

Savannah made a face like she was going to barf. "No. Just regular cow flesh."

"What about wheat?" asked a hopeful Harold.

"I had some brought in just for you," said Savannah.

* * *

After about twenty minutes and three pieces of raw cow flesh, one slice of watermelon, and one cookie and nearly an entire bag of wheat, the King returned.

"Did you get the attack all sorted?" I asked.

"I think so. These things are always risky. You can plot it out, think of the second- and third-order effects, but once the killing starts, all bets are off. I've seen some strange things happen when people think they are about to die...." The King's voice trailed off.

"So how are we to do this? To target and kill those two maniacs?" I asked.

"Where do you think Frederick is most likely to be?"

I shrugged. "Probably in the throne room where I saw him when I got captured. He thinks he's got this thing under control."

The King scowled. "He's sitting on my throne?"

"Yes."

"How presumptuous!" said Harold.

The King growled with rage. "Well, that will not last for long." The King paused. "He must know by now I have escaped. Even if he does remain in the throne room, he will have a heavy guard. A few traitorous endermen will be among them, but it will mostly consist of pillagers and perhaps some evokers and vindicators."

"We can take him. Just give me some diamond armor and some enchanted diamond weapons. I'll do it myself."

The King chuckled. "I bet you could, but I'm going to have twenty-five of my special forces soldiers come with me. They will lead the way. They should be able to cut down the guard in no time at all. We can stand back and guard the rear flank. If any enemy somehow manage break through the special forces, we will take care of them together."

"That sounds like fun, but do you think Frederick might just teleport away?"

The King nodded. "He could do that. But, I'm counting on the fact that he's a coward. He won't want to leave his guard. And by the time he realizes the guard has been defeated, he won't have time to teleport. And even if he tries, I've got this." The Ender King reached into his inventory and pulled out a giant pile of cobwebs. "I'm going to give some to each of my special forces soldiers. If any of them get close enough, they will wrap it around his ankles and wrists. If he's tied with this, he won't be able to teleport." The King paused again and thought for a moment. "And that's when we get to have our fun."

I looked at the King in horror. "You're not planning on torturing him are you?"

"I should, for what he did. But, I won't stoop to that. We'll just have a good old-fashioned public execution."

Everything was starting to get a little medieval. I didn't mind killing my enemy in the heat of battle, but an actual execution seemed a little morbid. But, I supposed if anyone deserved it, it was Frederick.

"Well, you're the King, so I guess you can decide about that stuff. What about the griefer?"

"With any luck, he'll be killed during the battle. I'm sure he won't come to rescue Frederick."

"I agree with you, King," said Harold.

"So, you don't have a specific plan for getting him? If he escapes, he might just do it again?" I said anxiously.

"Honestly, it would surprise me if he does escape. But we will deal with that when it comes to it. Most griefers are just cowards and run away when they realize the odds are against them. Unfortunately, since he's a player, I can't stop him from shimmering away from this realm. But, everyone knows that you can't leave the End and return to the Overworld until you kill the Ender Dragon. And he hasn't done that yet. Sure, his troops have killed dozens of Ender Dragons, but he hasn't. He will be stuck here until he does that."

"I guess there are some rules in Minecraft you just can't break," I said. "I suppose we have Notch to thank for that."

The King nodded. "I wish Notch and Herobrine would show up. It would help us out. But, they do tend to be standoffish."

I shrugged. "I don't know about Notch, but I did do Herobrine a solid a few months ago when I found his long-lost wife. Maybe he *will* show up?"

The King shook his head. "I wouldn't count on it."

Chapter 21

About fifteen minutes before the attack was to commence, we all teleported up to the cave of the young ender dragons. They were down to six young ender dragons. We heard the current full-sized Ender Dragon screaming in pain but still shooting fireballs at the illager forces.

Glacier came up to us. "There may be only six of us left, but we have dozens of potions we've recently brewed. We should be able to put a massive dent in the enemy army as the endermen make their final assault."

"Excellent," said the King before turning to Savannah and the General. "I'll leave it to you. This is your attack to lead. Once it looks like you have fully-engaged the pillagers, I will flip the redstone switch to summon Otis and his army and then Zeke and I will do what we need to do."

Savannah hugged her father again. I could tell she was fighting back tears. "Of course, Daddy. See you when it's all over and we've retaken the Palace."

The King stroked his daughter's hair. "Of course, we will. But if we don't, I'll look for you in the nectar."

Savannah sobbed briefly and then backed away nodding her head. She waved at us. Harold and I waved back.

The General approached the King and saluted. "Your Highness. I'll do everything in my power to win this battle and protect your daughter. If it looks like we've lost the day, we intend to transit to the Overworld to regroup."

The King nodded resolutely. "A fine idea. But only do that if it's completely hopeless. Zeke and I intend to capture Frederick and the griefer if possible. Once that is done, the illager army will give up and it should be an easy victory."

I'm not sure I shared the King's confidence, but maybe he was doing all this as part of an act. Showing his royal dominance in order to inspire his troops. I wasn't sure.

The Ender General saluted. "Yes, Your Highness. Would you like to address the troops prior to the battle?"

"Of course."

The Ender King walked over to the pile of end stone and walked up to the top of it. He looked out over the thousands of troops assembled before him.

"Men, this is the battle of your lifetime. The battle of my lifetime. Perhaps the most important battle in the last few centuries. We have never had an invasion of our realm be this successful. Of course, the outsiders never had the help of a traitor within the Palace."

All troops booed and chanted, "Death to Frederick." After the King let his troops chant for a few moments to get their energy up, he raised his hands calling for silence.

"Indeed, Baby Zeke and I intend to bring your chant to fruition. But what you need to do is battle the pillager forces with all your might. Your success against them will determine our success inside the Palace. The more pillagers you can pull away from the Palace, the more likely it is we will be able to capture and kill Frederick and the invading griefer."

The troops shouted with violent rage and joy. Some of the endermen teleported wildly around the room hooting and hollering. The King again raised his hands to call for calm.

"Hold the line. Follow Savannah and the General. Obey their commands. But if you find yourself basking in the glory of the end nectar, know that you are in the afterlife and have died of valiant death."

The troops then yelled the loudest they had yelled during the entire speech. I wasn't sure why they cheered their potential death so loudly, but they believed in their homeland. They would do anything to save it. I had to admire that.

The King then waved to his troops and walked down from the podium. He approached Savannah and the General. "They're all yours. Zeke and I will wait here."

Savannah and the General walked over to the dragons. Savannah hopped on the back of one dragon and the General onto another. Four ender soldiers mounted the remaining dragons. They each had ten lingering potions with various effects in baskets behind them on the dragons.

Savannah stood up on the back of the Dragon she was riding and addressed her soldiers. "Men. Assemble at the mouth of the cave. When I give the signal, rush out and charge the enemy. We will then fly ahead of your charging forces to drop our potions on the pillagers. Wait until we have a chance to do one strafing run with dragon fireballs and then engage the enemy with everything you have."

The troops roared yet again. They moved into position. The tension was high, but so was a desire to achieve the goal.

I started shaking with anticipation. I had never been involved in a battle of the scale. Even the battle at Herobrine's High Castle was nowhere close to this scale. *What kind of warrior was I if I had never been involved in such a battle? Did I really deserve my title?*

A few more seconds passed and then Savannah yelled, "Charge!" The ground shook under the feet of the advancing endermen. They rushed forward onto the plains between the Ender Dragon's Mountain and the Palace.

The pillagers, who had been concentrating their fire on the Ender Dragon above, suddenly looked shocked. They turned their attention toward the rapidly approaching horde of endermen. They sent dozens of ravagers toward the endermen. I saw vexes called forth by evokers. A few insane vindicators rushed toward the endermen as well.

At that moment the dragons took off. They quickly flew over the villager forces, dropping lingering potions of poison and weakness and harming on them. As they turned around to strafe the enemy line, thousands of pillagers emerged from the Palace running towards the enemy line to reinforce it.

The Ender King looked at me. "That's our cue. And Otis'."

"Hop on, Zeke," said Harold. "We will need all the speed we can get!"

I smiled at my loyal chicken steed and hopped on his back.

The King looked at the twenty-five special forces soldiers who had remained behind from the charge. He singled one out. "Conrad, the honor is yours. You will teleport to the portal room and inform Otis that I am free. Tell him to kill whoever gets in his way. Tell him to meet us in the throne room."

The King then removed the redstone communication device from his inventory, and flicked the switch.

After a few seconds, he said, "Go, Conrad." Conrad saluted his king without a word, and then vanished.

The Ender King smiled grimly. He looked at the remainder of his special forces troops. "Ready?"

They all saluted and shouted, "Yes, Your Highness."

The King then looked at me and Harold. "How about you?"

In unison, Harold and I responded, "Yes."

The Ender King put his hand on my shoulder, and we teleported to our destiny.

Chapter 22

We all materialized inside the throne room. The Ender King's prediction was correct. Frederick was still sitting in the throne, but looking worried. He was surrounded by fifteen pillagers, five vindicators, two evokers, and a handful of traitorous endermen.

Without a word the ender soldiers went to work with deadly efficiency. The pillagers shot their crossbows at them, striking only a few. The remainder of the endermen teleported to the pillagers and then began a slashing attack with their enchanted diamond swords. Several pillagers fell immediately.

A vindicator surprised one ender soldier and chopped one of his arms off. He fell to the ground writhing in pain, flashing red, and then disappearing into a puff of smoke.

I looked down at Harold. "We have to get in there."

"Aye, aye, Zeke." Harold dashed toward the vindicator who was about to hack at another unsuspecting ender soldier who was presently engaged in close quarter combat with a pillager.

We arrived just in time. I raised my sword and sliced the vindicator's non-weapon hand clean off. He turned to face me, rage in his eyes, and slashed at me with his ax. But, the loss of his other hand had thrown off his aim slightly and the sharp end of the ax passed just above my head. That was all I needed to thrust my sword upward into his armpit, severing his other arm. He screamed in pain, and then flashed red and disappeared into a puff of smoke.

Harold raced the two of us to the back of the room to regroup. By now half of the pillagers were dead. The ender soldiers were getting the upper hand, but then the remaining evokers went into action. One of them called forth evoker fangs underneath several of the ender soldiers, dealing severe damage to them, and killing a few of them. The other evoker called forth vexes which harassed of the ender soldiers, distracting them and allowing the pillagers to begin fighting back more effectively.

I looked to my side where I expected the Ender King to be but he was gone. "Harold, let's go after those evil evokers. If we can take them out, we can clean up the rest of this mess."

Harold rushed toward one of the evokers who was standing in the darkened corner of the room. The evoker summoned evoker fangs to attack us, but Harold was too quick, the fangs appearing just behind his footsteps as we raced toward the evoker.

By the time the evoker realized we were going to get to his position, it was too late for him to call vexes to his aid. I slashed at his throat, and scored a critical hit. That was it. He was done.

And that's when I saw the Ender King, he had Frederick in a headlock and was trying to get the cobweb restraints on him. But Frederick suddenly teleported out of his grasp to the other end of the room. But, the special forces soldiers were too quick. One teleported next to him and tossed cobwebs all over his legs.

When he tried to teleport again, he couldn't. Frederick screamed, "No. I am the true King!" He looked at the traitorous endermen who had been with him and screamed, "Defend your king!"

The endermen, realizing their rebellion was over, tossed down their swords and surrendered to the special forces.

"No!" he screamed.

Frederick's words and behavior disgusted me. I wanted to go over there at that very instant and kill him, but that honor was for the Ender King. Instead, I told Harold to go for the other evoker. The evoker's back was to us. He was calling forth evoker fangs and inflicting damage upon the soldiers. I held my sword out like I was in a jousting competition. Harold then ran as quickly as he could. When we arrived at the evoker's location, Harold was running at top speed, and my sword went all the way through the evoker, doing horrific damage.

He screamed and fell to the ground. But he still lived. He reached into his inventory for a potion of healing and removed the stopper to drink from it. But I was too fast, I slashed my sword, breaking the bottle.

"No, I'm dying," he screamed with rage.

"Good," said Harold. The evoker began to move his hands in a pattern and bubbles began to appear around him, but I was too quick. I sliced his head clean off, and that was the end of him.

I looked around the room and saw that the ender soldiers were finishing off the last of the enemy. Only ten ender soldiers remained, but the Ender King and I had survived, and Frederick was captured.

After the last of the illagers was dispatched, the Ender King stood in front of Frederick and said, "Your reign of treachery is over! Once we finish off the illager army, I will deal with you."

Frederick looked at me with rage. "If it wasn't for this meddling baby zombie, I would have succeeded."

The Ender King nodded his head. "You are probably correct, for once in your life."

I saw Frederick's eyes turn red with rage. "If I can't be King, then no one can!" he yelled. Then, with a quickness I didn't think possible, Frederick reached into his inventory, pulled out a trident, and was just about to throw it at the Ender King, when Otis broke down the door behind him. The sound of the door breaking distracted Frederick just long enough that he hesitated to throw the trident. When Otis saw what was happening, he and Bob raced to Frederick and chopped off his hand. The trident fell to the ground with a clattering sound.

Frederick howled with pain, and grabbed his bloody stump. "Another jockey? It can't be?"

Otis hopped off Bob and walked over to Frederick and slapped him in the face. "It can be, and it is. You should never have messed with us."

"My griefer friend will save me," Frederick whined.

"I doubt that," said Otis.

"Did you kill him?" I asked, hopefully.

Otis shook his head. "No, but he's on the run. My husk, spider, and skeleton army has chased him onto the plains. He won't get away."

At that moment a female husk jockey rushed in, jumped off her chicken and gave Otis a hug. "Thank Notch you're still alive."

Frederick blinked his eyes and shook his head. "Another one?"

The female baby husk looked at Frederick and said, "You bet your britches. It's a good thing you didn't hurt my man, or I would be hurting you."

Her man?

Otis blushed at the words from his girlfriend, Sandy. "Don't talk like that in front of strangers," he barked.

Sandy looked at him and gave him the stink eye. "Oh, don't you ever speak to me like that again."

I thought Otis might attempt to hold his ground but he soon realized he would never win this battle. He bowed his head slightly in submission and said, "Sorry, Sandy."

Sandy looked over at me and said, "Baby Zeke. Good to see you again."

I laughed. "Yeah, it sure is."

At that moment, an armored skeleton walked in. "The rest of the Palace is secured, Otis," he said.

"Thanks, J. T.," replied Otis.

I looked at the King. "Shouldn't we be hunting down the griefer now?"

"Yes," said the King before turning toward his soldiers. "Five of you men guard Frederick with your lives. Wrap him in cobwebs and put him into a cell from which he cannot teleport. Put him in the cell where they put me."

Five of the soldiers stepped forward and put their hands all over Frederick. They wrapped him in a shroud of cobwebs, and dragged him away.

The Ender King looked at Otis. "Now, show me where this griefer has gone."

Otis took his sword and picked some dirt out from under his fingernails. "Gladly," he said viciously.

Chapter 23

We followed Otis out of the throne room and up to the balcony that faced the plain between the Ender King's Palace and the Ender Dragon's Mountain. We scanned the area for a moment before Otis pointed his stubby little arm and said, "There!"

I followed the invisible line beginning with his tiny undead fingertip and saw that the griefer, mounted on the back of a ravager, was running away from the giant horde of husks, spiders, and skeletons Otis had brought with him. He was headed directly for the Ender Dragon's Mountain.

"There's no way he can get out of here," said the King. "The only way a player can leave the End is if he kills the Ender Dragon. Your army will catch up to him with no problem."

"Excellent," said Otis.

That's when I had a terrible thought. "But, isn't that where he is heading now? To find an ender dragon to kill?"

The Ender King looked at me with a curious and slightly worried glance. "What do you think he intends to do?"

I shook my head. "I can't know for sure, but what if he finds where all the young ender dragons are and then kills all of them. If he destroys their entire race, there would be nothing keeping him here, right? Isn't it possible that when they go extinct, a permanent return portal will manifest itself where he kills the final dragon and he can go back to the Overworld?"

A shocked and sickened look passed across the Ender King's face. "Not if I can help it!" He reached out and grabbed Otis and me on the shoulders and then looked at the five ender soldiers with us. "One of you teleport the husk jockey and the skeleton. We are going to the ender dragon training facility immediately."

Within a second, we materialized inside the Ender Dragon training area. But the griefer had beaten us there. He hopped off his ravager and pulled out a glowing diamond sword which must have been exceptionally enchanted. He rushed toward the one remaining young ender dragon, Glacier. Glacier was already starting to grow into the large size of the final Ender Dragon. During the transformation process, Glacier was defenseless. The griefer took full advantage of this.

The griefer rushed up to Glacier and began to hack at him. Glacier screamed in pain, unable to muster a fireball to shoot at the griefer. Sandy rushed toward the griefer and tried to slash his legs, but his enchanted diamond armor repelled her attack. He then slashed at her with his own sword, wounding her sufficiently that she had to retreat.

Otis screamed, "No!" and then he rushed toward the greifer. This time the griefer pulled out a crossbow from his inventory using his other hand and shot directly at Otis. The arrow hit Otis right in the chest and knocked him off Bob.

I screamed.

Bob screamed.

Harold screamed.

Sandy screamed.

J.T. screamed.

Only the Ender King did not scream.

The Ender King looked at me. "Tend to your friends. I'll handle this griefer."

The Ender King teleported to the side of the griefer and began to slash him with a sword. The five ender soldiers joined their king. I could tell they were doing serious damage the griefer, but the griefer ignored them, focusing all his energy on killing Glacier.

He slashed at Glacier with his sword and now, having dropped the crossbow and pulled out a second enchanted sword, he was doing double damage. It was going to be close. Would Glacier die first or would it be the griefer?

I pulled out potions of harming from my inventory and gave one each to Sandy and Otis to drink. They gulped them down. Almost instantly, I could see their health regenerating.

I turned and looked at the fight raging in front of me. J.T. had joined in, slashing at the griefer with his iron sword. Both the griefer and Glacier were beginning to flash red. I raced over to help the King deal final blow to the griefer, but at that moment, Glacier flashed red and disappeared into a puff of smoke.

"No!" I yelled.

A return portal appeared where Glacier had been only a second before, and the griefer fell forward into it, still flashing red and moaning in pain.

I reached out my sword to slash at him, but he disappeared before I could make contact, already back in the Overworld.

The Ender King screamed with rage, a guttural, wordless rage

"We'll get him," I said as Harold and I leapt into return portal.

Chapter 24

I knew that the lore said that when a player defeated the Ender Dragon and the player went through the return portal back to the Overworld, the player would return to the player's spawn point or bed. So, I assumed that Harold and I would appear in the griefer's house.

I was prepared for anything ... except what actually happened.

When we appeared in the Overworld, we were standing next to a bed inside of a house. I looked around quickly, my sword at the ready, but the griefer was nowhere to be seen.

Could he have already shimmered back to his own world? Ran away like the coward he is?

I looked down at Harold. I whispered, "Maybe I should hop off you for now? We can search the house more quickly if we separate."

After I hopped down from Harold's back, he looked at me. "But it could be very dangerous. Shouldn't we stick together?"

"Normally, I would say yes. But every second counts. If this griefer gets away, he may escape forever."

Harold nodded his head and began moving to the left while I went to the right. The griefer's house was gigantic. You could tell that he had been playing Minecraft for years. He had literally hundreds of chests all over the floors inside his house. It was so cluttered, that it was hard to move in between them. I opened one labeled "Weapons." Inside I found dozens of diamond swords, some with enchantments. There were some older pieces of iron weaponry, but it didn't look like they had been used in years. I grabbed a couple of diamond swords and tucked them into my inventory. Then, I shut the chest.

I continued on, searching through the kitchen, another storage room, and some sort of a room that had a lot of glass in it. It was pretty ugly. I could tell the griefer was not a designer and lacked any artistic sensibility. All he cared about was collecting and hording items. Items that he had stolen from others who had worked so hard for them.

When I turned another corner, I came face-to-face with Harold. My shoulders slumped a little bit. "You didn't see the griefer?"

Harold shook his head. "I think I looked everywhere."

At that moment the griefer jumped out from inside a chest and yelled, "Not everywhere!" and then he slashed at Harold, killing him! I saw a little piece of raw chicken meat floating where Harold had been only a moment earlier. His drop.

R.I.P.

Harold

I rushed over and screamed, "No!" I cradled the piece of chicken meat in my hands and put it in my inventory. I planned to give him a proper burial ... after I killed the griefer.

I looked at the griefer. "You monster!"

I pulled two diamond swords from my inventory, lunged at the griefer, and began slashing as hard as I could. The griefer appeared to have healed entirely from the flogging the Ender King had given him earlier. He must have imbibed some healing potions. There was no other way he could be completely healed so quickly.

Rage at the murder of my best friend and loyal steed coursed through my veins. I felt strength I'd never felt before. The world had taken on a red-ish tint. As I slashed the griever, using a sword in each hand, I could see fear in his eyes. He knew he had made a mistake by killing Harold. And now he was going to pay for it. I hacked at him repeatedly, forcing him to flee.

I followed closely behind until I cornered him, driving him back on his heels. In order to avoid my wrath, he stepped quickly to one side. His quick move caught me by surprise, and I took a couple steps forward, stepping on an unseen pressure plate! The plate was connected to TNT, which exploded and tossed me up in the air.

I landed with a thud somewhere inside the griefer's house. I was dizzy and disoriented. The blast had also tossed the griefer on his back, but he recovered more quickly than I did because he was farther away from the blast.

About ten seconds after the blast he was standing over me. He had a sword pointed at my throat. He was laughing.

"Any last words, Baby Zeke? The so-called Warrior of Minecraft?"

I would not give him the satisfaction. I shook my head and waited for the sword thrust to kill me.

But as I was shaking my head, I noticed a label on one of the chests out of the corner of my eyes, "Buckets of lava."

Just as the griefer was bringing the sword down on me, I mustered the strength to roll away from it. The sword stabbed into the wood where I had been only an instant earlier.

I rushed over to the chest and smashed it open. Dozens of buckets of lava were inside. I picked them up and threw each one at the griefer. Soon, the lava had engulfed him and he caught fire, like a zombie in the noonday sun.

He screamed in agony. "Put out the fire! Put out the fire!"

Of course, I did not put out the fire. I threw more and more buckets of lava until there were no more to throw. And by then, the griefer was all but dead. I stared at him with hate in my eyes, relishing the thought of his death in revenge for his murder of Harold.

He looked at me as he flashed red and said, "What did I do to deserve this? I didn't even have 'keep inventory' on."

I said and did nothing in response. He flashed red one last time and then disappeared into a puff of smoke.

After he was gone, and my desire for vengeance satisfied, the full force of what happened hit me. Harold was dead. I was a chicken jockey no longer. I was just a pathetic baby zombie. I fell to my knees and put my face in my hands and cried.

Chapter 25

After I cried for a few minutes, I felt a hand on one of my shoulders. I looked up and saw that it was Otis. "What happened, Zeke?"

I stared at Otis, tears streaming down my face. "He killed Harold. This is all that's left." I reached in my inventory and pulled out the small piece of raw chicken meat.

Bob, who was standing next to Otis, gasped. Tears fell from his eyes. He walked up to the piece of raw chicken meat and gave it a kiss. "Goodbye, dear friend."

"If only I could have been here to help you kill the griefer," said Otis.

I nodded my head, but now that the griefer was dead, it didn't even matter. Harold was gone. I'd even bring the griefer back to life if it would mean Harold could be alive again.

Smooch!

A few moments later the Ender King, Savannah, Sandy, and J.T. appeared.

Otis told them what happened to Harold. They all hung their heads in mourning.

"We need to give him a proper burial," said Sandy. "Was there somewhere he liked to spend time?"

I looked at Bob. Our eyes met. We knew where Harold would want to be for eternity. I looked at Sandy. "Yes. There is a small hill near our farm. It has a view of the wheat field and of the river. Harold loved wheat and he loved to drink water from the river. We should bury him there."

* * *

About a half hour later, the Ender King and Savannah had teleported us back to our farm. Before we left the griefer's house, we burned it to the ground. We didn't want anything left of his pathetic existence to stain Minecraft.

We all walked over to the grassy knoll where Harold loved to sit by himself and contemplate the world.

I took a shovel from my inventory and dug a small hole. Otis crafted a gravestone and wrote on it, "R.I.P. Harold, the greatest chicken steed who ever lived." Otis placed the gravestone next to the hole.

I brought out the small piece of chicken meat that Harold had dropped, the last earthly reminder of his existence in Minecraft. Sandy provided a small chest in which we laid the piece of chicken meat on some hay so it could have a nest for all eternity.

I closed the chest and was about to lower it into the hole when suddenly there was a blinding white light and Notch appeared!

"I've just learned about what has happened to Harold. Is that Harold's drop in the chest?"

I sighed. "Yes it is, Notch. Are you here to pay your respects?"

He shook his head. "I am not here to pay my respects."

Otis rushed over to Notch and grabbed his shirt. "You better pay your respects. While we were fighting the battle to maintain the Balance, you were nowhere to be seen. So get on your knees and pray for this piece of chicken meat!"

Although Notch could have killed Otis with a snap of his fingers, he delicately removed Otis' hand from his shirt. "Do not be angry. I saw the entire battle. Should I have been truly needed, I would have appeared. And that is why I have appeared now, because I am needed."

"Stop speaking in riddles, you freak!" yelled Otis. "Speak plainly."

Notch shook his head and walked over to the chest. He put it on the flat ground and punched it open to reveal Harold's piece of chicken meat. Notch then placed his hand upon the chicken meat and mumbled a few words that were incomprehensible to us. After a few seconds had passed, we heard clucking!

"Harold?" I said. I rushed over to the chest and there was a chicken inside of it! I reached down and picked it up. "Harold? Is that you?"

Harold looked at me like I was an idiot. "Of course, it is. But what am I doing in this chest? And why do I have such a bad headache?"

I started crying. "I'll tell you later."

Harold looked confused. "The griefer? Is he dead?"

I nodded my head and smiled. "He sure is."

Harold smiled. "That's all that matters then."

I shook my head. "No. All that matters is that you are alive."

Everyone cried, except Notch. He just stood there looking proud of his dominant powers.

After a minute of crying, we all stopped and stood around feeling a bit awkward. Thankfully, Notch broke the silence. He removed twelve ender dragon eggs from his inventory and said, "Ender King, please take these dozen ender dragon eggs back to the End. I was saddened to see that the griefer was able to exterminate the dragons. I will not let such a terrible action stand!"

The Ender King walked to Notch and took the eggs. "Thank you, Notch. I guess the Balance has been restored."

Notch sighed. "You know it is never truly in balance. There is always something going wrong or off kilter."

Off kilter? Who says that?

"No matter," I said, striking a dominant pose with my sword thrust into the air. "The Warrior is on the job."

There was silence as everyone looked at me, obviously in awe of my words. But, the silence was soon broken by laughter. First Otis, and then everyone else, even Notch.

But, it didn't matter. I was just glad Harold was there to join in and laugh at me too.

End of *Baby Zeke,* Book 11 – *Rebellion*

Book 12 – Revenge of the Husk

Chapter 1

I sat at the desk in my study, staring at the blank piece of paper in front of me. I held the quill at the ready in my decaying right hand, but I was having writer's block. As many times as I tried to start my next diary, the words wouldn't flow. I was uncharacteristically at a loss.

After I had been sitting at my desk, staring at the blank page for nearly thirty minutes, there was a quick, sharp knock on the door. I turned around and looked over my shoulder and was about to say, "Come in," but the door started opening anyway.

"What are you doing in here?" asked Otis. "Lurking?"

I sighed. "You realize you are supposed to wait for someone to give you permission *before* you open the door to his room, right?"

Otis snorted. "What? Do you have something to hide? I don't even know why we bother to have doors in this house."

"It's so that I don't have to listen to your snoring all night long."

Otis turned red and shook his fist at me. "I don't snore. And besides, if I did, what does it matter? You are a zombie. You zombies are low-key groaning all the time anyway, basically making snoring noises when you're awake."

"What are you talking about?"

Otis shrugged. "Never mind. Have you written anything yet?"

I shook my head and cast my eyes toward the floor. "I'm just not sure what to write for my next diary. I know my public has been eagerly expecting it."

Otis stuck a stubby finger in his throat to mime the action of making himself vomit. "Dude, seriously? '*Your* public'?"

"Yeah, *my* public. You know my diaries are successful bestsellers. I just want to give the readers a good story, but it has to be something actually from my life experience. I can't just make stuff up ... like some of the more unscrupulous mobs and players do."

Otis stood in the doorway and tapped his cracked lips for a moment and then said, "Why don't you just write about helping Jimmy Slade save Minecraft? We just finished helping him with that."

I shook my head. "I thought about that, but I already know that Jimmy is writing his own diary called the *Diary of a Surfer Villager*. He told me he would tell the whole story and send a copy to our dimension so we could publish it here. I don't want to repeat the same story that is already available somewhere else."

Otis shrugged his shoulders. "So what? Your readers are still buying your books. You need to start thinking more like a villager," said Otis, smashing a fist into his open hand for emphasis. "Get as many emeralds as you can *while* you can, even if that means repeating stories that are already in circulation. Come on, let's get greedy. You know I'm right."

"No, Otis, I will not exploit my public like that. I'm just trying to think of something else that was really interesting that I have done lately. But other than helping Jimmy Slade, there really hasn't been much."

Otis was about to say something annoying, I'm sure, when we heard a ruckus in the yard. Harold and Bob started clucking madly and screaming at each other.

"Run, Harold!" said Bob.

"Look out, Bob. It's going to kill you!" shouted Harold.

My eyes locked with Otis' eyes. We knew that our chickens were in danger. I dropped my quill and the two of us rushed out the front door of our house with our swords drawn.

"Stop that! Stop that you two," said a female player chasing after two cats who were in turn chasing after our two chickens.

Otis ran toward one of the cats and began to slash at it with his sword. But the player reached out her sword and blocked his attack. "Don't hurt my cats!"

Otis stared at her with rage in his eyes. "Then you need to stop them from killing our chickens! If our chickens get hurt, your cats aren't the only things I'm gonna kill."

The player immediately understood that Otis was serious. I rushed toward the other cat, ready to kill it myself if I had to. But at that moment the player removed two potions of slowness from her inventory and threw one onto each cat. Suddenly, the cats slowed and moved more like tired cows than hungry cats desperate to eat chicken flesh.

Harold and Bob noticed and ran over to the cats and kicked them before flapping away from the slow-motion claw strike attempted by each cat.

The player quickly gathered up her slow-motion felines and tucked one under each arm.

"You need to learn to control your cats better, girl," said Otis.

"That's right, player. What's this all about?" I asked.

The player shook her head and sighed. "It's not what you think. I was just passing through. I thought this farm was abandoned. I thought the two chickens were just wild chickens who were wandering around the area. I didn't know the farm belonged to a zombie pigman and a baby zombie...." The player's voice trailed off. She stared at us. She looked at the two chickens that were glaring at her. "Wait a minute ... are you Baby Zeke and Otis?!?"

"Of course they are," said Harold. "And I'm Harold and that's Bob."

The player's face suddenly wore a mask of shock and surprise. "Wow! The Warrior and his squad. Cool."

"Hey, girl, I'm not part of anybody's squad," said Otis. "I'm my own squad. By the Nether, I'm my own army!"

The player looked at Otis, a confused look on her face, and then laughed. "You act the same way Baby Zeke says you do in his books. I thought he was exaggerating to make his stories more interesting but ... no."

Otis snorted. "Have you bothered to read *my* diary? To get the real story about my tragic life before I met Zeke?"

The player shook her head. "Sorry ... I've been, um, busy. But it's on my to-do list."

Otis shook his head and turned and walked away, back to our house.

"Why do you have two cats?" I asked. "It seems like most players are content with just one."

The player shrugged. "I think cats rock. In fact, that's my name. CatsRock456. I just like cats. Don't judge."

"I will judge all I want," said Harold. "Those stupid cats nearly killed us."

"Yeah, sorry about that," said CatsRock456. "I try to control them, but sometimes their instincts take over."

"Well, it's a good thing they didn't kill Bob and Harold," I said. "I don't need to act all aggressive like Otis does, but he is right that we would've killed your cats to defend our chickens ... or to get revenge on their behalf."

The player nodded her head. "I totally understand. I would kill any creature or mob that I saw trying to kill my cats. It's a natural feeling."

"Okay, then, you can leave now," I said.

The player nodded her head. "Sorry about all this. If I were to come this way again, I will be sure to restrain my cats before I do. And, if you ever need any help on any future adventures, feel free to look me up. My house is located to the north over a couple of hills. Right near a river and surrounded by oak trees."

"Thanks for the offer. I doubt I'll ever take you up on it, but it's nice to know it's out there," I said.

And with that, CatsRock456 smiled and walked away.

After I was sure she was gone, I walked over to Harold and Bob. "You guys okay?"

"Just a little frightened," said Harold.

"Not just a *little* frightened. A *lot* frightened," said Bob, his beak chattering and his legs shivering with fear.

"I was going to peck them to protect you," said Harold.

Bob nodded his head. "That would be a nice gesture. But, it would've ended with me watching you die first by the teeth of a cat and then ... I would've been next. Cats are horrible, vicious creatures!"

"Seems like you guys are back to your normal selves," I said with a chuckle. "Why don't you go out to the storage shed and bring some wheat into the house. I will make you some warm porridge."

Harold and Bob had recently discovered that if you soak wheat in warm water it makes it mushy. They liked this porridge, as they called it, as much or more than just pecking at wheat seeds on the ground.

In light of their recent trauma, I thought I'd give them a treat.

"Really?" said Bob. "That is awesome."

"Yeah, Bob, let's go," said Harold.

I watched as the chickens walked in their bizarre way over to the storage shed to retrieve some wheat. I smiled. It had been an exciting few minutes, but it certainly wasn't enough to fill one of my diaries. I had to think a little more.

Chapter 2

The next day after eating breakfast and talking with Otis, Harold, and Bob for a few minutes in the hope of developing an idea for my next diary, I returned to my study. Again, I confronted the blank page, unable to think of anything worthy to tell my public. I was the Warrior, but nothing – other than my assistance with Jimmy Slade – had happened to me recently that would make for a good story. If I just wrote about my day-to-day life, everyone would realize just how boring it was.

The hours passed as I racked my undead, decaying brain for lively, full-fleshed ideas. I tapped my chin and scratched my hair. I shifted in my chair. I looked here and there. But there was no inspiration, and I muttered a swear.

* * *

Shortly before lunch, I heard what sounded like two large animals approaching my farm. I stood up and opened the door to my study and walked out to the living room. I saw Otis walking toward the front door. Before he opened it, he noticed me and asked, "You heard it too?"

I nodded my head. "Sounds like we have visitors."

Otis reached into his inventory and pulled out an enchanted golden sword. "They better not be up to any mischief."

"What happened to your diamond sword?" I asked, realizing that I couldn't recall having ever seen Otis with anything other than a diamond sword.

Otis shrugged. "Just trying to get in touch with my zombie pigman heritage a little more. Thought I'd try a traditional golden sword for a while."

Otis opened the front door and walked out into our yard. I checked my inventory to make sure my weapons were at the ready and then I followed him outside.

About ten blocks from our front door were two of the most peculiar players I'd ever seen. The first player was mounted upon a horse. Her armor was enchanted diamond, but it was painted with various shapes and patterns. From the top of her helmet, a large feather pointed skyward. Trailing behind and slightly to her left, I saw a male player riding a llama. He also wore diamond armor, painted with a series of interlocking circles.

I put up my hand. "That's far enough. State your business."

The female player sat astride her horse and looked down at me. "Baby Zeke, I presume?"

I nodded my head. "Who are you?"

Before she answered she dismounted her horse. The male player followed her lead and dismounted his llama. As she patted her horse's neck she said, "My name is Africa Unicorn. And this is my associate, Aaron."

Africa Unicorn? What does that even mean?

"Um, okay. And you were looking for me?"

Africa Unicorn nodded her head. I noticed now that the large feather sticking out of the top of her helmet looked a bit like the horn of a unicorn. "Yes, we were looking for you. We understand that you can be hired for missions."

"Of course he can be hired," said Otis. "As long as the price is right. Let's talk business."

I scowled at Otis. "I'll make the decisions about whether I can or cannot be hired, thank you very much." Otis stuck his tongue out at me.

Africa Unicorn and Aaron chuckled. "You guys are just like in your books," said Aaron. "I wasn't sure if your banter was really going to be like that."

"Well, it is. So get used to it, buddy," said Otis.

"I'm sure they will," I said. I looked at the two players and said, "What is it that you want? I don't take very many missions."

"And you would be a fool to take very many missions. But this is a *special* mission," said Africa Unicorn. "It involves a certain … flower."

"It's not Flowie, is it?" said Otis, trembling. I remembered that Otis had talked about a strange flower in his diary that had mesmerized him when he was staying with his mysterious trainer, Konichi Juan. (But, I don't want to spoil his diary if you haven't yet read it, so I won't mention any details.)

"Indeed, a tulip to be precise," said Africa Unicorn.

"Yeah, it sure is an amazing tulip!" said Aaron, awe in his voice.

I shook my head and rolled my eyes. "What are you talking about? How can a mission involve a tulip?!? They just sit in a pot or in the ground. They don't go anywhere."

"This is stupid. You had better not be making fun of us," said Otis with a threatening tone.

"How dare you say such a thing?" said Africa Unicorn. "Flowers are the *pinnacle* of beauty, and we are *deadly* serious."

Otis spat on the ground. "Whatever."

I rubbed my forehead. "Look, just tell me about this flower and we will make a decision."

"Very well," said Africa Unicorn. "Here's the situation. Aaron and I are tulip breeders. We've been rather disgusted by the mere four colors of tulips available in Minecraft. As you know there's only red, pink, white, and orange. Very boring, very plain."

Aaron nodded his head. "It's a terrible color palette."

I saw Otis rolling his eyes again but he said nothing.

"Anyhow, Aaron I have been breeding tulips for the past several years. We developed many hybrids, but nothing as gorgeous as our Semper Augustus tulip. It is red with stripes of white in each petal, like blood vessels. It is the *pinnacle* of beauty."

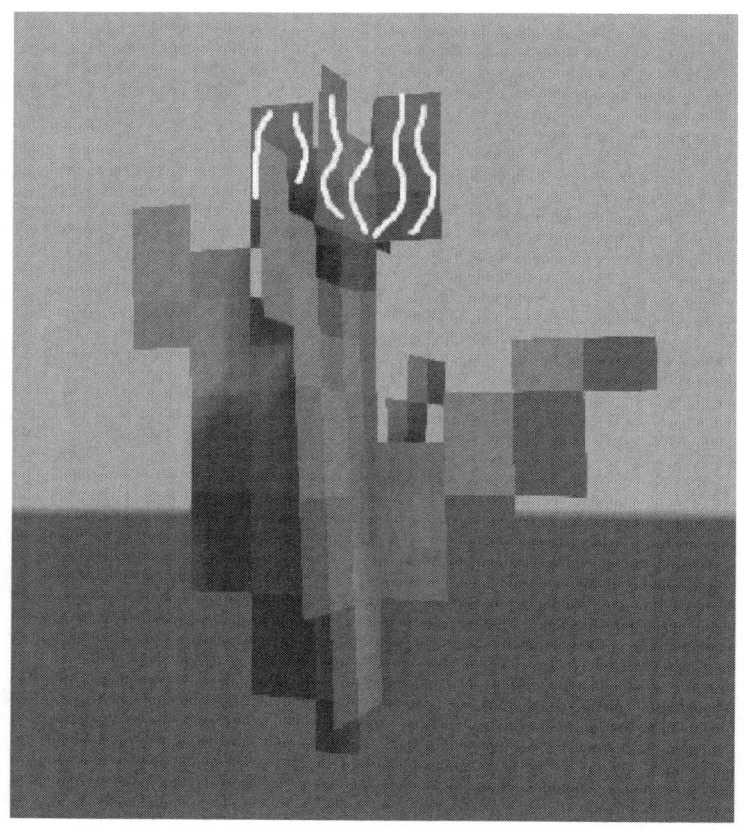

I had to admit, it did sound like a pretty impressive-looking flower. I had no idea how they had managed to breed such a creation, but at a minimum it was impressive, if the tulip truly looked as she had described.

"Okay, so you made a fancy flower. Why are you here talking to me?" I said.

"Our tulip has been stolen," said Aaron. "We want you to find it."

Otis couldn't take it anymore. He started laughing. Laughing so hard that he doubled over and was slapping his knees. Tiny bits of rotten flesh were falling off each kneecap because he was slapping them so hard. Africa Unicorn and Aaron stared at him incredulously. Finally, after about ten seconds, Otis stopped laughing and looked up. "You want Baby Zeke, the Warrior as he loves to call himself, to look for a flower? You are stupid. He's above that."

I didn't know he cared....

"Hold on a second, Otis. Let's hear them out," I said. "Are you sure it was stolen? Any ideas why or who would have taken it?"

"We are sure. We kept the flower in a locked greenhouse," said Africa Unicorn. "Other flower enthusiasts knew it was there. Many mobs, villagers, and players have even attempted to purchase it, but it was not for sale."

"So you think one of them took it?" I asked.

"One of them was likely behind it, but it was a professional thief who did the actual stealing," said Aaron.

"What makes you think that?" asked Otis, suddenly interested again.

"Precision," said Aaron. "The thief removed the bare minimum of blocks needed to gain entry to our fortified green house where we kept the tulip. It was done in the dead of night and there was no noise made. Only a pro could've done that."

"Exactly," said Africa Unicorn. "And there's something else. A small piece of fabric was caught on the thorn of one of our roses we were breeding in the same room. It was a light brown fabric and smelled of dust. We think a husk stole the tulip."

"What would a husk want with a fancy tulip?" asked Otis, incredulous.

The players both shrugged. "We don't think the husk actually wanted it. We think the husk took it to sell it to someone else or had been hired by someone to bring it to him or her," said Aaron.

I nodded my head. "So, you're thinking we should go to the desert biome to begin our investigation, right?" I asked.

"It seems like the logical thing to do," said Africa Unicorn. "I would do it myself, but husks don't have much trust in players. I thought you as the Great Warrior of Minecraft and a member of a mob species related to husks would have an easier time of investigating the theft."

"You're probably right about that," I said. I looked at Otis. "What's a fair price to charge these players?"

Otis squinted his eyes and looked at the players. "So, you say you've had some offers to purchase your fancy tulip, right?"

The players nodded.

"What is the highest bid you've ever had?"

The players shifted uncomfortably. They saw where this was going. "Umm, one thousand emeralds," said Aaron.

I thought Otis' decaying eyeballs were going to pop right out of their sockets. "That's crazy! And you didn't sell it?!?"

"Its beauty is priceless!" said Africa Unicorn.

Otis rubbed his hands together. "In that case, I'm sure you won't mind paying us two thousand emeralds to locate the flower."

Oh my Notch! So much money!

The two players looked uncomfortable. They retreated a ways and whispered to each other before returning.

"We propose the following: We will give you five hundred emeralds now and fifteen hundred emeralds upon delivery of the tulip to us," said Africa Unicorn. "Deal?"

"Deal," I said, cutting off Otis before he could say something stupid. "If you can deliver the five hundred emeralds today, we can start our search tomorrow."

I saw the look of relief pass across each of the player's faces. I could tell they were desperate to get back their tulip. Africa Unicorn reached into her inventory and pulled out pile after pile of emeralds until there was a stack of five hundred of them. As the pile grew Otis's eyes got bigger and bigger.

"That should be five hundred," said the player.

Otis rushed forward and began stuffing emeralds into his inventory.

"What are you doing?" I asked. "Those aren't your emeralds."

Otis laughed. "You know I'm the money man in this operation. You just do your 'Warrior' thing. I'll handle finances."

Chapter 3

Early the next morning, I readied my supplies. In addition to my usual travel supplies of rotten flesh – *yum!* – and a stockpile of weapons, I included a special, locking chest in which to place the tulip should I be able to recover it. I wanted to make sure it would be protected on my transport back to the two players who had hired me.

After a breakfast of some aged rotten flesh seasoned with chorus fruit, I saw Otis walk out of his bedroom. He looked at me with a determined expression and said, "Let's do this!"

I finished chewing a piece of my delicious rotten flesh breakfast and swallowed. "Yes, let's. Why don't you go tell the chickens we are ready? While you do that, I will make sure everything's buttoned up inside our house before we leave."

"You're so good at housekeeping," said Otis sarcastically. "I'll be right back with the chickens."

Otis walked out the door and I picked up my plate and washed it. Otis liked to break dirty plates outside and then recraft them, but I preferred the meditative process of cleaning a dish with soap and water.

Once the dishes were cleaned, dried, and put away, I surveyed the room to make sure there was nothing that would be a problem if we were gone for more than a couple days. I took our one house plant, an oak tree sapling, and put it out in the fenced backyard. As long as it rained every few days, the sapling should be fine.

Everything taken care of inside, I walked out the front door and locked it behind me. I stood in the front yard and watched as Otis and Harold walked back from the chicken coop. Bob was nowhere to be seen. "Where's Bob?" I asked as they approached.

Otis shook his head sadly. "Bob's feeling a little under the weather. He says he can't travel today, especially not in jockey formation."

"That's terrible," I said. "How are you feeling, Harold?"

Harold thumped his chest with his wing. "I feel fine. I think Bob just ate too much warm mushy wheat last night. His stomach is upset."

"Well, should we wait until tomorrow to leave?" I asked.

Otis shook his head. "The sooner we can find that tulip the sooner we can collect those other fifteen hundred emeralds. You and Harold set off on your own and Bob and I will meet up with you later."

I nodded my head. "Okay. This shouldn't be a very dangerous mission though it might be difficult to locate the tulip." I paused for a moment to think. "How about this? I'll go to the nearest husk village and look around. There is a desert villager village nearby called Obsidian Hot Springs. After I am done exploring the husk village, I will go to Obsidian Hot Springs and wait for you. There's a hotel called the Lava Flow Inn. If you are not in town when I arrive, I will get a room there. Look for me."

Otis nodded his head. "They let baby zombies in hotel rooms in that desert village?"

I took a deep breath and sighed. "I hadn't really thought about that. But, I am a celebrity after all. I'm sure they will make an exception for me."

Otis spat on the ground. "You and your celebrity. 'I'm the Warrior.' Bah. 'I'm so awesome.' Bah. It's so annoying."

"Why don't you get over it, Otis? You're always making fun of me. I didn't set off to be a famous celebrity and part of the Balance of the Four. It just sort of worked out that way."

"Yeah, Otis. Chill," said Harold.

"Bah! Whatever. You two get going. Bob and I will meet you at the village in a day or two."

I nodded my head and then I smirked. "I'll see how your girlfriend Sandy is doing when I'm at the husk village."

Otis shook his fist at me. "She's not my girlfriend. I mean, well ... I guess maybe she is."

"Just admit it, Otis," said Harold.

"Do you want me to give her any sort of message?" I asked.

Otis nodded. "Tell her she can pick out any gift she wants that's fifty emeralds or less. I think I will buy her something nice with the proceeds of this job."

"We have to find the tulip first," I said.

Otis shrugged. "We already have five hundred emeralds regardless of results. I'll just pull fifty emeralds out of that."

"But I'm doing all the work!" I whined.

"So what?" said Otis. "Didn't I tell you I was the money man?"

Chapter 4

About ten minutes later, Harold and I, joined in our jockey formation, set off for the husk village. The village was called Dust Junction. When I got there, I intended to stop at Sandy's house first to see if she knew anything about a stolen tulip or, perhaps, who might be interested in stealing one.

Even though the players seemed convinced that the tulip had been stolen by a professional thief, I did not want to jump to any conclusions so early in my investigation. But, my guess was that the husk had been hired since husks are not known for their appreciation of flowers given that they spawn and live in deserts for the most part.

"Harold, we can take our time getting to the husk village. Even if we mozy, we should arrive by mid-afternoon."

Harold nodded his head below me. "Good. I didn't feel like running ... certainly not with a bunch of decaying flesh on my back. And, by 'decaying flesh,' I of course mean you."

I rolled my eyes. "Yeah, I get it. Anyway, why don't we take the scenic route? We can travel along the Frothy River and through Sunflower Gulch. It should be nice."

Harold took in a deep breath before responding. "That sounds like a great idea. I wish we had a big river near our house. The little creek that runs past our house and into the nearby lake is not very impressive."

* * *

As we mozied toward Frothy River, we warily watched several players we noticed in the distance. Even though I was a famous celebrity in the world of Minecraft, there were still some players who did not know who I was. They would try to kill me to gain XP. I would always explain to them, as Harold and I were running away, that I was Baby Zeke, but that did not always work. And so, I have had to kill a handful of players over the years. Fortunately, none of the players we saw approached us and we arrived along the banks of the river without incident.

The Frothy River was the widest and fastest-moving river in the Overworld. Many players challenged themselves by attempting to row boats through the river's many sections of rapids. A few succeeded, but many failed. At best, they lost their boats; at worst, they lost their lives.

But, today, there were not any players in the river, so Harold and I enjoyed a leisurely stroll along the southern bank of the river.

"It is so peaceful here," said Harold.

"I agree," I said as I dismounted my steed and began to walk alongside him. "I think I'll walk for a little while. We have plenty of time."

The two of us walked along the edge of the river, observing the salmon swimming in the water and listening to the rumble of the water as it crashed against rocks. The turbulence caused by these collisions created bubbles and foam, giving the river a frothy white aspect and, hence, its name: Frothy River.

On occasion, we spotted a drowned lurking under the water. They regarded us with envy, able to walk in the sunlight without burning. At one point, a baby drowned swam near the surface of the river and waved at us. I smiled and waved back.

The baby drowned, having caught our attention, then grabbed a nearby salmon and sat astride it and rode it for a short distance under the water. Harold laughed heartily. "Look at that. A salmon jockey!"

I chuckled. "I guess you are right. Looks like fun."

Harold sighed. "I wish I could stay underwater for a long time. It would be fun to explore the watery realms. Maybe I could make friends with a squid?"

"Or an elder guardian?"

Harold shivered. "No, thank you. I'll leave those ocean monuments to players. I don't need to flex my dominance. I just want to look around without getting into a fight."

"A wise policy," I said. "Especially for a chicken."

The baby drowned had now been carried out of sight by the salmon. Harold and I continued walking along the bank for another thirty minutes until we came to the entrance to Sunflower Gulch. The entrance was framed by two large naturally-generated stone pillars. It was truly a wonder of the world. Once you passed through the pillars, all you saw was sunflowers and grass for hundreds of blocks.

"Harold, I think we'd best get back in jockey formation. Those sunflowers are so tall, if we got separated, I might not be able to see you!"

Harold laughed. "Yeah, it sometimes can be lame being so short."

I patted Harold on his head. "Maybe. But, if we weren't both short, we couldn't form a chicken jockey … one of the fastest and hardest to kill mobs in all of Minecraft."

"Meh," said Harold. "I'd rather be tall like an iron golem."

I laughed. "Suit yourself," I said as I jumped on Harold's back and we entered Sunflower Gulch.

Chapter 5

The sunflowers were dense, just as I had been told they would be. This was my first time visiting Sunflower Gulch, and I was not disappointed. Even riding on Harold's back, the flowers came up to my nose.

"It is so beautiful," I said in awe.

"Hmmmph. Whatever you say. I'm not seeing anything but green stalks and leaves. It's like a jungle biome down here," said Harold.

"Sorry, buddy. I'd let you ride on my back, if that were possible."

"Whatever. I'll complain to Notch the next time I see him."

We continued through the densely-packed flowers until I spotted a small hill in the distance. "Turn a little to the left. There is a hill up ahead. We can stop there for lunch and you can enjoy the view."

"Finally," said Harold.

About two minutes later, we arrived at the hill. I hopped off Harold's back and he took in the scene.

"Wow!" he said.

"Yeah, wow," I agreed.

The gulch itself was about one hundred blocks wide and was almost completely filled with sunflowers. From the vantage of the hilltop, we could see the path we had cut through the flowers. We also saw a few other paths, some more recent or more used than others, in the flowers.

"Who or what do you think made those other paths?" wondered Harold.

I shrugged. "Probably some players, or maybe some cows or mooshrooms or even a moobloom."

"Probably," agreed Harold.

I reached into my inventory and removed a small bag of wheat and put some grain on the ground for Harold to peck. I brought out a rotten flesh sandwich for myself. My mouth began to water. I quickly bit into the bread and the dank, moldy flesh.

"Sooooo. Gooood," I said, the delicious smell of rotten flesh wafting from my mouth.

I heard Harold retch before he moved a few steps away from me. "Ugh. Move downwind of me if you want to eat that dreck."

I chuckled. "Sorry. I forgot to check the wind." I stood up and moved so that the breeze blowing through the gulch would blow the smell of the rotten flesh away from Harold instead of directly up his nose.

After I finished my sandwich, I pulled out a bottle of water and took a long drink. I then offered the bottle to Harold. He grimaced. "You got another bottle? Something your nasty lips haven't touched?"

"Bro. Be nice," I said as I retrieved an unopened bottle and poured some of the water down into Harold's mouth.

Harold swallowed a couple of times and then said, "Thanks. Too bad I can't hold this bottle with my wings."

"No worries," I said as I tucked the bottle into my inventory. I was about to ask Harold if he was ready to go, when suddenly a small rock zoomed through the air and hit Harold in the center of his head!

"Oof," he groaned as he fell to the ground unconscious.

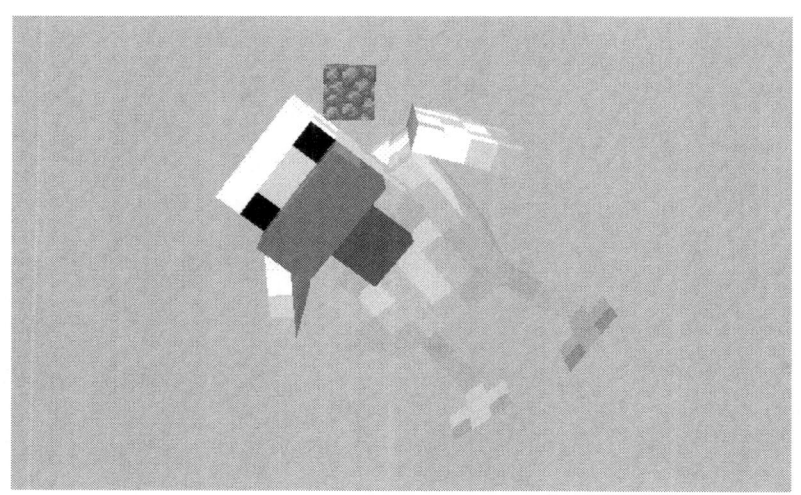

I quickly checked on him and, finding that he was still alive, pulled my diamond sword and yelled, "Show yourself, coward! How dare you ambush a defenseless chicken?"

I heard a rustling in the sunflowers and then suddenly a figure stood before me. "You?!?" I said in shock as I recognized him. But, my shock had slowed my reflexes and I didn't notice the mob sneaking up behind me. I was hit in the head from behind and lost consciousness.

Chapter 6

I woke up inside a cage in the back of a horse-drawn cart. My hands were tied securely behind my back. I looked around and saw an armored husk walking behind the cart and staring at me. I looked over my shoulder and saw another husk riding on the horse that was pulling the cart. We were on the edge of the grassland heading into the desert.

"Where's Harold? Where are you taking me?" I shouted.

The husk riding the horse snapped the reins and said, "Whoa." In response, the horse stopped. The husk hopped off the back of the horse and motioned to the other husk. "Hold the reins while I talk to our … guest."

The other husk chuckled and walked forward and held the reins. The second husk walked to the back of the cart and stared at me. "You recognize me, don't you?"

I squinted at him. My mind was still a little foggy from being bashed on the head, but then I remembered that I *had* recognized him before I lost consciousness. "It *is* you. You're the husk that wanted me to help you defeat Herobrine so that you could become famous and have meet and greets, right?"

The husk chuckled. He buffed his fingernails against his diamond chest plate. He wore a cloak over his armor giving the appearance of someone who was wealthy or perhaps even noble, though I doubted he was either.

"You have a good memory, Warrior. After you turned me away from your meet and greet and threw my emeralds back at me, I swore my revenge. If you didn't want to help me defeat Herobrine, then I will defeat and humiliate you."

He paused for a minute and then he smiled broadly, his dry decaying teeth a dark brown line inside his mouth. "And guess what? I *have* defeated you. Now I'm going to show you off to all of the husks in my village. Once they know how dominant I am, I will become the leader of the village. And after that, the leader of all husks. My fame will travel throughout the Overworld and all the realms of Minecraft. And you will be forgotten as the pathetic baby zombie you always have been."

Where does he get this stuff?

"I don't care about any of that. Where's Harold?" I demanded.

The husk chuckled again. "I left him unconscious on the ground in Sunflower Gulch. It has been nearly an hour, so he has probably been eaten by an ocelot by now. I'm sure you'll never see him again."

I started breathing quickly. I could not believe my friend might be dead. And, if he weren't dead, he was out there helpless.

"If Harold is dead, I'm going to kill you ... *slowly!*" I pulled on the ropes binding my wrists together but to no avail. "I'll use a potion of poison. You're not going to like it."

The husk shook his head. "Tsk tsk. I thought the Warrior was more noble than that. I thought you were above torture."

*Actually, I **was** above torture. I was just saying torturous things to try to get him to change his mind.*

"I'm not above anything if it will save my friends or get vengeance for their murder."

The husk shook his head sadly and reached into his inventory and pulled out an iron sword. He banged it against the bars of the cage in which I was trapped. The clanging sound rattled around in my ears. It gave me a headache. After about ten seconds, the husk stopped and tucked his sword back into his inventory.

"Enough of this posturing. You're never going free. I'm going to parade you around Minecraft for years."

Now it was my turn to laugh. "My friends will rescue me. You'll see."

"They won't be able to rescue you when I am the leader of thousands of husks in an army that will sweep across the Overworld and conquer everything in its path."

Seriously with this guy?

"You think you can conquer the Overworld? Become its emperor?"

"Funny you should use that word," said the husk as he pushed his purple cloak into the air so that it billowed majestically behind him. "You are correct. I shall be Emperor Cassius. Have you noticed my beautiful cloak? It is something an emperor would wear, don't you agree?"

"I don't believe this. I was just making the emperor stuff up as an insult. But you're seriously planning on doing that? Mere fame is not enough? You have to have *absolute power* too?"

Cassius looked at me with a disappointed expression. "See, that's the problem with all of you in the Balance. I mean, maybe Herobrine is an exception, but the rest of you just want to help everyone. You don't want any power for yourself. That's just lazy and stupid. If you have access to power, you need to make your own life better and *forget* about everyone else."

"That's terrible! I would *never* do such a thing."

Cassius nodded his head. "Of course *you* wouldn't. That's why you're in a cage and I'm standing outside of it." Cassius looked up at the other husk and said, "Get back here. We're leaving."

I could've said something else. Yelled at him or made a ruckus, but I decided not to. I needed to rest and recover my senses entirely after being knocked unconscious. I needed my strength for the moment when I would have my opportunity to strike. I *knew* it would come. It *had* to come.

Chapter 7

We passed into the desert and rode along a path for about an hour before coming to a village. I was surprised to see it was the village I had been traveling to. The village in which Otis' girlfriend, Sandy, lived.

Our entry into the town was greeted with curiosity. Several husks waved and said, "What are you doing, Cassius? What is in the cage?"

"Come to the central plaza of the village. I have an announcement to make. Spread the word."

Some of the husks were able to see me inside the cage. "A pathetic baby zombie? This better be good," said one of them.

"Yeah, baby zombies are stupid," said another.

Even though I was the Warrior in the Balance of Minecraft and I took it upon myself to value the lives of all Minecraft mobs, these husks were making it difficult for me right now.

So. Mean.

We slowly made our way toward the center of town with Cassius periodically announcing his request that members of the town come to the central plaza to hear his great announcement.

When we finally arrived at the center of town, about five minutes later, there was a crowd of several hundred gathered. I could only see in one direction out of the cage but judging by the noise, the entire plaza was filled. I hoped Sandy was there. Maybe she would get word to Otis about what had happened.

I heard another husk approach Cassius and say, "What is the meaning of this? You did not get approval from me for this announcement."

I heard Cassius growl a little bit. "Mayor Dustface, I don't have to get approval from you for every little thing I do."

Mayor Dustface gasped. "You certainly do. I am the mayor of this town. I control all aspects of life. You know that."

Cassius chuckled and then I heard the unmistakable sound of him drawing his sword and then the sound of the blade slicing through the air and then into flesh. This was followed by screams from the crowd and a *thump* as Mayor Dustface's head fell to the ground. I heard several husks shout, "Murderer! What is the meaning of this?"

Cassius yelled. "Silence! You are now my subjects. You will do everything I say."

"Why would we do that?" came a female husk's voice. I thought I recognized it. *Sandy?*

"I will show you why," said Cassius as he walked to the rear of the cage and unlocked it. He reached in and grabbed me by the scruff of my neck and brought me out and held me up like I was some sort of baby ocelot kitten. The crowd was unimpressed. Several of them started laughing.

"Silence!" yelled Cassius. He held me up higher in the air and said, "Zombie. Tell everyone here who you are."

I looked through the crowd hoping to see Sandy. I saw several baby female husks, but they all kind of look the same to me. I hoped one was Sandy.

Cassius poked me in the ribs with a stick. It really hurt. "Speak now! Tell them who you are."

"I am Baby Zeke. The Warrior in the Balance of Minecraft."

The crowd gasped. "What have you done, Cassius?" said someone in the crowd.

"What have I done? I have captured the Warrior. I am now the most powerful husk who ever lived. And you will bow to me. For I am your new Emperor. Emperor Cassius."

Several members of the crowd shouted, "Never!" A group of husks with swords and bows rushed toward Cassius, but he had this all planned. Several hundred husks in the crowd suddenly pulled out weapons and killed the handful of husks rushing toward Cassius.

Cassius surveyed the crowd, walking back and forth with his cloak flapping majestically in the breeze. "Any other challengers?"

The members of the crowd, seeing that Cassius had several hundred armed husks at his disposal and that he had captured me, decided not to do anything else.

"Excellent. In that case, I shall take the Warrior to our sister village across the mountains. Once they are my subjects, we will form a husk army and conquer the Overworld."

I saw the looks of trepidation on the faces of the majority of the husks. They did not want to be transformed into an invading army. They just wanted to be left alone to do their husk things, whatever they were. But now, they were under the yoke of a mad husk who was going to sacrifice their lives for his own self-serving plans.

I *had to* escape. I had to summon the other members of the Balance to somehow set all this right. But that took time and I would need my hands free. But, of course, they were tied behind me. I wasn't calling anyone. Not right now, anyway.

Cassius, who still had me by the scruff of the neck, walked back behind the cage and threw me in like a ragdoll before slamming the cage door behind me. He looked at the husk who had been trailing behind the cage for the entire trip. "Scabs? I want you to put together a detail of thirty of my finest husk warriors. We need to protect this cage. Now that I have revealed my plans, there are sure to be several traitors amongst us as there always are. We must be ready."

Scabs stood at attention and saluted. "Yes, Emperor Cassius. Your wish is my command."

It took Scabs only ten minutes to gather the requested soldiers. They surrounded the cart and horse and we left the village, the soldiers in a circular formation and I sitting forlornly in a cage while false Emperor Cassius sat astride his noble steed.

For some reason, I remembered the first minutes of my life after I spawned in a dark cave. A feeling of helplessness and uncertainty washed over me. If I'd been alone, I would've cried. Instead, I went to sleep and dreamed of my revenge.

Chapter 8

It took about four hours to make the journey to the next husk village. After we entered the village, Cassius once again played it as though he were going to make an interesting announcement. The soldiers who had been surrounding us while we traveled had snuck into town one by one before we rode in with the cage and horse.

Cassius made his announcement and was met with the same sort of resistance as in his home village. Once his thirty soldiers appeared, joined by another two dozen loyalists who were already present in the town, the town surrendered and pledged its fealty to Emperor Cassius.

"Excellent, my husks," Cassius said to the hundreds of assembled husk villagers. "My soldiers will teach you the ways of warfare and soon we will march upon the Overworld, enslaving those who surrender and killing those who will not."

I saw the terror in the eyes of the village husks. They realized the great consequence to their lives that Emperor Cassius would bring. I could tell they thought I was a powerless weakling. And, at this exact moment, I suppose I was. After all, how could the Warrior fall into the hands of a single husk?

Nevertheless, I was confident I would defeat Cassius. *But how?*

After the second husk village had been captured by Cassius' forces, he rode the horse and dragged the cart to a house on the edge of town, stopping near a medium-sized building that had the look of a warehouse. He dismounted his horse and went around to the back of the cage, opened it, and again grabbed me by the neck. He and Scabs dragged me into the building and tossed me onto the ground.

I was surprised to see inside the building there was very little. But what *was* there was fascinating. There were a dozen empty beds and an inactive nether portal.

"What's the big idea?" I asked.

Cassius smiled. "Oh, I'm going to take you down to the Nether. I want to share the news with all of the mobs down there, especially my zombified piglin cousins."

"Zombified piglins? Don't you mean zombie pigmen?"

"You haven't heard? They like to be called *zombified piglins* now. It's a new thing. Now that piglins have been revealed in the Nether by Notch, the pigmen realize that they are simply the undead relatives of the piglins."

"Otis is going to be surprised to learn this," I said.

"Otis is going to be *dead*. Sooner or later," said Cassius as though it were a foregone conclusion.

I stood up and rushed toward Cassius. Even though my hands were tied behind my back, I rammed him as hard as I could with my head, knocking him to the ground. I heard the air expel from his lungs as his ribcage slammed against the floor.

He recovered quickly, stood up, and slapped me across the face, knocking me back several blocks. One of my teeth fell out of my decaying gums and landed on the ground. I looked up from my nasty brown and black tooth at Cassius angrily. "You'll never get away with this. The other members of the Balance will stop you."

"Scabs, hold onto this fool!" ordered Cassius. Scabs grabbed me roughly. I tried to break away, but could not.

Cassius tapped his chin in thought. "I'm not sure that's true about the Balance. I think without you around, they aren't going to care. Sure, maybe the Ender King would, but not Herobrine. And, Notch ... well, he is too busy designing new biomes and mobs to really care."

"That's not true!" I said, still struggling against Scabs' grip on me. "You have no idea how the Balance works. If I'm gone, the Balance will become unbalanced and it could be catastrophic for Minecraft. The other members of the Balance will do *anything* to get me back."

Cassius shrugged. "I read your autobiography, Baby Zeke. I know that the Balance used to only be a balance of three: Notch, Herobrine, and the Ender King. You got added later. They will get along just fine without you."

"If you really believe that, then let me summon the members of the Balance. I just need a few minutes alone and when they show up ... we will sort this out," I said, finishing my sentence with a menacing tone while glaring at Cassius.

"You'd like that, wouldn't you?" said Cassius laughing. "But that is *not* going to happen. I'm sure they will all get wind of your capture soon enough. And that is when I shall be inducted into the Balance, replacing you as the *true* Warrior of Minecraft."

"You're insane!" I said. "You don't get to become a member of the Balance just because you capture somebody or kill somebody. You have to engage in struggle and be chosen by Minecraft itself."

Cassius walked up to me and flicked the tip of my nose with his finger. It really hurt. *What a freak!*

"You see, Baby Zeke, the problem is that you are stupid. Minecraft *has already* chosen me. Why else would it have allowed me to capture you?"

At that moment, I could feel Scabs' grip loosen just slightly. I turned around and saw that he had a look of shock and incomprehension on his face. He must have been thinking what I was thinking: Cassius was losing his grip on reality.

I took the opportunity to break free from Scabs and ram Cassius again, knocking him down. This time, it wasn't just the thump of his ribs I heard. I heard a *crack*. He screamed with rage and stood up and kicked me.

"Oof," I grunted as I fell to the ground.

Cassius turned his rage against Scabs. "Didn't I tell you to hold on to him?!?"

"I'm sorry, boss. He just slipped out. He's tiny."

Cassius pulled a sword out of his inventory and said, "I deserve a better servant than you! One who will call me emperor, not boss!" And then Cassius slashed at Scabs and chopped off his head.

Whoa!

After Scabs had flashed red and disappeared into a puff of smoke, I looked up at Cassius and said, "You're no warrior! You're just a murderous tyrant! You'll never be part of the Balance!"

Cassius looked down at me with anger. He was getting ready to yell something at me, but then he paused, drew back his boot, and kicked me in the head, knocking me out.

Chapter 9

The next thing I knew I was shocked awake as a bucket of cold water was dumped over my head. I shook my head a few times to clear the water away and blinked my eyes until I could see. Cassius stood in front of me laughing and holding the empty bucket. "You awake now?"

I spit water out of my mouth onto the ground. I coughed a couple times before I was able to speak. "I'm awake and ready to defeat you."

I heard laughter from multiple mobs coming from behind me. I turned around and saw that there were a dozen armored husks standing in the room.

"Thanks for entertaining the troops," said Cassius. "Maybe you can make them laugh some more?"

"I'm not planning on helping you out."

Cassius shrugged. "That's fine. You don't need to say or do anything to help me except exist. Once I show you off to the denizens of the Nether, they will join my Imperial Army. Together with my husk forces we will form a great hoard to swarm across the Overworld and kill everyone who does not bow before us."

Now it was my turn to laugh. "You really think that's going to work?" I asked. "You know that the Ender King will bring his Ender Army into the Overworld to defeat you. And that's even if Notch and Herobrine don't get involved."

Cassius smiled with a sly grin. "We'll see about that."

What did he have up his sleeve?

Cassius then raised his head and looked behind me at his soldiers. "Is the cart ready?"

One of them said, "It is, my Emperor. We've even brought two llamas to pull it through the Nether for us."

Cassius grinned. "Excellent. Knock down the outer wall and bring it in here. Then we will toss Baby Zeke inside."

I heard the sound of rocks breaking behind me. Soon, light from the outside was streaming brightly into the building. After the wall had been demolished,

I heard the footfalls of llama hooves and the creak of wooden wheels. Then a rough hand grabbed me by the neck, picked me up, and tossed me into the cage on the back of the cart before locking it shut.

Cassius approached and said, "Put on a good show for the kind people of the Nether. Just pretend you're a circus freak."

I decided not to respond. Every time I said something to challenge him, he said or did something mean back. I needed to think of a plan. A way to escape. But, right now ... I had no idea.

Once it became clear to Cassius that I wasn't going to respond to his evil, maniacal banter, he snorted and turned around. He walked up to the nether portal and activated it with a flint and steel. Then he turned around and addressed his troops.

"Husks. This is the most important moment of our plan. If we can convince our benighted brothers in the Nether to join us, we will form a group so large and so dominant that no force in the Overworld could defeat us. To stand a chance against us, it would take an army of the most dominant players, and even then we still likely would be victorious. The most important thing is for us to keep Baby Zeke in a cage. If any of you let him escape, it will mean your lives."

*Dude, this guy really thinks he is **all that**!*

The husk soldiers snapped to attention with frightening precision. They saluted their so-called Emperor and then as one shouted, "Oop! Oop!"

I started laughing. "That's your sound of celebration? Lame."

One of the husk soldiers poked me with the tip of his sword, drawing a little bit of blood. Cassius approached and, waving away the soldier, asked, "What's wrong with 'oop'?"

"I don't know. It sounds like a noise that a baby slime would make. Pretty weak and non-dominant."

"How dare you?!? It is a sound I have chosen myself. You cannot tell me that I am wrong. For I am Emperor Cassius."

I shook my head. "Emperor of what? Twelve husk soldiers and a couple of husk villages? Pretty pathetic?"

I saw one of the husk soldiers raise his sword, ready to strike me, but Cassius put out a hand and prevented him from doing it. "No, Crusty, we don't want him to be injured during our publicity parade.

Indeed, Emperor Cassius is truly merciful, even to his captives. Such mercy truly will convince others to join my empire."

Crusty the husk tucked his sword away and nodded his head before bowing before Cassius. "Yes, my great Emperor. Verily, you speak the truth."

These guys were totally brainwashed. They couldn't see that Cassius was a total idiot. They could not see that his plans would never succeed. But still ... with that kind of irrational, blind loyalty, maybe they could succeed.

"Let's go, men. I shall lead the way on my magnificent stallion. Crusty, you will hold the leads of the llamas attached to the cart. The rest of you form an honor guard on both sides of me with two of you walking behind the cart to ensure that Baby Zeke does not escape."

"Oop. Oop," they said as they took their places.

And with that, we entered the Nether.

Chapter 10

We materialized inside the Nether in the middle of a red netherwart forest. Notch had recently created this biome and implemented the update of which it was a part. Although I had been in this biome before when I was assisting Jimmy Slade, the *Surfer Villager*, it was clear that this particular Nether biome was completely new to the husk soldiers. I noticed them looking around in awe at the strange colors and bizarre plant life.

Noticing their curiosity, I thought that perhaps I could find a moment while they were distracted to exploit so that I could escape. Unfortunately, as long as my hands were tied behind my back and I was inside of the cage, I didn't think I would have an opportunity. I *had* to get out of the cage somehow.

"This place looks pretty cool," said one of the guards.

"Totally, man. So much more lush than the desert where we come from," said another.

"Everything's more lush than the desert, you fools," I said, trying to anger them in the hopes that they would do something stupid so that I could take advantage of it.

The two of them laughed at me. "We know what you're trying to do. Why don't you just sit back in your cage and enjoy the ride, you stinky little baby zombie?"

Meanies. So what if I stank?

Now that I knew they wouldn't fall for my trickery, I did sit down. But I didn't enjoy the ride.

* * *

About ten minutes later, we entered a large chamber made almost entirely of netherrack. There were several piglins milling about. They looked over at us with suspicion, gripping their crossbows more tightly, probably thinking we were there to steal their gold.

Behind them, I noticed a baby piglin riding a hoglin. It looked like he was having fun, oblivious to the tension now filling the chamber. I thought of Harold then. I missed him and hoped he somehow had escaped death.

Cassius called for a halt to our procession and dismounted his horse. "Ah! Hello there, my good piglins! How do you do?"

Several piglins surrounded a chest protectively and glared at Cassius. One of them said, "What do you want? Be on your way."

Cassius shook his head. "I mean you no harm. My men and I have something to show to your leader. I assume you have a king or queen, correct?"

The piglins continued to glare at him with suspicion but the same one who had spoken before said, "We have a Queen. Queen Piggy."

I noticed a couple of the husks stifling a giggle upon hearing the Queen's name. Fortunately, none of the piglins noticed.

"Queen Piggy. What a marvelous, regal, majestic name for a monarch," said Cassius without a hint of irony. "Indeed, then, I should very much like to meet her. I have something in the cage that I think she needs to see."

"What is it?" said the piglin who had been talking all along.

Cassius lifted a finger and wagged it. "Oh, no. Your queen must be the first one to see it. It is the polite thing to do."

The piglin tapped his chin for a moment and then said, "I'll tell you what. You wait here and I'll go tell Queen Piggy what you've said. If she wants to come see the contents of your cage, she will; otherwise, you will have to get lost."

Cassius nodded his head. "That's a fair deal, I suppose."

The piglin turned to the remaining piglins and ordered, "Guard the gold. If they come for it, kill them all. And … use the traps."

I didn't like the sound of that. I wondered what kind of traps they had. I had never heard of piglin traps. I could see a little bit of concern on Cassius' face as well. Maybe he was realizing gathering an army to conquer the Overworld was going to be a little more difficult than he thought.

After a few more minutes passed, we felt the ground shaking slightly. A few moments later we could hear the sound of dozens of feet marching toward us. Finally, we saw coming around the corner of a corridor two dozen armed piglins followed by a well-dressed female piglin being carried in an ornate sedan chair by four servants.

The armed piglins formed a semi-circle cutting off our movement. If things went south, the piglins would have superior numbers against Cassius and his soldiers.

Cassius bowed slightly to the queen and said, "Your Highness. Thank you for agreeing to meet with me."

The Piglin Queen stepped down from her sedan chair and walked a little closer to Cassius. "What is it that you have to show me? I was advised against coming to meet you, but piglins are a hospitable people. Anyone who enters my realm is my guest ... until they show themselves to be otherwise."

Cassius smiled. "Indeed, a wise and admirable policy. Queen Piggy, I have something to show you. But first, I will tell you this. I am *Emperor* Cassius. I intend to become the ruler of all of the Overworld and I have come to the Nether to seek allies to assist me in the conquest. I have come to you first."

The Queen looked askance at Cassius. "Emperor?!? I've heard nothing of any emperors. What grandiose nonsense is this?"

I noticed Cassius clenched his fist a couple of times, clearly angered by the Queen's words. But he needed her to join him in order to realize his plans, so he otherwise remained calm.

"Queen Piggy, it is true that there has been no universal declaration of my imperium at this point. However, I am well on my way to establishing such. All the husks in the Overworld are my soldiers now. But they are not enough to complete my conquest. I *do not* intend to become the Emperor of the Nether, only seek your allegiance."

I had to admit, Cassius was pretty slick. I bet he would be a great used mine cart salesman. Still, I could tell the Queen was becoming annoyed. "And what do I get out of such an alliance? If we join you, many of my people will surely perish in battle, for I do not believe the mobs and villagers of the Overworld would simply surrender."

"Agreed. And that is why you must look at the broader picture. You, Queen Piggy, will get fame and renown. You will become known as the greatest queen in the history of piglins. A queen of vision and destiny and military might. Is that not what all leaders seek?"

I could tell the flattery was working. The Queen paused for nearly ten seconds to contemplate his words before nodding her head. "I suppose that *is* true. But, what is this thing you have in your cage and how does it relate to your plans?"

Cassius smiled. "I wanted to show my potential allies *proof* of my power. For I easily have captured Baby Zeke, the Warrior of the Balance. He is in the cage as we speak."

A wave of shock passed through the assembled piglins and even the Queen herself gasped. "How is that possible? The Warrior's power is known throughout the realms. He even defeated Herobrine!"

Cassius walked toward the back of the cage. He unlocked it and reached inside and grabbed me by the scruff of the neck. He yanked me out of the cage and held me up like I was some sort of prize he'd won at a village fair. "Behold. The Warrior is nothing but a sniveling, pathetic baby zombie."

I tried to kick Cassius in the head, but he held me too far away. "I'm not sniveling! And I'm not pathetic!" I yelled, with my tiny legs dangling in the air. I suppose, being objective about it, I did look pathetic at the exact moment.

The Queen approached and looked at me closely. "By the Laws of Lava, it *is* Baby Zeke. Truly Cassius is worthy of being emperor of the Overworld if he was able to capture him." The piglin soldiers all cheered for their Queen and for Cassius.

"He didn't capture me!" I said. "I was on a mission. I was trying to locate a valuable tulip. And, while I was taking a break to eat lunch, he and one of his underlings snuck up behind me and hit me on the head with a rock like cowards."

The Queen looked at Cassius. "Is that true? That doesn't sound very honorable."

Cassius chuckled. He reached into his inventory and pulled out a pot with a tulip in it. **The** tulip. "You were looking for this, I presume?"

My mouth hung slack. My eyes bugged out. Anyone looking at me knew that the tulip in Cassius' hands was exactly what I had been looking for. "But ... how?"

Cassius chuckled. "I knew those two greedy players would go to you for help after I stole their tulip. It was easy. And I knew you were lame enough to take a job looking for a flower. And so, I just waited for my plan to come to fruition and ambush you on your journey. I didn't sneak up behind your back and hit you on the head, I manipulated you into a trap without you even knowing it."

I was crushed. I couldn't believe that Cassius had been able to conceive of something so diabolical and effective. Up until now, I didn't think he stood a chance at becoming emperor of the Overworld. Now ... I wasn't so sure.

Queen Piggy began to clap. "Bravo! Bravo! You truly are emperor material. I will follow you anywhere you wish to lead."

Cassius tucked the tulip back into his inventory. He bowed slightly to the queen and then said, "In that case, forevermore I shall be known to you and your people as Emperor Cassius. Agreed?"

The Queen nodded her head. "Agreed."

"For now, however, you don't need to do anything. Just continue with your standard military preparations and craft as many weapons as you can. I will be traveling through the Nether for probably another couple of days trying to gather more allies.

Once I know everyone is with me, we can make our plans for the invasion."

The Queen smiled. "Perfect." Then she looked at her guards. "Men, you may back away and let Emperor Cassius and his group pass from our land freely." The piglins complied.

Cassius held me up and turned my face toward his. "You see, Baby Zeke. You should never have turned me away from that meet and greet." Then he tossed me unceremoniously into the back of the cage and slammed the door shut.

The Queen and her soldiers laughed at me as "Emperor Cassius" mounted his horse and we moved away in search of additional allies.

Chapter 11

We continued our slow progress through the Nether, eventually finding ourselves traveling along a narrow pathway with a stream of lava running to our left. Although I noticed some curious eyes of blazes and magma cubes staring at us from hidden areas, none of them approached us.

Cassius seemed unconcerned by these eyes. He marched straight ahead as though he truly were an Emperor, protected by his divine right, knowing that not a soul would dare raise a hand against him because it would be against the natural order of things.

In other words, he was a lunatic.

Eventually, a couple of magma cubes hopped in front of Cassius' horse and said, "Hold on a minute there, horse-riding husk. What are you doing in the kingdom of the magma cubes?"

Cassius stopped his horse and smiled. "So I have arrived then? I have been looking for your kingdom."

The magma cubes squinted their orange and yellow eyes at him. "We'll ask the questions. Why do you have so many soldiers with you?"

"Oh, do not worry about them. We are not an invading force. My guards are here simply to keep what is in the cage from escaping."

The magma cubes looked behind Cassius and saw the cage but could not see into it. "What's in the cage?"

Cassius chuckled. "I can't tell you that, but I would like to give that information to your leader. Do you have a king or queen?"

The two magma cubes nodded their heads and bounced up and down excitedly. "We have both."

Cassius smiled and rubbed his hands together. "Would you mind fetching them for me? I would love to discuss something with them."

The magma cubes looked slightly concerned but one of them said, "I'll go and look for them. Why do you want to speak with them?"

"I have a proposition to make," said Cassius. "It involves the ... thing in the cage."

Thing? I'm gonna get you for that, Cassius.

"Okay, then, I'll be right back." One of the magma cubes hopped away while the other stood there, blocking our path. Everyone, including the magma cube, knew that he couldn't really block our path if we had decided to go forward. It was all symbolic. But Cassius honored the symbols. He knew that it was important to pretend like he cared in order to get more allies.

We all waited in silence for the magma cube to return with the King and Queen. Cassius stared at the lava stream passing by, the orange glow reflecting off his face making him look like some sort of evil demon illuminated by the corrupting fires of the Nether.

And so a few minutes passed before the magma cube returned followed by two magma cubes and a smaller child magma cube. The magma cube who had fetched the king and queen said, "Mr. Cassius. May I present King Mag and Queen Ma. And this is their son, Prince Trevor."

Cassius bowed slightly to the King and the Queen. "Thank you, Your Highnesses, for coming." And then he looked directly at Prince Trevor. "And you as well, young prince."

"I didn't want to come. My mom and dad made me," said Trevor.

The King and Queen looked back at their son and said, "Be quiet. We are handling official business." Trevor rolled his eyes but remained quiet.

King Mag looked at Cassius and said, "What's the occasion? I understand you wish to speak with us?"

"I surely do." And then Cassius explained, as he had to the Piglin Queen, about his plans to conquer the Overworld, his need for allies, and how he managed to capture me.

"I don't believe it! How could you capture the Warrior?" said King Mag, his body shaking slightly.

"Yes, and isn't the Warrior an ally of everyone in Minecraft?" asked Queen Ma.

I could see Cassius getting perturbed. "The Warrior *claims* to be an ally of all Minecraft, but he's just a selfish brat. I once spoke with him asking for his help and he turned me away like I was a piece of llama poop."

Trevor laughed. "He said poop."

"Shush, boy," said King Mag.

"Maybe he turned you away because he was busy with something more important?" suggested Queen Ma.

Now Cassius was really getting upset. He slammed his fist against his diamond chest plate and flourished his purple cloak. "There was nothing more important. He was just being rude. He was acting in a way unbecoming of the Warrior. That is why I captured him. That is why I show him to you now. To prove my strength and my vision for a better Minecraft. And that is why I ask you to join my alliance to conquer the Overworld."

King Mag and Queen Ma looked at each other, concern on their faces. "You know, you say you've captured the Warrior but you have never actually shown us what's in the cage. Are you sure he's back there?"

"How dare you doubt me?!?" shouted Cassius as he strode to the back of the cage and opened it. He reached in and yanked me out by the scruff of my neck yet again and shook me in front of their faces. "Satisfied?"

The shock on the faces of the royal magma cubes was plain. Their eyes and mouths were quivering.

"Yes, it is clear ... Emperor Cassius," said King Mag, submitting his fealty to Cassius and his evil plan. Queen Mag also lowered her eyes as a gesture of submission.

"What are you doing? We can't help this bully!" said Prince Trevor. "That's Baby Zeke! He's awesome!"

Cassius looked at Trevor with hatred in his eyes. "Is your son going to talk like this to me? Is he already a traitor?"

The king and queen turned to their son and said, "Be quiet, Trevor. Emperor Cassius is our ally now. We must obey him."

Trevor shook his head. "That's stupid!" he said before springing into the air and landing on top of Cassius. Trevor's contact shocked Cassius and knocked me free of his grasp. As Cassius struggled getting back to his feet, I said, "Trevor, jump on the rope around my wrists! I need to get free!"

Trevor looked at me as I rolled over so he could get a clear shot at the ropes. "But I might hurt you if I jump on them," shouted Trevor.

"Don't worry about it. Just break the ropes," I said.

Trevor bounced into the air and he was about to land on the ropes when Cassius smacked him in midair with the flat of his sword, sending Trevor out into the stream of lava. I looked over as he sank into the lava. I knew that magma cubes were immune to burning from lava, so at least he was still alive. But now he was *persona non grata* and could never be safe as long as Cassius controlled the kingdom of the magma cubes.

"Trevor!" screamed Queen Ma as tears formed in her eyes. "What have you done?"

King Mag looked at me with hatred in his eyes. "It is because of *you* that our only son is lost to us. You are no longer the Warrior in our eyes. We hate you!"

Dude, I didn't do anything.

"Your son will survive the lava," I said. "Don't sell your soul just because you're upset." I was going to say more, but those words were the last thing I remembered before Cassius kicked me in the head, knocking me out yet *again*.

Chapter 12

"Bro, can you stop kicking me in the head?!?" I said as I regained consciousness.

"If you just stop acting up, I wouldn't have to kick you. It's all your fault," said Cassius.

I rubbed the back of my head. I felt a small piece of decaying flesh fall off into my hand. I threw it at Cassius. But he ducked, and it fell into the stream of lava by which we were still standing. "You're not an Emperor. You're just a tyrant!"

Cassius shook his head. His husk soldiers laughed. The king and queen of the magma cubes looked concerned, but also looked at me with hatred because their son had to escape in the lava. I felt bad for them. They had been swindled by Cassius. That's what he was, *a swindler*. He wasn't a leader. He was a con man. But once he got enough people to believe his lies, he would become an Emperor. And he might even succeed in his insane plan to conquer the Overworld.

Cassius reached down and picked me up by the neck and tossed me in the back of the cage. He glared at me but said nothing as he slammed the door to the cage shut and locked it.

Cassius walked back up to the king and queen of the magma cubes. "Can you tell me where I might find the leader of the wither skeletons?"

King Mag nodded. "Keep following along this path and turn left when you see a bridge. The wither skeleton kingdom is the other side of it. But be careful, they don't trust strangers."

Cassius smiled and nodded his head. "Thank you. I'm sure when I display the Warrior to them, they will trust me. After all, they were allied with Herobrine before Baby Zeke defeated him."

* * *

There's really little point in discussing the wither skeletons or the blazes. They are generally evil creatures and immediately joined in with Cassius, not because they believed in him, but because they wanted an excuse to come to the Overworld and kill anything they could find. They all laughed at me. A couple of the wither skeletons spat on me.

They had no idea of the lengths to which I would go in order to save all of Minecraft, even them. And yet they were treating me like I was some sort of evil person. They couldn't see that Cassius was the truly evil one. They could not see that this was all going to end *very* badly.

The only hiccup Cassius had was with the ghasts. When we located the Ghast King, he allowed Cassius to explain his plan, but then said, "I don't think I am interested in participating. But we ghasts will not stand in your way. We prefer to stay in the Nether floating around and meowing."

Although I could tell Cassius was angry at the refusal, he also realized that he and his twelve husks were no match for the Ghast King and his personal bodyguards. Cassius bowed to the Ghast King. "I understand, King Marshmallow. Thank you for hearing me out. Should you wish to join us at a later date, please let me know."

King Marshmallow nodded his head and then looked at Cassius seriously and said, "You're not planning on conquering the Nether someday, are you?"

Cassius shook his head. "Oh, of course not. I would never conquer the Nether. I just want the Overworld to myself. But, I'm sure I will need allies down here to trade with."

"I can't think of what we ghasts would have to trade," said the Ghast King. "I suggest we simply agree to go our separate ways and live our lives without interference from the other."

I saw Cassius reach behind his back and cross his fingers. I knew that some people did that when they were about to tell a lie, believing that crossing their fingers would mean that the lie didn't count.

"That sounds like a perfectly reasonable idea. I say we *do* leave each other alone," said Cassius. He then uncrossed his fingers. I knew then that if he were to succeed in his imperial ambitions in the Overworld, he would return to the Nether and slaughter all the ghasts, exterminating their race.

"King Marshmallow!" I shouted. "Don't listen to him! He will come back and murder you and all of your people."

The Ghost King looked through the bars of the cage at me and then back at Cassius. "I hope for your sake, Cassius, that Baby Zeke is being overly dramatic and hysterical. But, if such an idea ever manifests inside your desiccated brain, I would advise you to reconsider it."

Cassius bowed deeply to the Ghost King. "King Marshmallow, I would *never* do such a thing. You have my word. We have now spoken leader to leader, royalty to royalty. My word is my bond."

"Liar!" I yelled. I was worried I was never going to get free, but at least I could try to get the word out about what Cassius truly was: An evil megalomaniac.

One of the husk soldiers reached into the cage and slapped me around. It hurt. I stopped talking. I had said what I needed to say.

The Ghost King began to float upwards. "Be on your way now, Cassius. If you wish to return for trade, we will be willing to discuss terms. But if you return for the reason Baby Zeke has said, you will die. Rest assured."

Chapter 13

About fifteen minutes after departing from the ghost kingdom, we encountered a zombie pigman wandering around by himself acting passive as neutral mobs like zombie pigmen tend to do when not threatened. (Otis, of course, being an exception to that rule since he always seemed to be hostile.)

Cassius hailed the wandering zombie pigman and said, "You there. Have you a king or a queen?"

The zombie pigman nodded. "We sure do. King Salami and Queen Prosciutto."

"Very good. Will you take me to them?" asked Cassius.

The pigman scratched his head. "I don't know. You and your crew look kind of scary. And what have you got in that cage?"

"I promise that we mean you and your people no harm," said Cassius. "What I have in the cage is a ... curiosity that I wish to show your king and queen."

*First I am a "thing," and now I am a "curiosity"?!? You are going to **get it**, Cassius!*

"Why can't you let me see it first?" asked the zombie pigman, moving toward the cage.

Cassius held out his hand to bid the zombie pigman to stop. "I'm afraid I can't do that. If your king and queen will let you stay, you can see it when they see it."

The zombie pigman thought about it for a minute and then said, "I guess that's acceptable. You don't have a bunch of TNT back there or anything, do you? Not planning on blowing up my leaders, are you?"

"Of course not."

I had to warn him. "Don't trust —" but I didn't get a chance to finish my sentence. One of the guards jammed the blunt end of a trident right into my head, knocking me out **yet again**. I was sure I was going to have brain damage from all this head smashing. Fortunately though, I had lived my entire life with a decayed and decaying brain, so a little additional brain damage wasn't really going to change much for me.

* * *

I regained consciousness as we arrived at the gates to the zombie pigman royal palace. The wagon stopped and we waited a few minutes until the gates opened and King Salami and Queen Prosciutto emerged. They wore polished golden armor and carried ceremonial golden swords in their right hands, but looked like they had not seen combat for years ... if ever. They approached Cassius. I would've shouted out to them, but I had been gagged while I was unconscious. I could not say anything.

"One of my subjects says that you have a curiosity to show us," said King Salami. "I'm sure that I would like to see it, but I am also sure that this cannot be the only reason for your visit. No husk has visited the kingdom of the zombified piglins in ages. You *must* have another motive."

Oh, that's right, they are called zombified piglins now. And this King Salami seemed pretty clever, having already seen through Cassius' ruse.

Cassius dismounted from his horse and bowed to the king and queen. "Your Highness, your perception of events is most admirable. Indeed, I do have an ulterior motive."

"Then get to it," said Queen Prosciutto. "We were playing a game of rock-paper-scissors. It's my favorite game, and I don't like to be interrupted."

"As you wish, Your Highness." And with that, Cassius explained his plan for conquest of the Overworld, his need for allies, and his desire to be the Emperor of all the realms of Minecraft.

"Sounds interesting," said King Salami, rubbing his chin. "I'll tell you what. If you promise to make the zombified piglins the second most important leaders behind you and your people, I will let my people join your army. For too long we have been ignored and vilified. We've been called by the disgusting epithet of 'zombie pigmen' and are now reclaiming our true name: zombified piglins. A war against the Overworld is just what we need."

Savage.

"I thank you for your wisdom," said Cassius. "And now that I have finished with my need for the Warrior to help negotiate these alliances in the Nether, I was wondering if you might let me execute him here, in front of your beautiful palace."

Execute?

The king and queen both chuckled. "Of course, you may," said Queen Prosciutto. "Goodie, goodie. An execution is much more fun than a game of rock-paper-scissors."

I began to struggle against the ropes restraining my hands behind me. I *had to* escape, even if that meant severing my decaying hands from my arms so that I could escape these ropes. I had to get to the Overworld and warn everyone. I had to call the other members of the Balance so that we could stop this insane action by Cassius.

But it was to no avail.

"Bring him to me," said Cassius to one of his soldiers.

The soldier opened the gate on the cage and grabbed me by the neck and pulled me out. I tried to go limp in his hand so that my weight would prevent him from taking me to Cassius, but I was merely a baby zombie, weighing little. The husk soldier laughed at me and lifted me in the air and tossed me to Cassius.

As I sailed through the air, it looked like Cassius was going to catch me, but then he stepped to the side and let me land with a ***thump*** on the ground. Everyone laughed at me.

I could not believe this. ***This*** *was how my life was going to end? Executed in the stinky bowels of the Nether? This **wasn't** right.*

Cassius picked me up and looked at one of his soldiers and said, "Drive a post into the ground. We will tie him to it and then shoot him full of arrows."

I could have panicked. I could have tried to squirm away, but I knew the odds were against me. Impossible odds. I would never escape. I could only hope to meet my death with honor and that I might respawn in a better place.

Cassius held me against the post while another of the soldiers wrapped ropes around me to secure me to the post so that I would be an easy target for the husk arrows.

Cassius looked over at the king and queen. "Would you like to participate? I could let you borrow a bow."

The two royals chuckled. "We always carry bows with us," said King Salami. "Never know when you will have to keep one of your subjects in line." He and his wife reached into their inventories and pulled out bows, ready to take a shot at me to help end my life.

I felt like crying, but I would not give Cassius the satisfaction of seeing me sad. I stood tall against the pillar. I looked Cassius directly in the eyes so that when he was defeated, as I knew he would be, he would recall how I mad-dogged him as I perished.

But, then something happened.

"Mind if I join in the fun?" said a voice that sounded very familiar. I looked toward it and saw a baby zombie pigman sitting on top of a chicken rushing toward me!

Otis?!?

Yes, it *was* Otis. He let fly with multiple crossbow shots, hitting two of the husk soldiers immediately. I saw his girlfriend, Sandy, riding atop her own chicken in a husk jockey formation, slash her sword at King Salami and Queen Prosciutto. The two royals screamed and ran away from the battle like little babies.

And then I saw something I had never seen before: A drowned jockey. Somehow he had made it into the Nether riding his chicken. The drowned jockey aimed his trident at Cassius and launched it through the air. Unfortunately, Cassius saw the trident and ducked, but the trident found home in the chest of one of the husk soldiers, ending him.

Otis rushed behind the post to which I had been tied and slashed at the ropes with his diamond sword, setting me free. He then tossed a sword to me and jumped off Bob before saying, "Hop onto Bob! He will take you to safety. I'll meet you there in a minute."

I tried to tell Otis I wouldn't leave him and the others, that I would fight too, but then he shoved me onto Bob's back and Bob rushed away into a crack in the wall. Behind the crack was a small alcove in which there was a chicken waiting for me. I would recognize him anywhere.

"Zeke! You're okay!" said Harold. I jumped off of Bob and rushed toward Harold and gave him a hug.

"I'm going back to help Otis," said Bob resolutely as he turned and rushed away.

"I'm so glad you're alive," I said.

"The feeling is mutual," said Harold, the mist of tears forming in his eyes.

"How did you make it out of Sunflower Gulch?" I asked.

"It's a long story. Right now, how do you feel about going out there in jockey formation and killing all of those husks?"

I smiled. I slashed the air with the sword that Otis had given me. "I'd feel great about it."

I hopped on Harold's back and we rushed back into the fray. About half the soldiers were already dead due to the good work of Otis, Sandy, and the baby drowned, but Cassius was still alive. He yelled toward the front of the zombified piglin palace. "Send out some soldiers! Are you not my allies?"

To my surprise, several dozen soldiers rushed out of the fortress and turned on me and the rest of the jockeys. Cassius took the lead and said, "Push them into that corridor from which they came! We will trap them inside and kill them one by one."

Unfortunately, there was no other way to go but the corridor. As we rushed down it, we looked for a place to stand and fight, but with over thirty soldiers coming our way, we needed more than swords and chickens to win the battle. I shouted to Otis. "How do we get out of here?"

Otis shook his head. "I don't know. We came from a different direction."

"No idea," said the baby drowned.

"Just keep going, boys," said Sandy with her dry raspy voice. "There's got to be a way out."

The soldiers pursued us, shooting arrows at us and narrowly missing us several times. We ran as fast as our chickens' legs would take us. The corridor kept getting narrower and narrower until we had to run through it single file. "We might have to mine our way out using pickaxes," I said.

"That will take too long," said Otis. "By the time we've made even a small passageway, they will catch up with us and kill us like silverfish trapped in a bucket."

We ran and ran, single file until suddenly Sandy, who was in the lead, said, "I think I found something!"

"What is it?" asked Otis.

"It's a trap door of some kind. You think I should open it?"

"Yes," I said. "They are right behind us. Hurry."

Sandy pushed open the door. We ran through and found ourselves in a large room with a full-sized door in the wall across the way. I looked around and said, "Is this a room in a stronghold of some kind?"

"I wouldn't know," said the baby drowned. "I'm more familiar with ocean monuments."

"Maybe it is a stronghold and maybe it isn't," said Otis. "But we have to seal this thing off once and for all or they are going to get us." He reached into his inventory and pulled out five blocks of TNT. He set them up by the trapdoor. He looked across the room to the other door. "Let's get to that door. We can shoot flaming arrows into the TNT to blow it up and seal this passage."

We rushed to the other door and made sure it would open. It opened into a passageway that clearly looked like it was inside a stronghold. I had never heard of a stronghold in the Nether. Somehow it seemed like we had returned to the Overworld without having to go through a Nether portal. I'd never experienced anything like it. It was very strange.

"Light it up, Otis," said Sandy.

"With pleasure," growled Otis, as he shot several flaming arrows into the TNT. We ran behind the door and shut it before rushing along the corridor until the massive explosion sent a shockwave through the air that knocked us and our chickens to the ground.

Chapter 14

After the shock wave from the explosion passed, we stood up and returned to the door to the room. We tried to open it, but the debris from the explosion was apparently pressed against it. We couldn't budge it no matter how hard we tried.

"They aren't getting through that way," said Otis smugly.

"No way sweetie. We got 'em good," said Sandy.

Otis turned bright red with embarrassment. "Not in front of my friend."

"I'll call you sweetie all I want in front of whomever I want. You'd better get used to it," said Sandy.

At the risk of invoking Otis's anger, I chuckled. Otis shot me a look, but said nothing. I looked over at Harold and said, "I'm glad you are still alive. How did you get out of Sunflower Gulch?"

"It was weird. After I regained consciousness, I knew you had been taken, but I was in a daze. I couldn't do anything except wander in circles. But, I was trapped beneath the sunflowers and could not see anything. Eventually, a player grabbed me. I thought he was going to kill me and eat me."

I gasped. "It's a good thing he didn't, or I would've got my revenge on him."

Harold nodded. "Fortunately, he turned out to be nice. His name was Theo and he was pretty dominant too. He had all sorts of high-level enchantments on his weapons and armor. He had a small house overlooking Sunflower Gulch. He told me that he had seen you and I being attacked by husks. He had no idea you were Baby Zeke."

"Why didn't he eat you?" I asked. "I mean, I don't want to dredge up your trauma or anything, but how would he know that you were my chicken?"

"He started asking me questions before he got to the point of eating me. He realized it was suspicious that a husk would attack a chicken jockey at all, much less tie him with ropes and toss him in the back of a cart. I explained who you were and Theo promised to keep me safe until help could arrive. I would've gone back to the house that very day, but I was still woozy from my head wound."

"So how did you end up here then?" I asked.

"That's thanks to me," said Sandy. "I was in the husk village that day when Cassius displayed you like a captive slave. I knew I could not free you at that moment with the numbers against me, but after you all left town, I rushed to your farm as quickly as I could to find Otis."

"Yeah, I was still at the farm tending to Bob's illness."

"Exactly," said Sandy. "Anyway, when I arrived, I told Otis that you had been captured and that I hadn't seen Harold anywhere. Otis knew you were heading towards Sunflower Gulch so he borrowed my chicken and rushed in that direction while I tended to Bob."

"You were a good nurse," said Bob.

"You're welcome," said Sandy.

Otis rolled his eyes. "Anyway, I went there as quickly as I could but could find nothing. Then, this random player arrived, riding a horse and carrying Harold on his saddle."

"Yeah, he was really helpful," said Harold. "Maybe you can meet him someday, Zeke?"

I nodded my head. "I'd like that, but first we have to get out of here."

"Can I finish my story?" said Otis bitterly.

It was my turn to roll my eyes. "Go ahead."

"Then, I met this guy," said Otis, pointing at the drowned baby zombie. "Tell him."

The baby drowned looked a bit embarrassed. "My name is Drake and this is my chicken, Spinner. I think you met my brother, Titus? He was the baby drowned riding the salmon when you walked by the stream."

I chuckled. "Oh, yeah. That was funny."

Drake smiled. "Anyway, after you left, he came back home and told me that he had just met Baby Zeke and Harold. I, of course, didn't believe him so I went to check it out myself. By the time I got there, you were gone but I stayed in the area for a while and that is when I saw Otis."

"How did you get here without burning to death?" I asked.

"We don't have time for that," said Otis. "Let's just say it involves a lot of swimming and building a nether portal near a body of water."

"Yeah, exactly," said Drake. "Plus, I know some underground rivers that pass near the drowned villages in the desert, so I could get there just as quickly as Otis and Sandy."

"Thanks, but how come you don't catch on fire in the Nether? I mean, I would think the heat would be too much for you," I said.

Drake smiled. "Enchanted armor. Special drowned zombie enchantment my great grandfather told me about."

I was shocked. I'd never heard of such a thing. "Tell me. What's the secret?"

Drake shook his head. "Sorry, man. I can't. I'm sworn to secrecy."

"I get it. Thanks for joining with Otis to help rescue me," I said.

"So, *anyway*," said Otis. "Bob recovered a few hours later and we set off to find you. We were following Cassius and his men and were just about to try to raid their storage warehouse when we saw them break open the wall and go into the Nether. We entered the portal a few minutes later, following at a discreet distance hoping to find an opening to rescue you without the husks noticing. We never got an opening. And, once we saw Cassius was going to execute you, we had to act. I wish we had greater numbers with us."

"Maybe you should've brought Theo with you," I said.

"In retrospect, you're probably right," said Otis. "But we just thought this husk was a loser who would be easily defeated."

"It's okay," I said. "I'm safe now. If I can get back to the surface, I can summon the Balance of the Four, and we can defeat Cassius before he is able to invade the Overworld. We just need to figure out a way to get out of the stronghold."

"Do you think it's weird that this stronghold was connected *directly* to the Nether?" asked Sandy. "I always thought strongholds only existed in the Overworld."

I nodded my head. "That is what I thought too. But maybe Notch made an update that we are unaware of? Or maybe strongholds do connect to the Nether and we just never knew it?"

"I don't care about all this metaphysical nonsense," said Otis. "Let's go. I'm sure we can find stairs leading up and out of this place. Maybe it connects with a cave system or something and we can get to the surface through a cave."

I nodded my head. "Let's get going."

Chapter 15

We began moving through the stronghold, trying to decipher its labyrinth so that we could get out. But we seemed only to be coming to dead-end after dead-end. Or, empty rooms of nothingness. After about fifteen minutes of this, Otis grew frustrated.

"This is stupid. This is the worst stronghold I've ever seen. The least we could do is find a library and get some enchantments or something."

"Or a fountain room," said Bob. "I could use a drink of water."

"You're ridiculous, Bob," said Sandy's chicken.

"Don't you ever get thirsty, Speedy?" asked Bob of Sandy's chicken.

Speedy?

"Not very often. I live in the desert of husk country. We don't drink water much."

As we turned the corner we saw a pack of three zombies. They saw us and began to moan and lurch toward us.

"Hey guys. Can you tell us how to get out of here to the surface?" I asked, happy to see some fellow zombies.

"We will not help you," said one of them.

"Why not, bro? One zombie to another, know what I'm sayin'?"

"You don't deserve help, Zeke. You let us die when you spawned."

What was he talking about?

And then ... I remembered. On the day that I spawned, I was in a cave with three adult zombies, one of whom burned to death before my very eyes. The others had remained inside the cave, hiding from the sunlight as I left.

"So you respawned in a stronghold? I guess that is cool," I said, trying to defuse the situation.

"We have not respawned. We are the ghosts of your sin," said one of them as they came closer and closer to me.

"Ghosts of your sin?!?" said Otis. "How ridiculous. Let me take care of these guys." Without awaiting a response from me, Otis pulled a sword and walked up the zombies and slashed at them. But to his surprise, his sword passed through them as though they were *not even there!*

"Oh no! They *are* ghosts!" said Bob, his beak quivering.

"That can't be! Maybe Otis just missed," said Sandy.

"I never miss, woman. They really *are* ghosts."

"I want to go back to the water. This is crazy," said Drake, stroking Spinner's neck to keep him calm.

"Well, if they are ghosts, they can't really hurt us, can they? Not physically anyway," said Harold, trying to be logical.

"Good point," I said. "Why don't we try something?" I walked up to the three zombies approaching me and stuck my arm into one of their bodies. I felt no pain and was uninjured. The three ghost zombies kept walking forward, passed all of us, and then walked right into the wall, disappearing from view.

"Netherrack. What's going on?" I said.

"I've never seen anything like it," said Sandy. "I didn't even believe in ghosts ... until now."

"Yeah, it's creepy!" said Drake.

"Well, I *still* don't believe in them," said Otis gruffly. "This is some sort of illusion or magic or something."

"You're probably right, sweetie," said Sandy. "Some illusioner is probably messing with us."

"Could be," I said, "but those three adult zombie ghosts knew exactly what happened when I spawned. That's creepy."

"Bah," said Otis. "Anyone who read your stupid diary would know that stuff happened. I'm sure some illusioner who read it is probably hiding around the corner giggling right now."

"I don't hear any giggling," said Bob.

"Shut up," said Otis.

"Let's just forget about it," I said. "We need to focus on getting out of here."

Chapter 16

The next ten minutes were uneventful. We finally found a staircase and were able to climb up a level, but then once again got lost in the labyrinth of the stronghold. However, we did manage to find a library. After clearing it of cobwebs, we located a chest.

"There better be something in here," said Otis as he punched the chest open.

"What's inside?" I asked.

Otis shook his head. "A bunch of junk. Six loaves of bread and a few iron ingots. What a rip-off."

"We might need bread soon," said Bob. "We can't seem to find a way out of this labyrinth, and I'm getting hungry."

"Whatever," said Otis bitterly.

"Speaking of food, why don't we rest for a moment and have a snack?" I said. "If we pull some books out of the shelves, we can make ourselves a place to sit down."

Everyone seemed willing to relax for a bit. We dumped some books on the ground and sat down on the makeshift benches. I pulled out a rotten flesh sandwich from my inventory. The chickens were disgusted by it. The four chickens found a spot on the ground a few blocks away from us baby zombies and pecked at the bread Otis had found in the chest.

After finishing our snack, we were just about to resume our search for the exit to the stronghold when the door to the library swung open. We all grabbed our weapons, ready for action. But that wasn't necessary. It was an old friend.

"Herobrine!" I shouted. "Finally, another member of the Balance is here."

Herobrine laughed at me. "You know I've always hated you. You know that I didn't want you to join the Balance. And now is my chance to put an end to it."

I stood up and took a defensive stance, gripping my sword tightly. "What do you mean? I thought we were friends now? I mean, I found your long-lost wife and everything."

"I could've found her without your help. You're just lucky sometimes. You are no Warrior, that's for sure."

"My man," said Otis with a chuckle. "That's what I've been saying all along."

Herobrine snapped his head toward Otis, his white eyes glowing with hatred. "Shut up, you wimpy zombified piglin!"

"Oh, no! You did **not** just say that. I don't care about these newfangled terms. I'm a zombie pigman. Period! Forever and always."

"Shut up," said Herobrine as he threw a pile of cobwebs on Otis, entangling him.

"What's the big idea?" asked Otis as he struggled to get free of the cobwebs. "I thought we both agreed Baby Zeke is annoying?"

Herobrine did not respond but looked back at me. "When Cassius came to me a few weeks ago and told me his plan to capture and humiliate you, I could not wait to join."

I gasped. "You're telling me you're in cahoots with that fool calling himself an 'Emperor'? I didn't think you were so gullible!"

Herobrine chuckled. "I don't care what he calls himself. All I care about is that you'll be dead and the Balance of the *Three* will return."

I knew it was now or never. The only way that we could defeat Herobrine – maybe – was with a surprise attack. I leveled my sword and rushed toward Herobrine. A surprised look crossed his face as I slid on the ground and slashed at his legs. But my sword went *right through* his legs as if they weren't even there.

Another illusion?

I looked back at Herobrine ... or his apparition ... or whatever it was. "What is happening?" I said in shock.

Herobrine laughed maniacally and then vanished.

Otis finally tore all the cobwebs off his body and stood up and stomped the ground. "Netherrack. If that wasn't Herobrine, who or what was it?"

"I don't know, but this stronghold, if that is what it really is, is weird," I said.

"It sure is," said Sandy. "We need to get out of here ASAP."

And that's when I remembered. "Say, if we are in a real stronghold, that means there's an end portal somewhere, right?"

"Yeah," said Otis.

"So, if we can find it, we can travel to the End and get the Ender King to help us."

"But aren't we going to need eyes of ender to activate the portal?" said Harold. "Twelve, right?"

"You are right. Let me see," I said as I dug around in my inventory. "I've got three."

Otis, Sandy, and Drake searched their inventories and found five more between them.

"That makes eight," I said. "We'd better hope that four of the eyes have already been placed on the portal or we are not going to be able to get to the End."

"I don't want to go through the end nectar again," said Bob. "I hate it so much."

"I know, Bob," I said. "But, if we can't find a way out of this maze, the best thing we can do is get to the End."

Bob shivered with terror but nodded his head. "I understand."

"What's end nectar?" asked Speedy.

"Yeah, I've never heard of it," said Spinner.

Harold shook his head. "It is something whose horrors mere words cannot describe. The less you know, the better." Speedy and Spinner's eyes got wide with terror, but they said nothing.

"Come on," I said. "Let's find that end portal."

Chapter 17

The eight of us kept wandering around the stronghold. It was actually starting to get a little embarrassing about how impossible it was for us to find our way out. Sure, we found a library at least, but we couldn't find the exit and we couldn't find the end portal.

"This is so stupid!" shouted Otis as he punched the wall of the corridor in which we were walking. "Ouch!"

"What did you expect by punching a wall, you fool?" said Sandy. "Your hand is probably broken now."

"So what if it is?" said Otis, reaching into his inventory with his other hand to pull out a potion of harming so that it would heal him. He pulled the stopper and drank it. Within a few seconds he started flexing his fingers again. "Good to go."

"You're gnarly," said Drake with admiration.

Sandy shook her head. "What a waste of a potion of harming! You need to control your temper."

"What if I don't?"

"Then you can find yourself a new girlfriend."

"Burn," said Bob.

Otis shook his finger at Bob. "You better be careful or I'm going to roast you. *Literally*."

I'm sure the bickering would have continued indefinitely if we hadn't heard a voice in the distance. "Help!" It called. "Help!"

I looked at my companions. "Did you all hear that?"

They nodded. "Probably just another one of those stupid illusions."

"Maybe, or maybe someone really does need help. Let's go," I said.

I could tell the others, especially Otis, were not very enthusiastic about following the voice. But, regardless of what was going to happen, I was still the Warrior and if someone needed my help, I was going to try to give it to them. If it turned out to be another one of those strange ghosts or illusions, then so be it.

We followed the sound of the voice for about a minute, taking a few wrong turns before we finally zeroed its location. It turned out the voice was that of a player who was locked inside of a prison cell.

"Are you real?" asked Otis.

"Um, yeah?" said the confused player.

"Let me just check," said Otis as he shoved a stick into the player's gut. The player doubled over in pain.

"Why did you do that?" he said as he grasped his stomach. "Ouch!"

Satisfied, Otis put the stick back into his inventory. "It's a long story. Let's just say that you are the first solid creature we have seen in quite some time."

The player, still confused, said, "Okay. So, can you let me out?"

Otis approached the door of the cell. "I don't know. Whose side are you on?"

"I'm not on anybody's side. I'm just a player, trying to make a living, gain XP, level up. You know."

Otis squinted at him. "Is that so? How did you end up in here?"

The player took a deep breath and sighed. "It's a bit embarrassing."

"We got time," said Otis, crossing his arms.

"Yeah, we do," said Sandy. Drake and I nodded our heads. All four chickens stared at the player with their glassy black eyes, awaiting his explanation.

"Well, I was exploring a cave system. I was mining here and there. Occasionally lava would come out of a hole, and I would patch it. Other times, water would come out, and I would patch it. I wasn't finding much of value so ... well, I decided to risk it and mine straight down just to see what I might find. Somehow, I opened up a hole and fell through. It was a deep hole and dark. I fell so far that I thought I was going to slam against the ground and splatter to my death. But instead, I saw a purple rectangle directly beneath me and passed through it and ended up here in this prison cell."

"Is that true?" I asked with astonishment. "You fell through a nether portal and into this cell?!?"

The player nodded his head. "As far as I know, that's exactly what happened."

I looked at Otis, Sandy, and Drake. "What do you guys think? Should we let him out?"

"I don't care," said Otis.

"Let him out," said Drake. "Maybe he can help us find the end portal."

The player smiled. "I probably can. I heard some mobs down here talking about it about an hour ago."

I quickly reached over and opened the cell door to free the player. "Really? What did they say?"

"They said that they found an end portal nearby. I think it might be down at the end of this long corridor," said the player pointing. "That's the direction from which they came."

"What's your name anyway, player?" I asked.

"My name's DJ. What's yours?"

"You're telling me you don't know who the Warrior is?" said Otis in a sarcastic voice pretending to be shocked. "Oh my Notch, Baby Zeke, you're not famous enough for this guy to know who you are."

I rolled my eyes. "Shut up, Otis."

"And I'm Sandy."

"And I'm Drake."

The player had a strange look on his face. He looked back and forth at the four of us and then focused his gaze at Otis. "Otis? The zombie pigman jockey?"

"Yeah, what about it?"

The player reached into his inventory and pulled out a copy of Otis's diary. "Your diary is my favorite book I've ever read. I keep it with me all the time. It's *so* inspirational. Could I have your autograph?"

I thought Otis was going to cry. He had to turn around and pretend like he was blowing some snot from his nose onto the ground but I knew he was just wiping the tears away from his eyes. When he turned back around he said gruffly, "Sure, I'll autograph it for you. Do you have a quill?"

DJ reached into his inventory and pulled out a quill. He handed the quill and the diary to Otis. Otis opened the cover of the book and wrote some words inside and then handed it back to DJ along with the quill.

DJ lovingly took the book and then opened it. He read the words and I saw tears forming in his eyes. He wiped them away and looked at Otis. "Thank you," he said before tucking the diary back into his inventory.

"What did you write, Otis?" asked Bob.

"None of your business," said Otis.

"Do you want my autograph too?" I asked.

DJ shook his head. "Your diary is awesome and all, but it just doesn't speak to me the way Otis' diary does."

Otis chuckled. "Ha ha. Burn."

"It wasn't a burn," I said. "He just has different taste in literature than most other players."

"Whatever," said Otis. "Anyway, DJ, do you want to come with us to find the end portal?"

"You know, I'd like to, but I got the sense that you are on another dangerous adventure. And I want to make sure I can get this diary back to my special shulker box so that it doesn't get damaged."

"Do you know another way out of here?" I asked.

DJ shook his head. "I don't, not unless I can find that nether portal again. Besides, I don't have enough XP or strong weapons to go to the End yet and face the Ender Dragon. There must be another way out, right?"

"I hope so, but we haven't been able to find it," said Drake.

"I think I'll still go on by myself and see what I can find," said DJ.

"Suit yourself," I said. "Thanks for the hint about the location of the end portal."

"No problem," said DJ. He smiled and waved at us as he walked away.

Chapter 18

Our group walked in the direction DJ had indicted. The corridor was indeed long, and it took us two minutes to arrive at its end where it branched into a T-shaped intersection. There was a door straight ahead. Otis punched it open and lo and behold there was an end portal inside!

We rushed up the stairs and examined the portal. To our great misfortune, there were only three eyes of ender already placed. That meant we were just one eye short.

"Netherrack," said Otis. "One measly eye!!!"

"Let's just place the eyes we have and maybe we can find an ender pearl in a chest somewhere," I said. "I've got some blaze powder so once we have an ender pearl, we can craft the final eye of ender."

We placed our eyes and stared at the one block missing an eye. If we could just activate this portal we could get to the End and alert the Ender King about

Cassius' plot. He could contact Notch and the real Herobrine, and we could put an end to this false Emperor once and for all.

Our group left the portal room and began to walk down one of the corridors we had never gone down before in the hope of locating a chest. We had been searching for about five minutes when I heard a voice behind us.

"Took you long enough," it said. I'd recognize that voice anywhere. *Cassius*.

"How did you manage to get through our little roadblock?" I asked.

Cassius laughed. "That little pile of rubble you left? Not a problem when you have hundreds of soldiers at your disposal to help clear it."

"It looks like you are on your own now though," said Otis with menace. "Let's see how well you can defend yourself." Otis drew his sword and rushed toward Cassius. Cassius stood his ground. In fact, he didn't even move. Maybe Otis would stand a chance? Or maybe this is a trap?

Otis slashed his sword right across Cassius' stomach. But the sword went right through him. He was another illusion!

Otis threw his sword on the ground. "No! This isn't fair!"

"Come on, Otis, let's ignore this illusion and get moving," said Sandy.

"You'll never get out of this stronghold," said the false Cassius. "Never, ever, ever."

We all ignored the illusion and kept moving forward. The false Cassius stood and watched us leave, his evil, bellowing laughter echoing throughout the stronghold.

Chapter 19

We wandered around for several hours, but had been unable to locate even one ender pearl that we needed in order to craft the final eye of ender to activate the end portal. We did however find one chest in a room. Although it did not contain an ender pearl, it did contain some good loot, including a golden apple, a diamond, and an enchanted book with an enchantment of sharpness V and unbreaking III.

When he saw the enchantments, Otis snatched the book from my hands. "That one's mine."

"But I found it," I said. "Those are good enchantments."

Otis shrugged as he tucked the book into his inventory. "Yeah, but you're already 'the Warrior.' Let me have something awesome for a change."

"So you're finally admitting it's cool that I'm the Warrior?" I said. I had been waiting years to hear him say this to me. It felt good.

Otis snorted. "Not even. It's just that other people — stupid people — think you are cooler than me. I want some enchantments that people think are cool."

Drake approached and said, "Is he always like this?"

"He sure is," said Sandy laughing.

Otis grunted and growled, but did not contradict Sandy. "Whatever. Anyways, I get the anvil first thing when we get home. I want to use these enchantments ASAP."

After we finished dividing up the loot in the chest, I saw Harold sit down and put his face in his wings. He looked sad. I walked over to him and said, "What's wrong, Buddy?"

Harold shook his head. "This just all seems so hopeless. We can't find a way to the surface and we can't find what we need to get to the End. It seems like we're trapped in here ... on purpose. Like some young villager trapping a silverfish so he can watch it struggle. We're the silverfish."

Dark.

"I'm sure we'll get out of here," I said, trying to boost Harold's confidence but not entirely sure I believed my own words.

"Yeah, I'm sure we will," said Bob. "We've gotten out of worse situations."

"Well, I've never been in any serious danger during my life," said Spinner, "but I feel like the Warrior will get us out of here."

"Of course he will," said Speedy.

Harold seemed to brighten a little bit when his fellow chickens shared their more positive outlooks. He stood up and said, "Okay. I think I'm better now. I just needed a moment."

"Come on, let's get going," said Otis. "We have to find an ender pearl."

Another couple of hours passed as we wandered around. Drake had been keeping a map of our path so we could find our way back to the end portal room once we did find an ender pearl. The map was getting increasingly complicated, and he was having to use additional pieces of parchment to draw it.

We turned a corner and saw a door ahead. "Maybe this will be a library?" said Harold hopefully.

"That would be nice," I said. "There's always a chest inside of a library in a stronghold."

We walked up to the door and I was about to punch it open when I heard voices inside the room. I put my finger to my lips to indicate silence before quietly crouching down so that we could not be seen through the window in the door.

"Oh man, that was hysterical when you made Herobrine appear," said a cackling voice that must have belonged to a witch.

"Yeah, it sure was," said a masculine voice. "But, my favorite was the three zombies. I thought Zeke was going to pee himself."

And then voices broke out into laughter. It sounded like there were between three and five individuals in the room. I looked at my fellow undead babies and said, "These must be the idiots who have been making our stay in this stronghold so miserable. Let's go in there and get them."

Otis pulled his sword from his inventory. "I'm ready."

"Hold onto your britches a sec," said Sandy. "If these folk are the ones who have been sending the illusions after us, we need to question them. At least, keep *one of them* alive."

"Good point," said Drake, as he readied his trident.

"Let's do this," I said. "I'll kick the door open and each of us should take one of them. If there's more than four, each of us should take a kill shot. If there's less than four, I'll call out the name of the creature we should let live. Got it?"

Everyone nodded.

I turned around and looked at the chickens. "You guys stay by the door. If it looks like we are going to need to fight in jockey formation, get to your jockey as quickly as you can. Understood?" The chickens all nodded their heads, stoic expressions on their faces.

"All right guys," I continued. "I'm going to push open the door now. Let's do this thing." I kicked the door as hard as I could and it flew open.

Inside the room, we saw five mobs, two witches and three illusioners. "Keep one of the illusioners alive!" I shouted. "Kill the rest!"

Otis and I rushed toward the two closest mobs because we were using our swords. I slashed at a witch who was completely taken by surprise. She didn't even have time to get any of her splash potions out. She died quickly.

Otis rushed toward one of the illusioners and slashed him violently with his sword. Even while being attacked, the illusioner began to move his hands as though he were going to cast a spell, but Otis chopped one of his arms off. The illusioner slumped to the ground on his knees before flashing red and disappearing in a puff of smoke.

"Two down," growled Otis.

Drake and Sandy each had ranged weapons. Drake tossed his trident, which found home in an illusioner's chest. It didn't kill him immediately, but did knock him to the ground, rendering him unable to fight.

Sandy shot arrows in rapid succession at the second witch who was trying to hide in the corner of the room. All but one of Sandy's arrows found home, ending the witch's life quickly.

Now there was only one mob left uninjured: an illusioner. The four of us approached the uninjured illusioner as he was beginning to cast a spell.

"You had better stop casting that spell right now," I said. "Or you'll be dead." The illusioner looked for a moment as though he were going to continue casting his spell, but then he thought better of it and put his hands at his sides.

"Tie him up, Drake," I ordered. Drake rushed behind the illusioner and bound his hands with rope behind his back.

Then, Drake walked over to the wounded illusioner and yanked his trident out of his chest. The mortally wounded illusioner stared at him. "How could you? How did you find us?" Drake looked over at me and raised an eyebrow. I nodded my head. Instead of giving the illusioner an answer, Drake thrust the trident back into his chest, killing him.

The battle over, our chickens entered the room. All eight of us stared at the illusioner. "Talk," said Otis.

The illusioner, a look of terror on his face, shook his head. "I can't talk. If I do, my family will be in danger."

"What are you talking about?" I asked. "All illusioners are pure evil. You don't care about anything ... not even your own family."

The illusioner looked at me like I was a monster. "I *do care* about my family. But you are correct about the 'pure evil' thing otherwise."

"What are you doing in here? Did Cassius put you up to this?" I asked.

Judging by the illusioner's expression, the answer to my question was definitely *yes*. But he wouldn't say anything. He held his lips closed tightly and shook his head. I could respect that he wanted to defend his family.

I decided to try another tactic. "Look, I'm willing to set you free if you just tell me where I can find an ender pearl or an eye of ender."

The illusioner shrugged. "I don't know. I didn't design this maze."

"What do you mean ... *designed*?" asked Sandy. "Aren't strongholds spawned at random?"

The illusioner's eyes suddenly got wide. He realized he had already said too much. "Yeah ... hurrr ... spawned. That's what I meant."

Otis grabbed the illusioner's cloak and pulled him close so that he was only a hand's width from his face. "That's not what you meant at all. Are we even in a stronghold?"

We never got an answer. Suddenly, a block in the ceiling came loose and landed directly on top of the illusioner, crushing him to death.

Otis jumped back in shock. "Netherrack!"

"I don't think that block fell out accidently," said Drake in shock. "Does this sort of stuff happen to you guys all the time?"

I took a deep breath and sighed. "Unfortunately, it does." I paused for a moment and thought about what we could do now. "Look, obviously we cannot get any information from these mobs anymore. Let's keep searching for an ender pearl. There must be one somewhere in this stronghold or maze or whatever it is."

"I think our troubles are over," said Harold excitedly.

We all turned to look at him. "What are you talking about?" I asked.

Harold pointed with his wing at the drop pile of one of the witches. "Look. The witch dropped an ender pearl."

My eyes bugged out when I saw it. "I didn't know witches could drop ender pearls. I thought only endermen could."

Harold shrugged. "I guess not. That sure looks like an ender pearl to me."

Sandy rushed over and grabbed the ender pearl. She held it in her hand and spun it around to look at it from all sides. "Sure looks like a genuine, rootin' tootin' ender pearl to me."

I tapped Drake on the shoulder. "You're in the lead. Follow your map back to the end portal room. Once we get there, I will craft an eye of ender using my blaze powder and we can get out of here."

Chapter 20

We arrived back at the end portal room without incident. When we entered the room, we were surprised to see DJ sitting on the stairs leading to the end portal. As we walked in, he looked up with a smile. "Oh, good. I thought maybe you already had gone through the portal."

"How could we have gone through the portal? It's not even active," said Otis. "What are you, some kind a noob?"

"I'm not a noob. I just thought maybe you had gone through and someone had come in here and taken one of the eyes of ender or something."

"Couldn't you find a way out?" I asked.

DJ shook his head. "I looked for a couple of hours and then gave up. I decided I would go to the End to see you guys. Since you know the Ender King, I figured I'd be safe even though I don't quite have the weapons and armor I should have before venturing to the End."

"Well, now you can travel with us," I said. "We found an ender pearl, so I can craft the final eye of ender right now and then we can get going."

"Awesome!" said DJ.

At that moment, I realized I didn't have a crafting table! "Hey DJ, any chance you have a crafting table with you?"

DJ smiled and reached into his inventory and set a crafting table down on the floor. "Of course, only a noob wouldn't have one."

*Wait. Was he calling **me** a noob?*

I pulled out the blaze powder and the ender pearl from my inventory and put them on the crafting table. Within a few seconds, the final eye of ender was staring me in the face. I grabbed the eye and rushed up to the portal and put the eye in the one empty slot. The portal activated immediately.

I walked back down the stairs and looked at everyone. "All right then. We're good to go. For those of you who don't know, we will have to pass through the end nectar. It will be tough. The end nectar is as though you're being suffocated by a bunch of goo. You will think you're about to die, but you are not. Just try to remain calm."

I noticed that everyone who had never entered an end portal before was shivering. Even DJ. I tried to reassure him. "You are the exception, DJ. For some reason, players don't feel the end nectar." DJ suddenly looked relieved.

"Everybody, follow me," I said. "Once we get to the End and inform the Ender King about what has been happening, Cassius' days will be numbered."

We all lined up and then jumped through the end portal. I waited for the strange suffocating feeling of the end nectar to envelop me, but it never happened. Instead, I fell. I fell into the darkness of an abyss. I could hear my companions screaming as they fell.

"This is just like when I fell from the cave into the stronghold!" shouted DJ.

"Are we going to die?" yelled Harold.

"Quit your sniveling," said Otis. "We'll figure this out."

And then, after about ten seconds, we landed on something soft and squishy. We all started to laugh with relief. We were alive!

Suddenly, several hundred torches were ignited and held aloft in the hands of various nether mobs. They stood in a circle surrounding us. And now, under the light of the torches, I could see that we had landed on dozens of slime cubes! Having broken our fall, the slimes now bounced away. We all looked around confused.

And then, I saw him. Cassius.

"What's the big idea?" I demanded.

Cassius began laughing hysterically. All the mobs standing around joined in. After about ten or fifteen seconds, Cassius stopped laughing long enough to say, "You're so *precious,* Baby Zeke. The rest of you babies as well. All of your chest thumping and rhetoric about how you are the Warrior. And then, all that work you did to escape only to find out you were trapped the whole time."

"What are you talking about?" I said.

"The maze," said Cassius. "I let you escape into the fake stronghold to torture you. And, you put on a show for my new allies. I wanted to show them how powerless and stupid you truly were. And you proved me correct."

"You've been watching us this entire time?!?" said Otis.

"Of course. Thanks for the entertainment," said Cassius. "You were my favorite."

Without warning, Otis pulled his sword from his inventory and rushed toward Cassius, but two wither skeletons suddenly jumped in front of Cassius and smacked Otis in the head with their shields. Otis landed on the ground, dazed.

"Thank you," said Cassius to the wither skeletons. The two bowed wordlessly, their bones clicking before backing away and standing at his side, ready to protect their emperor. "I see you've met my new bodyguards," said Cassius to Otis.

"So you really did it?" I said. "You got all the nether mobs to join your fool's errand."

"It's no fool's errand," said Cassius bitterly. "They joined because it makes sense for them. They're sick of being ignored and viewed as residents of the least important realm of Minecraft. The Overworld's going to learn."

The nether mobs cheered. "Oop! Oop!"

"The Overworld will defeat you!" yelled Drake. Then, he caught fire, the heat of the Nether had finally become too much for his enchanted armor.

Cassius just stood staring at him, watching him burn.

I wasn't sure what to do. I could've thrown water on Drake but that would've been only a brief respite. Better that he die quickly and in as little pain as possible. I thought about getting out my sword and chopping his head off just to stop his misery.

But DJ thought faster. He suddenly reached into his inventory and quickly built a nether portal and activated it with a flint and steel. Before Cassius could stop him, DJ grabbed Drake and his chicken, Spinner, and kicked them into the portal saying, "I hope this opens up near some water."

"How dare you!" bellowed Cassius. "That was my entertainment."

"Run, DJ! Get out of here," I said.

DJ stood indecisive in front of the nether portal. I could tell he wanted to stay and help us, but he also saw the dozens of arrows flying through the air toward his body. He leapt into the nether portal and disappeared.

"Destroy that portal!" demanded Cassius. Two husks ran immediately to the nether portal and hacked it into bits, preventing our own escape. They then tossed the remains of the portal into a nearby lava stream to prevent anyone from using it ever again.

Cassius kicked the ground and screamed with rage. But then, he took a deep breath and gathered himself. "Their escape is of no moment. We still have the Warrior in his two little sidekicks. It will be a triple execution."

Again, the nether mobs cheered their stupid cheer. "Oop! Oop!"

The three of us and our chickens tried to run away, but we were surrounded. And soon we were captured and tied to posts. All of the mobs of the Nether stood at distance, preparing their ranged weapons to use in our execution.

I looked to my right and left and saw Sandy and Otis. They were tied to their posts, seated upon their chickens. Just as I had been tied seated upon Harold. "I'm sorry everybody. I wasn't able to save you."

Sandy said nothing but Otis said, "That's all right, Zeke. It was a good life. We did a lot of noble things.

And, even though I get annoyed when you call yourself 'the Warrior,' it is pretty cool that you got to be part of the Balance."

I smiled at Otis. His words meant a lot to me.

"Barf," said Cassius, eliciting an eruption of laughter from his force of murderous mobs. "Do any of you have any last words before we commence the execution?"

I wasn't going to give him the satisfaction. I just shook my head and stared at him. No one else had anything to say.

Cassius shrugged. "In that case, let the execution begin."

As the mobs took their positions to shoot at us with arrows, I stared at the lava lake just to my right. Even though lava was extremely hot and very dangerous, there was something mesmerizing about how it flowed. I stared at it, letting my consciousness drift, hoping that I wouldn't feel any pain from the arrows.

But then, in the swirling pattern of the lava, I saw something. A movement. And then I saw another one. And then, I saw the eyes of a magma cube.

Trevor?

At that moment the magma cube hopped out of the lava and landed directly in front of us. "Don't kill the Warrior! You are evil!"

"Hold your fire," said Cassius to the assembled mobs. "You little sneak. You interrupted my entertainment. I'm going to kill you now. Right in front of your parents!"

"No!" cried Queen Ma. "He's our only child!"

Cassius sneered at her. "He should've thought of that when he betrayed me earlier. There is no age limit on execution for traitors in my empire."

I couldn't believe what I was hearing. What a monster!

As Cassius strode toward Trevor to carry out the sentence of death, suddenly several hundred ender soldiers materialized right in front of me! One of them, who I knew could be no one other than the Ender King, grabbed Cassius by the neck and held his sword to his chest.

"Your little rebellion is over," said the Ender King.

Cassius screamed with rage. "How can this be?!? How can you know about this?!?"

The Ender King slammed Cassius to the ground and stepped on his neck to prevent him from escaping.

"Silence, scum!" The Ender King then looked up at all the nether mobs with fire and fierceness glowing in his eyes. "If you disperse now, none of you will die. But if you linger, my troops will execute every last one of you."

"Come on boys," said one of the husk soldiers. "We can take them."

An ender soldier teleported to the husk who was speaking, slashed him multiple times with a sword and killed him before teleporting away without a word. That was all the message the rest of the mobs needed. They quickly ran away leaving Cassius to his fate.

"Free Baby Zeke and his companions," said the Ender King. Several soldiers quickly obeyed.

I rushed over to the Ender King. "Am I glad to see you. How did you know where to find us?"

"That magma cube there, Trevor. He found a nether portal and came up to the Overworld. He bounced around until he found an enderman who delivered a message to me in the End. At first, I didn't believe it. But, when I tried to find you at your house, it was empty. Then I knew, everything Trevor had told my subject was true."

I looked at Trevor with gratitude in my eyes. "How can I ever repay you?"

"Can you promise not to kill my parents for being traitors to Minecraft?"

Dang. That kid's words cut deep.

I looked at King Mag and Queen Ma. "Will the two of you ever betray Minecraft again?" I asked.

They both quivered their cubes and said, "No. Never."

I turned back to Trevor. "It is agreed. As long as they remain loyal to Minecraft, I will have no cause to harm them."

A look of relief passed over Trevor's face. "Excellent. Thank you," he said before bouncing to his parents and giving them what passed for a tender hug among magma cubes.

"What should we do with Cassius?" asked Sandy.

"I'm gonna cut him up into little pieces," said Otis, cleaning under his fingernails with the point of his sword.

"No, you aren't," said the Ender King. "It is true that he must be executed for his crimes against Minecraft, but we don't have to turn into savages."

"But I *like* to be savage," said Otis.

"No, Ender King. Spare me," begged Cassius while the King's foot was still upon his neck. "I can be useful. I'm persuasive. Surely, there is use for those skills in your palace."

The Ender King shook his head. "You've already revealed your true nature. And it is abhorrent to me and anyone who loves Minecraft. And for that, I must pass the sentence of death upon you."

The Ender King looked at two of his soldiers and snapped his fingers. They walked over to where Cassius was pinned to the ground. One grabbed his legs while the other grabbed his arms before the

Ender King lifted his foot. The two ender soldiers lifted Cassius and walked to the edge of the lava lake.

"Just a second," I said as I walked up to Cassius.

"What do you want?" he said defiantly.

"Just this," I said, reaching into his inventory and retrieving the fancy tulip that he had used to bait his trap. "I'm going to give this back to the players who hired me. Baby Zeke always completes his missions."

"I hate you," said Cassius. "And, for your information, talking about yourself in the third person is stupid."

I rolled my eyes and then looked at the Ender King. "All done."

The King nodded. "Proceed, men."

"No!" screamed Cassius as he realized he was about to die. "No!" But, his cries fell upon deaf ears. The two soldiers, without another word, tossed Cassius into the lava.

Chapter 21

After Cassius was disposed of, the ender soldiers built a nether portal in order to allow us to travel back to the Overworld. We appeared on the surface less than a thirty-minute walk from our farm.

"Do you want to come to our farm to have a snack or anything?" I asked the Ender King.

He smiled. "I don't think so. I need to return to my realm. I have a feeling that Cassius' ideas are going to spread and cause problems for everyone. The fact that he was able to raise such a large army so quickly suggests that there are some problems in Minecraft that need addressing."

"Like what?" said Otis. "I will *address* them with my sword."

The Ender King smiled wryly and shook his head. "Not everything can be solved with violence, Otis. Cassius exposed the fact that the nether mobs are discontent. We need to make sure that life in the world of Minecraft is more than just spawning and wandering around waiting to get into a fight. Cassius' success reveals that many mobs are yearning for something more meaningful in life."

"But *killing* is my life," said Otis. "Why can't other people be like me?"

I shook my head. "If only everyone were so simple-minded." Otis shook his fist at me but said nothing.

"Do you think Drake survived?" asked Bob. "I really liked his chicken, Spinner."

I shrugged. "I hope so. He did seem pretty cool. It would be helpful to have an ally so at home in the water. Plus, DJ went through the same portal. I'm sure he would have helped Drake to survive."

"Speedy and I had better get going," said Sandy. "The husk kingdom is going to be in disarray now that Cassius has been killed and all his followers have been dispersed. I'll do my best to help restore order."

I nodded my head. "If you need the Balance to help you, let me know. Now that I'm free again, I can summon everyone and we can come up with a plan."

For once, Otis did not make fun of me for you discussing the Balance.

"Of course, we will," said the Ender King. "But now, my men and I must return to the End. Goodbye." And with that, the Ender King and his soldiers teleported away.

Sandy and Otis walked a few blocks away and whispered some words to each other. Then Sandy gave Otis a kiss on the cheek, and he pretended like he did not like it, but I could tell he did. After that, Sandy galloped away on top of her chicken Speedy.

As Otis, Bob, Harold, and I made our way back toward our farm, Otis looked at me and said, "I guess you won't have writer's block anymore. My guess is you will be writing this adventure down in your next diary."

I chuckled. "You better believe it."

End of *Baby Zeke,* Book 12 – *Revenge of the Husk*

A Note from Dr. Block

Thank you so much for reading Volume II of the *Complete Baby Zeke* collection. I hope you enjoyed it. If you have a moment, **please leave a review where you bought it or on your favorite book review site** and let me know what you thought.

If you would like to be notified when I release new books, the best way is to sign up for my email list at www.drblockbooks.com. You'll also get access to TWO FREE short stories – one about Baby Zeke and one about Jimmy – when you do. If email isn't your thing, you can follow any of my social media accounts. I'm on Instagram, Facebook, and Twitter @drblockbooks and I also have an official Goodreads profile you can follow or friend.Thank you for reading my books!

Sincerely,
Dr. Block

If you want to find out what Baby Zeke gets up to next, be sure to read *Baby Zeke 13: A New Enemy*.

Be sure to check out my *Surfer Villager* series (*recommended for **ages 9 and up***).

Made in the USA
Columbia, SC
12 May 2021